The Melancholy History of Soledad Prison

HARPER'S
MAGAZINE
PRESS

The Melancholy History of Soledad Prison *In Which*

a Utopian Scheme Turns Bedlam

Min S. Yee

HARPER'S MAGAZINE PRESS

Published in Association with Harper & Row, New York

CRC 1/76

Library of Congress Cataloging in Publication Data

Yee, Min S.
  The melancholy history of Soledad Prison.
  1. Soledad Correctional Training Facility.
2. Jackson, George, 1941–1971. 3. Prison Riots—
California—Case Studies. I. Title.
HV9475.C3S68 1973   365'.9794'76   72-12097
ISBN 0-06-129800-X

for MARCIA,
with my love and gratitude

Take away the sign 人 [*man*] from the sign 囚 for *prison*,

Add to it 或 [*probability*], that makes the word 國 [*nation*].

Take the head-particle from the sign 患 for *misfortune:*

That gives the word 忠 [*fidelity*].

Add the sign 亻 for *man* (standing) to the sign 憂 for *worry*.

That gives the word 優 [*quality*].

Take away the *bamboo* top 竹 from the sign 籠 for *prison*,

That gives you 龍 [*dragon*].

People who come out of prison can build up the country.
Misfortune is a test of people's fidelity.
Those who protest at injustice are people of true merit.
When the prison doors are opened, the real dragon will fly out.
                    —*from Ho Chi Minh's* PRISON WRITINGS

Contents

Acknowledgments

A man's life and his work bear the imprint of family, friends and associates. My life certainly bears that imprint and it is here that I publicly thank them for their friendship, love, instruction and help: Wo-gang and Jin-shee Yee, Grace Herde Hatfield, Alice Fletcher, Mary Brent Townsend, Dee and June Jenkins, Fred and Lillian Ying, the Gates family, Bill Brinkley, Nathan Kudatsky, Bill Bennett, Maylon and Anne Hepp, Dick Christman, Tom Archibald, Helene Joyce Yee, Loren Fessler, Frank McCulloch, Lawrence Chang, Blake and Kit Holcomb, Jim and Susan Newcomer, Harry and Joan Thayer, Dick and Carol Waldman, Jay and Betsy Taylor, Herb and Cornelia Levin, Bill Page, Dale Enger, Prescott Low, Ed Querzoli, the Mc-Sweeney family, Marty Fassler, Bob Shaw, Dan and Beth Siegel, Jack Thomas, Tom Winship, Bill and Susie Cardoso, Donald A. Johnson, Allan and Marjorie Reed, Holly and Woody Camp, Rod Gander, Midge Keator, John Edward Hill, Hannah Kerner, Dave Fuller, Jo Ann Silverstein, Pat Bell, Susie Gerard, Paige Cogswell, Maurice Chuck, Frank Chin, George Woo, Alan Copeland, Dee

Gorton, Ron Alexander, Nikki Arai and my family, Marcia Reed, Keetja, Tai Reed, Min Lorentz, Clyde and Philos.

This book required the help of many friends and associates. To them and to others unnamed I want formally to express my gratitude. To the inmates of Soledad and San Quentin prisons, men who are more concerned about the truth than they are about their safety, for consenting to talk on and off the record. To the parents and families of many deceased inmates. To Robert Jordan, Jr., inmate at Folsom Prison. To the attorneys—John Hill, Floyd Silliman, Rich Silver, John Thorne, Fay Stender, Salle Soladay, Melvin Belli, Charles Cohler, Joel Kirshenbaum, Patti Roberts, David Kirkpatrick, Edwin Caldwell, Doug Vaughn, Phil Ryan—for informative points and counter points. To Tim Findley, of the *San Francisco Chronicle* and *Rolling Stone,* a fine reporter and writer who knows more about the California prison system and its workings than anyone, save inmates and staff. To the San Francisco area journalists who covered these events and shared their information—Gerry Lubenow and Lala Coleman of *Newsweek,* Bo Burlingham of *Ramparts,* Wally Turner and Earl Caldwell of the *New York Times,* Bill Marmon and Karsten Prager of *Time,* Roy Aarons of the *Washington Post,* Alice Yarish of the *Pacific Sun,* Jeanine Yeomans and Edie Lederer of the Associated Press, Rick Davis of KNXT-TV, Los Angeles, Bud Lembke and Phil Hager of the *Los Angeles Times,* Paul Avery of the *San Francisco Chronicle* and Eve Pell, Joe Durden Smith and David Grunwald —for thoughts, exchanges of information and assistance once the prisons' doors started slamming on all of us. To two very competent private investigators, Hal Lipset and David Fechheimer, for tracking down the Branson story. To Phil Guthrie, public information officer of the California Department of Corrections, who has a difficult job but tries hard to help. To the CDC guards, employees and staff members, who shall remain nameless, for unspecified editorial assistance. To my friends Hannah Kerner and Carol Harmon, for typing the manuscript.

To Mary Clemmey, Greg Armstrong, Steve Lerner, Libby Edwards, Frank Rundle, Donna Benton, Mark Dowie, Paige Cogswell, Transitions to Freedom, Connections, the Prison Law Project, and the Delancey Street Foundation for editorial help. To Kathleen Hyde and Marjorie Horvitz, production editor and copy editor at Harper's, for valuable editorial assistance. And last, but really foremost, to Larry Freundlich of Harper's Magazine Press for listening to a long story, believing in it and helping edit the manuscript.

M. S. Y.
Mill Valley

The Melancholy History of Soledad Prison

The Model Prison

The air is clear in the Salinas Valley. The winter rains that drench the gently rolling Monterey County farmlands stop in January and run off the rocky slopes of the Santa Lucia Mountains, settling the dust along the Gabilan foothills. A long, narrow valley that stretches more than a hundred miles, the Salinas is a flat green-and-brown patchwork of lettuce, corn, alfalfa and barley fields threaded by California Highway 101.

In the center of the valley, just south of John Steinbeck's birthplace, unobtrusive among the leafy alfalfa and stalks of California corn, squats Soledad Prison, three stories of drab beige brick and mortar, whose innermost cells—the maximum security Adjustment Center—are cut off from the farmlands outside by a series of nine lock-and-key, electronically controlled doors and gates.

Carefully conceived, meticulously planned and precisely organized, the prison was built in the late 1940s and early 1950s by a state appropriation of ten and a half million dollars. Soledad was California's "model prison," the showplace of liberal prison reforms which began with the inauguration of Earl Warren as governor in 1942.

During his first term as governor (Warren served three terms, from 1942 to 1953. In 1946, he was the nominee of both the Democratic and the Republican parties. In 1953, he was appointed by President Eisenhower as Chief Justice of the Supreme Court.), Warren ordered a thorough and secret investigation of the state's prison system. The details of the reports shocked even the experienced Warren, who, until his election as governor, had been a crusading district attorney and state attorney general. He had visited prisons many times. He knew that conditions were bad but the detailed accounts of depravity and sadism and squalor which were commonplace in the state's penal institutions convinced him that the system had to be discarded and completely reorganized. "Scandal after scandal and a sordid record of mismanagement," Warren's investigators told him.

Officials were compensating for money shortages by cutting food supplies. Prisoners who complained about their food were stretched across racks and "unmercifully flogged" with truncheons. Those who broke prison rules were shackled and chained and left hanging from cold, dank walls at Folsom. For more serious infractions, inmates were thrown into dark, solitary dungeons, given two buckets for toilet facilities, and forgotten for months at a time. Many committed suicide. Many more went mad.

Warren released the report to the press. A week later, on January 27, 1944, he called a special session of the state legislature to ask for a complete reorganization of the state's penal, parole and investigatory systems. With an aroused and angry public behind him, the governor got much of what he wanted. Senate Bill No. 1 that year empowered the California Department of Corrections (CDC) to oversee the prison system, the Adult Authority to function as the state parole board, and the Department of Justice to serve as the investigative branch of state government.

To accomplish his reforms, Warren chose Richard A. McGee, an ex-college administrator who carried impressive reformist credentials. McGee, then forty-six, had been director of education in the

U.S. Bureau of Prisons and had won some admiring press for having organized and opened Riker's Island penitentiary in New York City. When he was asked to come to California, McGee had just completed his fourth year as Washington State director of public institutions, a job which included supervision of prisons and other state facilities. Warren named McGee director of the CDC and placed the parole board under his direction as well.

McGee faced a difficult task. Besides the thorny personnel problems of reorganization, the state's prison population was increasing in geometric proportions. When McGee took over on May 1, 1944, San Quentin and Folsom were already filled. The state inmate population stood at 5,711, and officials expected a huge postwar influx. One estimate on the governor's desk predicted that 54,000 men would be behind bars by 1985. "If we cannot house 5,000 properly now," Warren asked, "what will we do then?"

The new director of the CDC seemed well suited to handle what he simplistically described as the "twin evils" of prison life: idleness and overcrowding. At Folsom, idleness had been combated by rock-busting convict labor gangs who worked at a nearby stone quarry. That wasn't McGee's idea of combating "idle hands." The new director established educational programs with competent instructors, opened vocational training shops in auto repair and furniture making and started some very basic programs in counseling and psychiatric rehabilitation.

"Rehabilitation" became a key word. With the guidance of reformers and professional penologists, a change in the sentencing laws created the "indeterminate sentence." Under the new punishment system, someone convicted of second degree burglary, for example, would receive an indeterminate sentence of six months to life. That was surely "indeterminate," but the reformers felt that if a prisoner behaved himself, rehabilitated himself, he would be released shortly after serving the minimum sentence. However, if an inmate broke prison rules, was insubordinate and refused to rehabilitate himself despite the educational and vocational programs available to him, then he would be required to remain in prison longer. Conceivably, he might be forced to stay until he served his full life term, but no one foresaw that as being a realistic consideration.

To implement the new indeterminate-sentence law, the Adult Authority parole board, traveling from prison to prison, would periodically review an inmate's progress toward rehabilitation by interviewing the prisoner and by reading over his record to see what guards and counselors had to say about his behavior.

Along with the new reforms came a new terminology. Henceforth, guards would be called "correctional officers." The term lent dignity. Prisons would be called "correctional training facilities." Convicts or prisoners would be called "inmates" and "residents," men who were "housed" or "in custody" instead of being "imprisoned" or "incarcerated." The rehabilitative processes of education, vocational training and counseling would be called "treatment." "Correctional officers" were in charge of "custody." "Counselors" were concerned with "treatment." If the inmates broke rules and had to be punished with closer confinement, they would no longer be placed in dungeons but in "adjustment centers," the Orwellian term for maximum security cellblocks which were built to house the most recalcitrant of inmates. Solitary-confinement or isolation cells were called "quiet cells." Sometimes, against the intention of the new palliative jargon, a "quiet cell" was called a "strip cell" because the cell was bare, stripped of heat, light, all furniture, running water and adequate ventilation.

The aim of the new system was to change attitudes. Before McGee took over, a guard's job was to keep prisoners locked up, to make them behave, to teach them work habits, and to keep the prison quiet and its trouble out of the newspapers. "If all this was done," one warden said then, "the law was appeased, society was satisfied and the prisoner was presumed to have reformed and would go forth to sin no more."

McGee knew this to be untrue. His reports showed that the guards could barely accomplish what was expected of them under the old system. Their failure was a failure of the entire prison system and this tarnished record was annually reported in the recidivism rates—the numbers of ex-convicts being returned to prison for later crimes—which were among the highest in the nation. The new director tried to teach his men that rehabilitation could not be forced on an inmate. For true rehabilitation, the prisoner's attitude had to be changed before his behavior would change. This insight, in large measure, was responsible for the passage of the indeterminate-sentence laws.

To change the attitudes of prisoners, McGee first had to change the attitudes of his guards. The changes would have to go far beyond a simple change of title. As one of McGee's protégés explained it, "The old-time guard, gun-guard or turnkey could force behavior but he couldn't improve attitudes. In fact, he was apt to make situations worse." While the correctional officer was still responsible for the custody of the prisoners under his charge, he was now supposed to give the convict as much "freedom" as possible to offset the debilitating boredom of cell life. The new "correctional officer" was to do this "by his own impact and fair treatment practices through leadership rather than resorting to severe punishments." The new correctional officers were, of course, the same old guards.

That other evil twin in the prison system, overcrowding, was an entirely different problem. When McGee assumed office, there were 5,711 inmates in California prisons. Twenty-five years later, shortly after McGee retired, there were 28,795 men behind bars. Indeed, more men were confined in state prisons in California than in all federal prisons combined. California held the rather dubious distinction of controlling the world's third largest prison system, after the Soviet Union and China.

Prison populations in all federal penitentiaries and all other prisons in the then forty-seven other states increased according to general population trends, from 127,938 to 172,187 inmates, a 35 percent rise, while the nation's general population rose about 40 percent. In California, the trends were reversed. The numbers of inmates grew in almost meteoric proportions in comparison to general population growths, jumping from 5,700 to nearly 29,000—an increase of 505 percent while the state population doubled.

There was another, more subtle, change. In 1944, when the liberal reforms went into effect, white inmates totaled 68 percent of prison population. Seventeen percent of the inmates were black. Twenty-five years later, 54 percent were white while 28 percent were black. During the entire period, blacks comprised less than 6 percent of the state's general population.

	California Population	Percentage of Blacks in California	State Prison Population	Percentage of Blacks in California Prisons
1944	9,000,000	5.0	5,711	17
1969	19,800,000	5.6	28,795	28

In 1944, when McGee became director, the state's three penal institutions—San Quentin, Folsom and the California Institution for Men—were already filled to capacity. Folsom Prison was so jammed that inmates constructed shanties in the prison yard and were living in what one old-timer recalled as a "raucous shantytown of filth and degradation."

In May 1946, the CDC purchased a 936-acre farm in the Salinas Valley. Weeks later, a warden, two guards and six convicts moved onto the site, setting up quarters in the wooden farmhouse that came with the property. The farm became a work camp adjunct to San Quentin, taking in the overflow of inmates. During the first few months, prisoners constructed a series of army barracks to handle the additional inmates who were being transferred there from Quentin and, later, from the other two prisons. But soon even the Soledad barracks overflowed and it became obvious to the CDC that an entirely new prison would be needed.

California appropriated $10.5 million for this new prison project, estimating that the new structure would house 1,500 inmates. The new Soledad prison would be the first step forward since the waves of shock and scandal washed over the department just a few years earlier. Within the higher echelons of the CDC, hopes were strong for rehabilitation and reform.

"This new institution of modern design," CDC planners declared, "will be California's model." The visionaries emphasized that Soledad, "since its inception, will place primary emphasis on a program of academic and vocational training while the overall program emphasis will be on the correction of educational and job skill deficiencies in younger offenders."

At Soledad, each inmate would have his own private cell. Prisoners in medium security status would have keys to their own cells although the prison itself would maintain a separate electronic locking system. Within each wing there would be an honor system for lights out on the three-storied tiers. Men on the first tier, or floor, locked in at 7:30 P.M., men on the second floor at 9 P.M. and men on the third at 11. Games—checkers, chess and dominoes, the favorite among inmates—would be available. One large room in each wing was set aside for television viewing. A radio system was installed, with earphone plug-in units for each cell, even in the more dangerous units in maximum security. A large gymnasium, complete with sports equipment for basketball, volleyball, weight lifting and the like, was open during planned recreational hours. At night, the gym would be used for first-run movies.

CDC planners explained their penal philosophy just before they opened Soledad for public inspection. "The policy of the California State Board of Prison Directors is based upon the concept that there can be no regeneration except in freedom. Rehabilitation, therefore, must come from within the individual, and not through coercion. With this principle in mind, the rehabilitation program of the State Board of Prison Directors contemplates not only important educational and vocational factors, but also, by and through classification and segregation, a gradual release from custodial restraint, and corresponding increase in personal responsibility and freedom of choice."

At the new Soledad model, the correctional programmers went even further. The Soledad experience, they declared in no uncertain libertarian terms, will be a "community-living approach" whereby "inmates and staff work together and discuss problems and responsibilities at regular meetings.

"The new prison," they concluded, "has been designed to permit the most modern rehabilitation procedures. Inmates are constructively employed in the agricultural and industrial operations of the institution."

Surrounded by flower beds and meandering walkways, Soledad Prison was completed in the fall of 1951 and opened for public inspection on November 24 of that year. Visitors were impressed. They remarked about the cleanness of the place, the neatly trimmed lawns, the farmscape of alfalfa and corn, even the mountain ranges which flanked both sides of the prison. It was indeed, as the Spanish name implied, a place of solitude.

When the visitors left, the prisoners went to work. Within a few months, Soledad inmates were turning out institutional clothing, seeding new field crops, slaughtering pigs and selling surplus milk and dairy products to a nearby mental institution, the Agnew State Hospital.

At first, due to a lack of competent instructors, educational programs started slowly. Until McGee's reforms, much of the teaching chores at other state prisons were handled by inmates who simply claimed they were familiar enough with a subject to teach it. McGee insisted on hiring civilian instructors. The Soledad program in education began with basic courses in English and mathematics. However, within a few years there were nine classes covering grades one through four, sixteen classes of elementary math, twelve of elementary language arts and a complete high school curriculum.

Eventually, prison officials turned the high school program over to the Monterey County Office of Education, whose educators helped design the courses and, as a side activity, helped fill the shelves of the new prison library. The high school curriculum included eight history and government courses, seven math classes, eight literature sections, three science subjects, and skill courses such as typing and drafting.

In 1972, about 300 prisoners received high school diplomas, some 250 men earned elementary school diplomas and another hundred were given literacy certificates.

The vocational shops were also humming. The program started slowly but gradually prisoners were able to choose from nineteen occupational offerings: meat cutting, shoe repair, welding, baking, landscape gardening, dry cleaning, upholstery, sheet metal work, body and fender, auto mechanics, machine shop, cooking, masonry, milling and cabinetry, appliance repair, horticulture, electronics and offset printing.

It didn't seem to matter that, with perhaps the exception of offset printing and auto repair, most of the vocational training courses were antiquated and not applicable to skills required in contemporary society. The men were, after all, not idle. Nor did it seem to matter that it sometimes took up to eighteen months on a waiting list for an inmate to get the vocational training he wanted. In the meantime, he could work and learn something else. He couldn't be idle if he wanted to shorten his indeterminate sentence.

If the inmate didn't want vocational training, he could go to work in the industries program, putting desks together, stamping license plates, canning food, sewing the national and state flags, or pulling off rolls of toilet paper. "Industries Work Helps Reduce Idleness—the grinding boredom of enforced idleness is the prime cause of many destructive prison riots," said the reformist literature. The industries work program provided an "outlet, where the inmates can do something meaningful, which will be of potential value in their future." Besides, the convicts were paid—from seven cents to twenty-five cents an hour, depending on their job.

Not much has changed in Soledad's operation. The hog ranch furnishes the prison about six tons of pork a month. Sixteen tons of alfalfa and corn are produced annually. Drab gray and beige desks are shipped to the state capital at Sacramento, where they are used by government offices. Twelve million automobiles and trucks bear twenty-four million California license plates and renewal stickers.

And hundreds of rolls of toilet paper are pulled from paper converters every hour.

With a collage of floral walkways, baseball diamonds, gymnasiums, movie theaters, classrooms and private cells, the noble dream of prison reform began. And with a simple, almost naïve reliance upon the mere fact that the rehabilitative machinery was started, the reformist visionaries sat back and waited for the fruits of their labor.

It did seem unusual, however, that in a quarter century, more and more black men were among the prison population, "souls on ice," as former Soledad inmate Eldridge Cleaver put it. But the color of a man's skin had never seemed a problem to the reformers, even as late as the mid-1960s—even after the Montgomery bus crusade, the Mississippi civil rights murders and the black ghetto riots of Watts, Harlem, San Francisco and Oakland.

Down in the Salinas Valley, the rising cries of racial injustice seemed muffled among the ripening fields of produce. Behind the thick steel gates and electronically controlled doors, life in Soledad Prison continued, with an unswerving reliance on the rehabilitative machinery of the reformist dream.

With the civil rights movement clamoring outside the prison walls, it would not have been unexpected to find commensurate black reaction on the inside. For insubordination and troublemaking, there was always the indeterminate sentence and beyond that the Adjustment Center and isolation cells. Some reformers dared to believe the problem was in hand.

II

Conditions of a Shocking and Debased Nature

Robert Jordan had been sitting there in the darkness for some time.

The isolation cell was small, only six feet by eight. But the lack of ventilation and light was what bothered him first. He sat as close as he could to the inner cell door, a sliding row of bars, because the rear and side walls of the cell were flecked with the urine and excrement of former occupants. There were no windows to open, no lights to turn on. Three feet away, a steel flap covered the only window. The window could let in some light but guards kept it closed.

Twice a day, a guard opened the steel outer door, crossed the short vestibule and slid some food and a small white Styrofoam cup of water through a slot in the inner cell door. Twice a day, another guard flushed Jordan's toilet, a circular hole in the concrete floor, from outside the cell. Sometimes they left the outer door open while he ate. The guards never forgot to serve the food, but they sometimes forgot to flush the toilet or to leave the outer cell door open. He ate with his hands but he had trouble keeping them clean because sometimes he ran out of his daily ration of toilet paper and there was no washbasin in the cell. Sometimes he couldn't eat because the smell was so bad.

Jordan was supposed to sleep on a four-and-a-half-by-five-and-a-half-foot stiff canvas mat on the floor but he preferred to sleep on the concrete, pulling the mat over his body. He was over six feet tall and part of his legs would be on the floor anyway. There was no heat in the cell and he had no blanket. He found that he could clean off part of the cell floor, the front end, by scraping up the excrement and vomit with his hands and throwing the stuff down the hole in the floor.

He could sit on the concrete floor during the day but he had to be careful about that. Some time ago, a prison doctor had cut out some hemorrhoids and told him that sitting on concrete had caused them. There were no chairs. Anyway, he preferred to sleep during the day. It was cold at night and he slept fitfully. He kept warm by running in place. It helped to pass the time. Whenever a new arrival was locked in next door, Jordan would ask about news from the outside, about politics, about friends, even about Vietnam. That helped to pass the time too.

Relieving himself was a more difficult process. He knew in which corner the circular hole was and he didn't have far to go, seven feet at most. Still, in the dark, he had to move carefully, first feeling the walls, noticing when the first flecks of excrement there reached his fingertips, lightly tracing his bare feet, one after the other, over the floor in front of him, feeling for waste particles.

Jordan decided to complain.

Robert Jordan is black. His dark eyes, set in a pleasant, narrow face with high cheekbones, peer out impassively from behind a pair of horn-rimmed glasses. Considered amiable and articulate by his friends, his attorney, a federal court judge, and even some of his jailers, Jordan was in Soledad Prison serving a six-month-to-ten-year sentence after pleading guilty to burglary charges in Santa Monica. At twenty-six, he had served more than six years of his sentence and during that time had been sent to the "strip cell" about two dozen times for various disciplinary infractions. When he tried to file a petition in court against these conditions a guard tore the petition up.

Sometimes he spent weeks and months in the strip cell, losing all track of time. It was enough to make men commit suicide, and some did.

This last time was briefer than in the past—twelve days without washing, showering, shaving, brushing his teeth, reading, writing, listening to a radio, or wiping himself. He ate, but during the last three days pieces of his teeth were falling out. He asked for a doctor. The guards laughed.

When the twelve days were up and Jordan was returned to the "hole," basic isolation, where he had writing implements, he wrote letters and filed petitions to all the courts and federal agencies that might conceivably hear his case. He was charging cruel and unusual punishment. A fairly able jailhouse lawyer after nearly seven years of imprisonment, Jordan filed petitions for writs of habeas corpus, mandates and injunctions to the Monterey County Superior Court, the California State Supreme Court, the Federal Court in San Francisco, the Public Health Service and H.E.W.

The government agencies said they were powerless. The state courts denied all his petitions. However, in an unprecedented move, the Federal Court in San Francisco decided to hear the case. It would be the first time a federal tribunal had investigated state prison conditions. U.S. District Court Chief Judge George B. Harris was aware of the implications of his decisions. "We went into the case most carefully," Harris said years later. "Jordan's petition came before the state supreme court and was denied almost out of hand." Harris was apprehensive when the case began. "It was . . . real touchy. A federal tribunal crossing the threshold into the state arena. We went into it most carefully."

The state of California, however, did not want to go to trial. In a brief filed by the state attorney general, Jordan's complaint was described as a "sham," a "frivolous" petition that was "no more than an attempt to harass and annoy the defendants," who were the Soledad Prison officials.

Judge Harris, however, pressed forward. "It certainly was a case that warranted more than passing attention." Harris remembers going into the affair "primarily because Jordan wrote a good habeas corpus." That might have been the judge's justification but Harris, a roguish liberal even before Harry Truman appointed him to the federal bench, had for some years been concerned about prison conditions. Aware that Jordan, as a convict and an indigent, needed an attorney to continue the case, Judge Harris appointed a young lawyer named Charles B. Cohler. Cohler had recently been graduated near the top of his law school class. The landmark case would be the young attorney's first courtroom trial.

After a series of interviews with Jordan and other Soledad inmates, Cohler answered the state's request for a dismissal. "The congeries of horrors," Cohler wrote, "cry out for a trial. There is a veritable flood of tendered evidence which puts Edgar Allan Poe's imagination to shame." The state of California, he added, "would appear to be trying to avoid a factual inquiry into pre-medieval prison conditions by resorting to medieval legal theory. . . .

"A trial," Cohler concluded, "is imperative." Judge Harris agreed.

The case went to trial on August 9, 1966. In hearings that spanned two weeks, the court heard testimony from six inmates and fourteen prison officials. "The whole picture," Judge Harris said later, "was one of despair. Of course, the testimony was shocking but let's face it, these inmates were telling the absolute truth."

The first inmate witness, a convicted Chicano burglar named Alfonson Henry Esparza, said he was placed in a strip cell whose walls and floor were covered with human waste. He didn't know the exact location of the waste matter because the cell was totally dark. But he could smell it. "A nauseating odor, a repuking odor," Esparza said. The Chicano inmate said the problem was that guards did not provide enough toilet paper. "They hand you a small piece and that's your fix for the day."

Other inmate witnesses testified that prison guards provided little or no water to inmates in isolation. The allotment was one Styrofoam cup of water during daylight and one cup at night. There were no washbasins in the cells so guards did not need to provide soap, towels or toothbrushes. Inmates were permitted to shower once every three weeks. One after another, the witnesses quietly and matter-of-factly told how they were forced to endure the same conditions of filth, darkness and near-starvation. Whenever they complained, guards would beat them and shoot tear gas into their cells. When they were slow to follow any of the guards' orders, the punishment was swift and harsh.

The punishment for one inmate who was making "too much noise" was confiscation of his clothing and canvas mat. A guard walked up to his cell and told him to take off his clothes and throw them out of his cell along with his sleeping mat. The prisoner, a black inmate named Warren William Wells, refused. "I'm thinking, 'Wow, man!' because this is in November and it's pretty damned cold and there's no window, there's no ventilation and there's no heating system. 'Wow!' I says to the guards. 'It's pretty cold back here.' They said, 'We don't care. Just give us your clothes. If you don't, we're going to tear-gas you.' " The black inmate thought about that for a moment. Then, because he had never been tear-gassed before and was not aware what tear-gassing could do to a man within the narrow confines of a cell, Wells refused to hand over his clothing. Instead, the prisoner grabbed his canvas mat and draped it over his head. A guard quickly unlocked his outer cell door, ran in and began spraying the tear gas through the bars on the inner cell door. "All of a sudden," said Wells, "I was smelling that sweet bitter smell. I found out quick that the canvas ain't going to do me no good and I threw it off. Then I reached through the bars and tried to pull the gas mask off his face to show that if it was good for me, it was good for him, too.

"When I did that, he panicked and shot me in the face with it. And I just grabbed my eyes because when it hits you in the face, it's like somebody is going to gouge your eyeballs out and your chest is burning all to hell and your throat feels raw, like you drank raw alcohol and the hair under your armpits and your rectum starts to burn and your testicles start to burn." Wells finally said he quit. They could have the damned clothes.

The aftereffects were almost as bad. Tear gas, even on the outside, will hang from trees and walls for days, continuing to sting and burn anyone who walks nearby. Wells, confined as he was, knew "there was no place to go and run and get away from there." When he panicked and screamed in pain, the guard returned and told him they'd shoot again. Wells was trying to relieve himself of the pain by screaming. He started having convulsions. That prompted a guard on a later shift to call the prison hospital for a medic, a civilian employee called a medical technical assistant, MTA for short. The MTA arrived about two hours later. "How are you?" he asks. The MTA is smiling. "Wow, man," Wells thought to himself, "this guy is sadistic." Furious, Wells said nothing to the medic. "He's all right," the MTA said, and left. A month later, on Christmas Eve, Wells was released from strip cell status.

By the time Jordan himself appeared as the last inmate witness, descriptions of the strip cell conditions in Soledad's O-wing were becoming redundant. Jordan testified that he was placed in the cell naked, that it was completely dark, that his cell reeked from the urine and feces of former occupants, that he vomited twice and cleaned that up with his own hands, that he was not allowed to wash or shower, that some days his toilet—the circular hole in the cement floor—was not flushed.

Up to that point, the court had not heard about the disciplining of inmates through a restricted diet of something the prisoners called R.D. R.D., a reddish-brown cube that is served cold, looks like a piece of meat loaf. Cons say it smells worse "than the men's urinal at Grand Central Station" and tastes worse than a rotten egg. Whenever inmates complained about it, prison officials trotted out a nutritional expert to describe in serious medical jargon that a chunk of R.D. met the minimum daily health requirements of vitamin, protein and calorie content.

After Jordan brought attention to R.D., Soledad officials rebutted by stating that while the restricted diet was perhaps not palatable, it was adequate enough to keep a prisoner alive.

The most damaging testimony in the case came from the prison officials themselves: the warden, Cletus J. Fitzharris; the chief medical officer, Dr. Edward Kunkel; and the chief psychiatrist, Dr. Raymond L. Hack.

Cletus James Fitzharris, sixty-one, had been warden of Soledad since 1964. A gangling, broad-shouldered man, the warden rarely ventured into the confines of the prison itself, and was recognized by only a handful of trusted prisoners who worked as clerks in the front office. When Fitzharris arrived at Soledad the first time, in 1947, the place was little more than a row of surplus army barracks hastily constructed around a farmhouse and serving as a temporary prison facility to ease the crowded conditions at San Quentin. Fitzharris stayed for seven years. By the time he left, transferred to San Quentin as an associate warden, the Soledad facility had been constructed and was achieving its reputation as the state's model prison. Fitzharris returned to Soledad as warden in March 1964, after a year at San Quentin and nine years as a member of the state parole board. On the witness stand at his own trial, *Jordan* v. *Fitzharris,* the defendant could reflect on more than nine years at Soledad and more than twenty-five years as an administrator in the California prison system.

Warden Fitzharris began his testimony by telling the court that some inmates required too much time and attention from the prison staff. The real tragedy of prison life, which he had learned in over two decades, was having these "high echelon people working on these hoodlums." Fitzharris wanted his staff to concentrate on "development programs," to work with "the more amenable people." He didn't spell out what these programs were, but he made it plain that he'd had a bellyful of "hoodlums."

The questioning turned to prison conditions in O-wing. Well, said

Fitzharris, he had already improved conditions in O-wing. "They painted the upstairs and it looked so nice." He had ordered his guards to provide water pitchers and water basins in the cells. And although this order was issued *after* the federal court demanded a hearing in the case, Fitzharris did not want the court to think the increased water allotment was "a result of the judge appointing counsel" to Jordan.

Fitzharris was visibly relieved when his own attorney, Assistant Attorney General Robert Granucci, began asking questions. Cohler had made Fitzharris seem awkward and incompetent. The warden fared worse, however, under friendly questioning.

The assistant attorney general smiled at the warden and asked whether Fitzharris's use of the strip cells was a proper means of controlling inmates. "I don't know," the warden mused in the first of two comments which would weigh heavily in Judge Harris's later decision. "I just don't know what is the proper means. The best we have so far."

Granucci walked to the defense table and picked up a heavy volume entitled *A Manual of Correctional Standards*. The manual, published by the American Correctional Association, was largely written by penologists of the California Department of Corrections. Walking back to the witness stand, the state attorney asked Fitzharris if he tried to conform with those standards in Soledad. "Yes, sir," the warden promptly answered. "I would hope, though, that we can go beyond those standards and do something even better."

"In what way?" Fitzharris was asked.

"I don't know," the warden answered. "Nobody's happy with having to treat human beings like this, but some human beings can't be treated otherwise, that we know of." Fitzharris shrugged and, dismissed, left the witness stand. He did not deny that horrible conditions existed in his prison. He simply did not know what to do about them. Fitzharris admitted that "in many many instances we were in violation of the [CDC] director's rules," but, he quickly added, these disciplinary functions were taken at lower levels, by guards and counselors who "knew all the bums in the place."

Dr. Edward Kunkel, the chief medical officer at Soledad, was a codefendant because Jordan had charged that he had been denied adequate medical care. Kunkel, a retired Navy captain, had been Soledad's CMO for eleven years. He testified that his visits to inmate cells were a matter of routine. In fact, the doctor told the court, "When I'm not on vacation, I visit each and every cell every Monday morning." It wasn't the length of Dr. Kunkel's vacations that disturbed Jordan's attorney. Cohler wanted to know how much time the doctor spent inspecting cells. The doctor said plenty of time but Cohler produced O-wing visiting logs which showed that the physician must have inspected 108 cells in a period of eight minutes. Dr. Kunkel thought the log, which he signed himself, was wrong. Cohler produced other logs. The doctor thought those were wrong too.

Judge Harris was more concerned about the doctor's attitude about prisons in general. The judge was uneasy because Dr. Kunkel kept referring to "incorrigibles" whenever he talked about inmates. Judge Harris took over the questioning himself, asking the doctor to define an "incorrigible." "An incorrigible," Kunkel answered, "is one that the psychiatrists have given up on, we have given up on and everybody else has and there is not much hope for him."

"In short, doctor," the judge summarized, "your definition contemplates a complete abandonment of any hope, isn't that correct, sir? Do you think that is a breakdown of the individual or a breakdown of the prison system?"

"I don't think it's a breakdown of the prison system," Kunkel replied.

The judge switched to another tack. "What have been your studies in penology, doctor?" he asked.

"In penology?" the doctor asked, a bit surprised.

"Yes," Harris said firmly.

"Only some of the books that I have read in my experience at the institution."

"What are the books, doctor?" the judge continued. Dr. Kunkel said he read the books they gave him when he came in to work about eleven years ago. Harris asked if he had "kept abreast of the current literature in penology." The doctor said not completely. Harris asked Kunkel if he would state to the court what, if any, studies he had made recently in penology. Kunkel replied wanly that he hadn't made any. "And yet," snapped Harris, "you assume to characterize an individual as an incorrigible. Isn't that true?" Yes, said Kunkel, but that was because the men were in trouble all the time and weren't trying to help themselves. He admitted, however, that "they are all human beings."

Dr. Raymond Hack, a retired Air Force officer, was the chief psychiatrist at the prison, but he worked only part time. The prison cited budgeting problems as the reason why they could not afford to hire a full-time psychiatrist. There were no other part-time psychiatrists for nearly three thousand inmates. As in the questioning of Warden Fitzharris and Dr. Kunkel, Judge Harris was mostly concerned about the man's philosophy of penology. Hack was prepared for such questions. He said it was all rather simple. There are two kinds of people in the world, the good and the evil, those who lived by "the standard constructive code" and those who lived by the standard "destructive code."

When the court expressed great interest in this, Hack rose from his chair, walked to a blackboard which had been provided and, in chautauqua evangelical style, lectured on the ethical history of the human race. "In the million and a half to two million years that the human race has been in existence," the psychiatrist began, "we have developed two ways of living." Hack carefully drew a line down the center of the blackboard. "We have developed a system for living which I refer to—and others of us, particularly at our institution— as the standard constructive code. Originally, this was developed out of the taboos of tribal society. As we know, for some five thousand five hundred years or so, these original unwritten laws or taboos have been written and developed through a series of historical legal structures from the Code of Hammurabi to the current California code—which is our minimum standards.

"Now," Dr. Hack continued, with the full attention of the court, "there has been and there continues to be people who live on another system for living, the antisocial or destructive code." The problem inmates which Soledad and other prisons were confronted with, Dr. Hack explained, were this kind of destructive-code people. They were the kind of people who had "what I call 'the third form of illness of mankind.' That is, they are neither physically nor mentally ill—the first two forms of the sicknesses of mankind. It's a kind of social disease. I like to call them 'socialization disorders,' " the chief psychiatrist offered. "This whole group is what I look upon as the expert group of miseries of mankind."

Back on the witness stand, Dr. Hack's roughest questioning came when the judge himself pressed the psychiatrist about strip cell conditions. The judge asked the psychiatrist to assume that Hack himself was in a strip cell.

"All right, doctor," said Harris. "Do you concede that there isn't any light in the cell?"

"Yes," said Hack.

"Mindful of the conditions under which a man is confined in the cell in question, how do you propose he maintain his personal bodily cleanliness, his hands and the like?"

"He is provided with toilet tissue. He is supposed to be removed to be showered."

"When and how often?"

"Every five days."

"So," said the judge, "for a period of five days, his body and his hands would be the subject of some degree of contamination. Isn't that correct?"

"Yes," said Hack, "but as—"

"Is that correct, doctor, or is it not?" Harris repeated.

"For a period of five days he possibly might be quite soiled," Hack conceded.

"Yes," said Harris, "and quite contaminated."

"Yes," said Hack.

"Let's confine ourselves to the cell in question, to the degree of light, to the lack of cleanliness, to the lack of apparent facilities for a man to either bathe or wash his hands. I address the question again to you, doctor, mindful of your constant surveillance. Did you at any time during the course of your career make a recommendation regarding any device or facility that might be used by the inmate?"

"No device or facilities."

"Is it not true," the judge asked finally, "notwithstanding the stench or smell, many of these inmates were permitted to and forced to eat their meals in that stench and odor?"

"I don't know as they were forced to," Dr. Hack allowed. "It is true that if they were going to eat, that they might have to eat under those circumstances."

It was time for final arguments. Cohler reminded the court that the case had come a long way since Jordan was smuggled a pencil and paper to write a letter out about conditions within Soledad. It had come a long way, too, from when the state called the civil rights suit a "sham" and described it as "frivolous." Summarizing the testimony from his witnesses, Cohler asked the court for injunctive relief from the strip cell conditions and $100,000 in monetary damages. He noted that whatever the court's ruling, the decision would affect other prisoners at other California prisons.

Arguing for the prison system, Granucci conceded that "We are not dealing with what is penologically the most advanced concept," although he refrained from advancing what might have been more "advanced." The only question to be decided, said the deputy attorney general, was whether Jordan suffered cruel and unusual punishment.

Granucci recalled Judge Harris's remarking that the state of California should welcome "an inquiry into prison conditions in order that the truth may be known." He said the state wouldn't "go so far as to say we welcomed this trial," but it had entered the proceedings (on federal court order) and now was worried about the possibility of the court granting damages to Jordan. "To award damages here not only undermines the prison discipline but it makes the prison administrators and custodial officers leery about imposing discipline" for fear that any inmate "has a good chance of collecting money from his custodial officers. . . .

"Wouldn't it be a wonderful world if there weren't any prisons?" Granucci concluded. "Wouldn't it be a wonderful world even if there wasn't any need for an Adjustment Center in any prison? Wouldn't it be a wonderful world if there was no need to control anybody because there was no such thing as uncontrollable violence? Well, we are never going to see such a world, not in this life."

Two weeks after the final arguments, Chief Judge Harris handed down his decision.

He began cautiously. "It may be noted," he wrote, "that this is the first occasion that the United States District Court in this circuit has undertaken to inquire into the procedures and practices of a state penal institution in a proceeding of this kind."

Harris turned then to the legal definitions of "cruel and unusual punishment." He found three. A punishment is cruel and unusual when it is greatly "disproportionate to the offense for which it is imposed," when it goes beyond "what is necessary to achieve a legitimate aim," or when it "is of such character as to shock the general conscience or be intolerable to fundamental fairness." On the basis of the third, and last, Harris decided, "such a judgment must be made in the light of developing concepts of elemental decency."

Of Jordan's testimony, the chief judge observed that the plaintiff "testified categorically concerning the practices engaged in by the defendants. He was subjected to a lengthy and searching cross-examination by the two attorneys representing the defendants. His testimony is clear and convincing. [Harris didn't need to add that the inmates offered to take truth serum or lie detector tests.] It is evident . . . that he was required to eat the meager prison fare in the stench and filth that surrounded him, together with the accompanying odors that ordinarily permeated the cell."

In two moving paragraphs, Judge Harris summed it all up:

"When, as it appears in the case at bar, the responsible prison authorities in the case of the strip cells have abandoned elemental concepts of decency by permitting conditions of a shocking and debased nature, then the courts must intervene—and intervene promptly—to restore the primal rules of a civilized community in accord with the mandate of the Constitution of the United States.

"In the opinion of the court, the type of confinement depicted in the foregoing summary of the inmate's testimony results in a slow-burning fire of resentment on the part of the inmates until it finally explodes in open revolt. Requiring man or beast to live, eat and sleep under the degrading conditions pointed out in the testimony creates a condition that inevitably does violence to elemental concepts of decency."

Harris went on to note that guards and prison officials made no effort to remedy the situation even after persistent and violent complaints from inmates. He granted Jordan injunctive relief from such conditions but declined purposely to specify the "precise procedures" which Soledad officials needed to adopt "to meet the demands of the Constitution." Noting caustically that California penal "authorities" had written the *Manual of Correctional Standards,* he suggested that Soledad officials follow the manual. He refused to award any monetary damages to Jordan.

The court verdict was a stunning defeat for the administrators of the California prison system, but few in power took it seriously. In Sacramento, the state prison director, Richard A. McGee, had his own notions about Judge Harris's decision. When appointed by Governor Warren in 1944, McGee was supposed to have been the archetypal administrator of the prison reform movement in California. Now he stated flatly that prisons would continue to use the strip cells. "We have no intention of stopping their use." The judge merely said "the conditions were improper," McGee said, and concluded, "Strip cells are considered humane. We don't use the dark dungeons or handcuff them and hang them to the wall as they once did at Folsom. There are regulations against torture. I can't get too excited over this."

In a way, McGee was right. Soledad officials stood convicted but they had merely had their hands slapped. More water was provided. A few extra squares of toilet paper were added. But the strip cells remained, complete with their canvas mats, the hole-in-the-floor commode, the darkness, the stench and the filth. As the prison director said, "the judge didn't do anything for him [Jordan] except to comment on conditions."

Jordan was not allowed to return to Soledad. When federal marshals drove Jordan to the prison, a deputy warden met the plaintiff and told him that he had been transferred to San Quentin. "Because of the publicity given this case," the deputy warden explained to reporters, "Jordan has become a *cause célèbre*. He would be, at Soledad, a focal point for leadership—not that he is seeking it, but it might be thrust upon him." Jordan was transferred to San Quentin and after a year and seven months he was released.

Six months later, in October 1968, he was arrested in Santa Monica and charged with attempted murder, kidnap and rape.* He pleaded not guilty but was convicted and is now serving a life sentence at Folsom. His appeal on the conviction is pending.

He was quiet, almost shy when I asked him to reflect on his case. Once again, he was confined in the Adjustment Center, but he was not on isolation status. In the intervening years, he said he had become "politicized." He was not hopeful about getting out. "I see a long way to go," he said simply.

* The reader must understand that if I believed the charges I would not be quoting Jordan's reflections on justice and human dignity.

He folded his hands over his neatly starched blue denims and talked about his case against Soledad officials and prison conditions in general. "For some reason that I really don't understand," he said, "the masses of the American people disbelieve the reports that come out of prisons about the treatment we receive. It's a curious anomaly that reports of the 'tiger cages' in Vietnam send shock waves to all levels of our society, while conditions proven in a court of law, convicting Soledad as a collection of 'tiger cages,' is virtually ignored.

"And no one closely questions the mentalities—the psychiatric makeup—of those in positions of authority. Military officials, politicians, correctional officials all have similar mentalities. They all profess to believe in justice and are the first to dispense injustices. They are the first to cry for law and order and the first to engage in lawless activities. They are the first to profess belief in human dignity and individual freedom and the first to perpetrate gross indignities and deny freedom to their fellow human beings.

"When a man is struggling for simple human dignity and respect, when his every waking moment is one of bare survival, he doesn't have time for rehabilitation or anything else. People forget that we are human beings and that we are men. We ask only to be treated as such. I don't believe that's asking too much."

Jordan said neither he nor his attorney had wanted to appeal for monetary damages, even though they won the case, because they preferred to make certain that Judge Harris's decision would not be overturned. "I was afraid that if we went after the money it would look like I was just trying to make some money. And who knows what would have happened on appeal? At the time, I was satisfied with the decision."

If he were to go through it again, however, Jordan would appeal for the money. "The penal authorities there and in other California prisons have no respect for law or justice or even the judicial process. The only emotion they have is fear, fear that they will lose their life savings, fear that they will lose their jobs, fear that they will end up behind bars themselves. What's needed to bring about genuine change is for some court of law to administer a stern blow to the hierarchy of the penal system in the form of massive monetary damages. If the judge had said, 'Give the man fifty thousand dollars'—or even fifty dollars—that would have people in Sacramento jumping up and down on one spot."

As it turned out, little or nothing was changed as a result of Jordan's court victory. The Department of Corrections continues to use strip cells. Men are still thrown in the "hole" for reasons ranging from a disciplinary infraction to a guard's whim. There is supposed to be more ventilation and light. There is supposed to be more heat in winter. There are supposed to be standard toilet facilities. The cells are supposed to be clean. And yet, Soledad and other prisons are still defying the court's order. Strip cells are not clean. Ventilation and light are a matter of a guard's discretion. Guards still forget to take the men out of the cells for showers and shaves. And the food is, oftentimes, "quite soiled."

"Actually," said Judge Harris, reflecting on the case, "the problems at Soledad transcended our limited investigation." He told me there were many questions about prison conditions and prison procedures which he wanted to look into but the court "had neither the money nor the power to pursue those matters. . . . *Jordan* v. *Fitzharris* might well be considered simply the initial investigation that brought forth the conditions at Soledad as it existed. Soledad was a model prison. What went wrong? I don't know. Why did it change? I don't know the answer to that, either."

III

January 13: Anatomy of an Execution

The guts of Soledad Prison is the "main line," a long corridor which Warden Fitzharris describes as "a quarter mile of madness." Branching off from it, like steel steps from a telephone pole, are the prison's various housing wings, dining halls, classrooms, its gymnasium and hospital. The prison's maximum security block, O-wing, also protrudes from the main line. Like the other wings, O-wing—called the Adjustment Center or A/C—is three tiers high. Each floor is a double row of small one-man cells, back to back.

While Soledad's 2,500 main-liners shuffle back and forth in a daily routine of reveille, showers, mess hall, vocational training, industry shops and classrooms, O-wing inmates are locked in their six-by-nine-foot cells, surrounded by three sides of solid wall and a row of floor-to-ceiling bars covered with heavy steel mesh. Food trays are shoved through a three-by-ten-inch slot. Thirty minutes a day, on some days, inmates are let out onto a tier corridor to exercise. During the exercise period the men take turns going through a double-locked sally port, a completely barred inspection cage, before they're cleared to take showers. There had been daily recreational periods for basketball, handball and punching bags in a small, narrow exercise yard adjacent to the wing itself. The outdoor yard was closed and integrated exercise periods ended, however, with the fatal stabbing of a black inmate named Clarence Causey in April 1968.

The circumstances surrounding the Causey death have never been made public. Indeed, very little that has happened in Soledad is known to the public. "They murdered Causey," said Thomas Meneweather, a lean black con who is a judo expert. What Meneweather meant, explained another black inmate, is that the guards "set up" Causey to be killed. Normally, when prisoners are released for tier exercise in integrated groups, prison policy had been to make certain that the number of black inmates equaled the number of whites and Chicanos. This precaution minimized the dangers to a minority participant, whether white or black. It is generally assumed in prison that guards can "get" any inmate through a variety of methods.

Murders and crippling assaults are a matter of routine. Weapons, mostly chunks of sharpened metal called "shanks," are easily acquired. Sometimes zip guns are used. A contract is cheap. A setup is easy. The legal tender can be—and many times is—cigarettes. Five packs will fetch a welding rod, smuggled in from the industry shops, to construct a weapon. A carton and a half will buy a piece of iron stiff enough and sharp enough to cut a man's backbone. For three cartons of cigarettes, you can buy a man's life.

"We make them down here in the cell," an inmate told me. "Take the match heads from a couple of books of matches. Mash that into a powder. Then we take the rims off the pencils or we use steel from an ink pen for the barrel. Sometimes we use the razor stock, whatever we can get hold of, and we reinforce that with plastic. We get toothpaste tubes, Crest and those things, and we make a mold and heat this and melt it down to make the bullets. Then we put the whole thing together and all we have to do is put a match to the match heads in the stem—and fire."

A setup is easiest as an arrangement of odds. Pick whom you want hurt or dead and place him in an enclosed area where his enemies or hit men are, and make sure that the would-be attackers have shanks. It works and it doesn't. Someone had two tries on a lanky black con named Arthur Anderson but missed both times. The first try was a zip gun blast into his cell but the bullet missed. The second time two whites tried to knife him but he fought them off. Anderson didn't count a third attempt because his would-be killers refused to cooperate. By remote control a guard had opened Anderson's cell door while nine white inmates were out on the corridor exercising. "They knew what was supposed to happen," Anderson sighed, "but they wasn't attacking for that pack of bulls. Sometimes, they don't like to be used."

"Me, myself," Anderson said, pointing a thumb to his chest, "police couldn't get me to put down nobody. 'Cause, I mean, he's the oppressor and I'm the oppressed." Anderson said the system among guards and prisoners is different in federal penitentiaries. There is very little factionalism. And federal guards seem to be more conscientious about things like searching for weapons. "Here," said Anderson, "they have a shakedown or something, they see a knife and they'll leave it. You feel that when the police go in there and he sees a knife in a cell, he's supposed to take it. I mean, they got this little place here—they call it max row—and it's more guys stabbed and cut up in here than all the other sections in this prison."

And the outside never hears about them. In Causey's case, the Soledad guards were aware, when they assigned Causey to exercise with five inmates from the Chicano group, of the virulent rancor between Causey, a "troublemaking Negro," and a number of Mexican-Americans in the wing. "The guards watched the killing," said Meneweather. "They watched with undisguised pleasure until Causey fell in a pool of his own blood. Then they sounded the alarm." Two Chicano prisoners were later tried for the Causey death and acquitted. They and the white guards testified that Causey—129 pounds on a five-foot-three-inch frame—attacked the six Chicanos with an ink pen but the men overpowered Causey, took the pen away from him and somehow, in the process, Causey was stabbed to death. It was a simple case of self-defense.

Asked about it three years later, a CDC official confirmed that Causey was assaulted by inmates. Five prisoners were out on the tier corridor exercising with Causey and four of the group attacked him. One guard said he saw two weapons and sounded the alarm, but by then Causey had been stabbed a number of times. The wounded black inmate had run toward the officer's area and collapsed at the front end of the corridor, where he died.

Causey was stabbed to death during a regular exercise period. Since "race was not considered a problem" at Soledad, it wasn't unusual that the guard's confidential incident report to CDC head-quarters in Sacramento neglected to mention that the attackers were white and the deceased black, or that racial tensions existed in O-wing.

Sometimes the guards themselves are responsible for an inmate's death. Eight months after Causey was stabbed, a black con named William A. Powell was slain in O-wing. Powell, an "insubordinate nigger," had refused to come out of his cell so that guards could, ostensibly, search his cell for weapons. The guards brought out tear gas guns, pumped enough into Powell's cell to knock him unconscious and dragged him out. When Powell regained consciousness, he began arguing and struggling. Three correctional officers, using the butt end of a gas gun, a billy club and a flashlight, smashed Powell back into a state of unconscious submission, according to inmates who said they saw the beating. Along with the thud of the weapons, prisoners on the tier heard the guards screaming racial slurs and curses. "They was so carried away," said an inmate witness, "they even forgot we were watching." Powell was carried to the prison hospital. Later that day, when some of the blacks asked about Powell's condition, the guards remained silent. The men noticed, however, that the guards were "nicer," letting the inmates stay out longer during the exercise period, passing out extra food and water rations. Days later, the prisoners were told that Powell died of a heart attack. An inmate who was working in the prison hospital when Powell was taken there said the battered black died from skull fractures. He had seen the medical reports. "We wrote the NAACP in San Francisco," one inmate said, "but none of the letters got out."

The official prison version of Powell's death was different. It stated that guards wanted to search Powell's cell because two shanks had been found on the tier that week. When asked to step out of his cell, Powell refused. Guards said they then asked an inmate to "reason with" Powell and gave the black con some time to "think it over." Powell still refused. The guards said they finally resorted to tear gas but claimed that the tear gas canisters they fired into Powell's cell had no effect on the adamant prisoner. Somehow, four guards "got him out." A search was made of the cell. Nothing was found. The official incident report said that Powell "developed some trouble breathing" as he was being carried to the officers' area. The guards applied artificial respiration and Powell began to breathe normally. He was taken to the prison hospital. At 2:20 P.M. that day, December 18, 1968, Soledad's civilian medical officer, Dr. Daniel Boone, checked on Powell and found him to be "O.K." Two hours later, when Dr. Boone made another check, he discovered that Powell had died. An official postmortem showed only one abnormality: a congestion in Powell's lungs. There was no follow-up investigation. No charges were considered, not even a reprimand.

Because of the Causey and Powell deaths, racial antagonism in O-wing was intense. Vengeance for violence and death to "snitches" are the two cornerstones of the convict code. The blacks in O-wing swore revenge. Aware of this, the guards stopped integrated exercises. The outdoor exercise yard, which had been used for basketball and handball, was closed. It was a time to tighten security. Henceforth, only one inmate at a time would be allowed out to exercise. Setups would have to cease. Still, the prisoners were plainly worried. Whites, aware that the blacks were intent on revenge, feared for their lives.

The blacks worried too. They were afraid the guards would arrange for more killings of their racial brothers. Tensions within the prison continued unabated.

By the summer of 1969, mutual fears and racial animosities between blacks and whites had increased to such intensity that five O-wing black prisoners tried to take their complaints and fears to court. Led by W. L. Nolen, a prison boxing champion who was quickly becoming politicized, the group filed civil suits against Warden Fitzharris, the Department of Corrections and several guards. The petitions filed by Nolen's group went much further than the case Robert Jordan had presented to the court. The Nolen suits charged that the guards were aware of "existing social and racial conflicts"; that the guards helped foment more racial strife by helping their white inmate "confederates" through "direct harassment in ways not actionable in court." Nolen meant that his charges would be hard to prove, like leaving a cell door open "to endanger the lives of the plaintiffs." Also hard to prove was the fact that the guards made "false disciplinary reports" to keep blacks on max row in the "hole" for longer periods of time.

The prisoners also petitioned the court to order O-wing guards to assign food porters from both races. This, they said, would stop the white porters from dumping "urine, excrement, cleanser and other inedible substances in the foodstuffs to be consumed by blacks." The blacks, of course, refused to eat the food—and went hungry.

At the same time, Nolen filed a separate civil suit against Fitzharris and his subordinates, charging Soledad officials with cruel and unusual punishment. In the suit, Nolen recalled that just months earlier he had been attacked by a group of "white Nazi-sympathizing inmates" while he was exercising on a tier corridor. He said prison guards watched the affair "indifferently," until they saw that he was winning. Then they jumped into the fight, pummeled Nolen to the ground and dragged the black con to a strip cell. The attack, he declared, was planned by guards with the "purposeful intent" of entering yet another bad conduct report in his file to "further arouse the hostility" of the Adult Authority parole board. He reminded the court that the parole officials are "guided solely by the reports and recommendations of the prison officials."

The last allegation in Nolen's suit was even more damaging to the prison. He swore that Soledad officials were "willfully creating and maintaining situations that creates and poses dangers to plaintiff [Nolen himself] and other members of his race." Nolen said he "feared for his life." The case never came to trial; four months after he wrote the petition Nolen was shot to death by an O-wing guard. Two other black inmates, one of whom signed Nolen's petition, were also shot to death.

The killing of W. L. Nolen, on January 13, 1970, began an incredible chain of tragedies that led the California prison system to disaster. The initial consequence was the first killing of a guard in Soledad history, a revenge murder, and from there the poison spread. In the nineteen months following the January 13 incident, at least forty persons were killed as a result of events and circumstances in the California prison system. Of the forty, nineteen murders are directly linked to the series of tragedies which began with the shooting of W. L. Nolen. For the killing of seven guards, two CDC staff members and a Marin County judge, twenty-one blacks and two whites, all inmates, have been charged. No CDC guards or staff have been charged with the shooting deaths of seven black inmates.

These men died:

W. L. Nolen, black inmate, shot by white guard, O. G. Miller.
Cleveland Edwards, black inmate, shot by white guard, O. G. Miller.
Alvin Miller, black inmate, shot by white guard, O. G. Miller.
John V. Mills, white guard, beaten and shoved to his death; George Jackson, Fleeta Drumgo and John Clutchette, three black inmates, charged, acquitted.

William Shull, white guard, stabbed to death; seven blacks charged, three went to trial, all acquitted.

Robert J. McCarthy, white guard, stabbed to death; Hugo Pinell, black inmate, charged.

Kenneth Conant, white prison administrator, stabbed to death; two whites charged.

William Christmas, black inmate, shot to death at the Marin Civic Center.

James McClain, black inmate, shot to death at Marin.

Jonathan Jackson, black youth, shot to death at Marin.

Harold J. Haley, white judge, shot to death at Marin; Ruchell Magee and Angela Davis charged; Davis acquitted, Magee on trial as this is written.

Richard L. McComas, guard lieutenant, gun suicide, after about a hundred Soledad inmates were transferred to Deuel; reportedly committed suicide because he feared for the lives of his men.

Leo Davis, white guard, stabbed to death while guarding a "snitch" who testified in the murder of guard Shull.

Paul Krasenes, white guard, stabbed and strangled to death.

Frank DeLeon, white guard, stabbed and shot to death.

Jere Graham, white guard, stabbed and shot to death; five blacks—Hugo Pinell, Fleeta Drumgo, John Larry Spain, David Johnson and Willie Tate—and two whites—an inmate named Luis Talamantes and an attorney named Stephen Bingham—charged with the three guards' deaths and the two stabbing deaths of:

John Lynn,

Ronald Kane.

George Jackson, shot to death by two white guards.

James Carr, considered George Jackson's closest friend on the outside, shot to death on lawn of his home; two whites charged.

Four other people were critically wounded in two of the above incidents but they survived:

Gary Thomas, assistant district attorney, Marin County, paralyzed from the waist down by gunshot wound to spinal column.

Kenneth McCray, white guard, throat slashed from ear to ear.

Charles Breckenridge, white guard, throat slashed badly.

Urbano Rubiaco, white guard, minor throat slashes, deep stab wounds to throat.

A great deal of blood has been running in the corridors and cells and yards of the state prison system. CDC officials say eighteen other inmates and a white guard were murdered in the same period of time for reasons ranging from racial conflicts to gambling debts to homosexual jealousies.

How did all this happen? How did it begin? What were the conditions and circumstances under which a militant black leader like Nolen was shot and killed in the first place? Why was most of the evidence suppressed? Why is it that even now state investigators, district attorneys and prison officials quickly gloss over and cover up the shooting deaths of other black inmates but bring the full power of penal, investigatory, judicial and media forces to bear in the deaths of prison guards? Why is it that the circumstances surrounding the death of an inmate, black or white, can be suppressed and forgotten while the killing of a guard cannot be hushed up or forgotten? And finally, what beatings, what killings, what fecal-infested food, what dark filthy isolation, what parole refusal, what lies, what other indignities and what insight led or compelled the blacks to lash out and kill seven white guards?

The answers begin at Soledad, with conditions of "a shocking and debased nature" as confirmed by a federal court; with bigoted guards who found it easy to practice both the subtler and the crasser forms of white racism, pitting white against black to foment racial hostilities; with a largely inept and lethargic administration which didn't know and didn't care what happened outside its own air-conditioned offices; with a listless CDC headquarters in Sacramento which was ineffectual in controlling either its various prison administrations or its individual guards; with judicial processes that—except for one brief honest moment—supported racism and oppressive conditions in the prison system by refusing to hear inmate petitioners and by refusing to guarantee due process of law for all inmates; with investigatory practices (some flagrantly illegal) which sought out evidence to support guard theories and twisted the truth to prove them but found it

easy to overlook, forget and suppress evidence to the contrary. All
these forces rushed to a cataclysm on January 13, 1970, when a corpulent white guard named Opie G. Miller squeezed off a shot that
struck the breastbone of W. L. Nolen, a politicized black inmate
who, for years, had been a close friend and comrade of a black
convict named George Jackson.

W. L. Nolen entered Soledad Prison in October 1963, after his
conviction as a participant in a grocery store robbery in Oakland. He
wasn't there long before he was transferred to Folsom and then to
San Quentin, in a routine, called "bus therapy" by the cons, by which
troublesome inmates are switched from prison to prison. It was in
San Quentin that Nolen met Jackson. As the two men became
politicized by what they observed and what they read, they cooperated in black awareness discussions and Marxist study groups. According to prison officials, both were involved in racial fights. Not much
else is known about Nolen's time at Quentin except that he won a
boxing title. He was transferred back to Soledad in February 1968.
Soledad officials say Nolen was "given a chance" on the main line,
mixing with the general population, but he was soon locked in the
Adjustment Center for threatening a white inmate with a knife. "The
officers in the Adjustment Center considered him a black racist,"
said Deputy Warden William Black. "I don't think he was a member
of any one organization but he was certainly a militant."

The Soledad Catholic chaplain, Father Gerad Lasko, remembered
Nolen as angrily militant but "a rather likable fellow." "He told me
a long time ago he didn't expect to get out of prison alive," Lasko
said. Nolen was convinced that the only way he could get out alive
would have been a reversal of the robbery conviction that put him in
prison in the first place. He had filed suits claiming that he was
mistakenly identified as a participant in the robbery and offered
alibi witnesses that he was elsewhere. He was serving the seventh
year of a five-year-to-life sentence and a higher court was considering
his appeal when he was shot and killed.

W. L.'s father, O. C. Nolen, said the robbery conviction "never was exactly proven." O. C., a tall, husky businessman, goes by his initials. ("They don't stand for nothin'. Just somethin' we do back in Arkansas.") With his wife, Addie, Nolen lives in a modest second-story stucco walk-up in East Oakland, a middle-class black section of tract homes laid out on square lawns jammed together on square blocks. O. C., his massive shoulders hunched over as he shuffled photographs and letters from his son, sat on a light brown sofa which was covered with clear protective vinyl. Addie Nolen, a lean woman of fifty with an oval face, light skin and deep-set eyes, sat on a wide vinyl-covered easy chair. She is a laundress.

O. C., who had been working as a bonderizer in a chemical plant, talked slowly and deliberately about his son, their migration from Arkansas to California and his son's troubles in school and out on the street. There was a succession of street fights and W. L. was sent to reform school. Once out of junvenile hall, Nolen had trouble re-entering school. "They wasn't too particular about kids that been in juvenile goin' back into school," said O. C. "They said that he would be behind in his studies and that it would make him be with kids that is not his equal." In the process, the young Nolen had an argument with his high school principal. The principal said Nolen had threatened him and the youth was expelled from school for the last time. He was sixteen. Against his expulsion orders, Nolen returned to the high school campus. School officials called the police and Nolen was sent back to reform school. He stayed in juvenile for two years. Several months after he was out he was arrested for the grocery store robbery and sent to Soledad on an indeterminate sentence, five years to life. He was nineteen.

"We visited him in Soledad," said Addie Nolen. "That is, whenever they would let us," she quickly added.

"No, we would visit him once a month," said O. C., "with the exception of sometimes they had restricted us visits. And we had some bad experience of visiting whiles he was down there. One time we went out on a visit and they had him chained, and with some kind of leather jacket on. They had his hands handcuffed to this jacket and had him brought in clanking shackles. I don't know why they did that. We was all inside of the buildin'. And they had a guard sit right down with us—a man, a special man sit right down with us to hear everything we said.

"And there was times we had been down and couldn't see him. They had him in what they call the 'hole,' where they use the extreme punishment. They had him in the hole for some time but that was because W. L. was a very frank-speakin' person. He didn't cut any corners about anything that he thought. After he come out and we saw him, he didn't 'laborate on it too much. He said that there was some mix-up with the guards and they had had arguments. This was about, yeah, about six months before he was shot."

The Nolens last saw their son in November, about two months before he was killed. "They let us stay the full visiting time," said Nolen's father. During this last visit, the young Nolen told his parents his life was in danger.

"W. L. explained to us," said O. C., "that the guards was out to get him. He said this in words. He said that they had been fixin' to open up a place where he did get killed. Here's how he said it to me. He says, 'Look, Dad, I'm not worried about it but they are trying to figure a way to get rid of me.' W. L. said, 'Now, they is gonna open up a yard out there and they gonna put me out there.' He was thinkin' they were gonna give somebody a weapon to try to get to him to do away with him. But he wasn't afraid of comin' in contact with a single individual even though they might have a weapon. That wasn't what he was afraid of at all. But he said, 'If they succeed in doin' away with me, I just want you to know what happened.' Isn't that what he said, Addie? That's exactly what he said. I said, 'Aw, I don't believe nothin' like that.' He said, 'Well, I'm not worried about it but this is what you can expect.' "

"That was in November," said Mrs. Nolen. "After Thanksgiving.

'Cause that's the last chance we got to see him because he was writin'
us and told us that our visitin' privilege was taken away from us. We
couldn't go back to see him. Then he got killed."

Nolen's principal antagonist among the prisoners was Billie D.
("Buzzard") Harris, a twenty-three-year-old white supremacist who
was serving time for grand theft and assault on a prisoner. A stocky,
barrel-chested kid from San Jose, Harris had grown up in Wilson,
Oklahoma, where he got as far as the eighth grade and no farther.
Before entering Soledad, he had worked as a beekeeper. The blacks
on max row called Harris the "chief nigger-baiter-in-residence." His
white friends in the prison's "Aryan Brotherhood" said Harris had
a "long chaw of hate for the niggers."

Even to guards Harris had been an aggressive, insubordinate con.
Periodic shakedowns of his cell yielded razor blades, needles, glass,
mirrors, and pieces of steel. He had been in numerous fights, many
of them racial brawls. In Folsom, he and six other whites had ganged
up on three blacks and beat them mercilessly. His outbursts against
guards included throwing urine and fecal matter and cursing and
threatening them. "Come down here and check my door," he yelled
at one O-wing guard, "and I will kick your ass." During one cell
shakedown, he twice slugged a guard in the chest, then stepped
back and taunted, "You come and get me, you son of a bitch."

Harris held particular hatred for the O-wing guards because,
according to him, they were lazy. "They want to get a job down there
so they don't have nothing to do. They just keep us locked up and
exercise a half hour and they lock us back up and their day is over,
except for the feeding."

Sometimes, said Harris, a guard would try to make friends with
him. " 'Yeah,' they'd say, 'I can't stand them niggers either.' " But
these whispered confessions of racial hatred were never uttered
during disciplinary hearings or in counseling groups. There, in those
group sessions, said Harris, "they would talk about how you are not

supposed to dislike colored kids or 'pity the Negro.' They did that inside the committee but outside, if they seen you and you were talking to them, they would make little sly remarks."

Although Harris hated Nolen, the Okie held a grudging respect for the black inmate leader. "I know he had respect," Harris said of Nolen. "I even give him respect even though to me he was nothing, you know. But I give him respect because he was, you know, he was a man. He had the respect coming that he put forth." Harris admired the way Nolen disturbed the guards. "They'd get mad," Harris recalled, "and tell him something and he would tell them something and they'd argue." Harris said the guards would jump on Nolen when the black was assigned as a tier tender, fabricating incidents like "not picking up the trash quick enough" or "being too slow in mopping. . . .

"Like I didn't even like him," Harris explained. "He's nothing to me, you know, but I will tell you he did clean the tier pretty quick. Because at that time there was maybe three other darkies down there and they kept putting him back out there working so he must have been doing a pretty good job."

Harris said the guards singled Nolen "out of his race. They did mess over him. Like they would go out and give him a bad recommendation in committee or [parole] board or anything, kept shooting him down and keeping him down there. Just little things to harass him. The main thing is Nolen didn't really never let nobody push him around." The guards even went so far as to insist that Nolen eat faster. Harris watched once when three O-wing guards tried to set Nolen up. Letting Nolen and an armed white inmate out on the tier at the same time, the guards stood back in the officers' area, smiling, to witness the expected fight. No fight materialized. A state official who later heard the story challenged Harris's version. "Why would they have three other guards just standing up there all smiles?" the official asked. "I had a mirror," Harris answered. "I could see them."

The importance of Harris's statements, of course, is that, with his fierce hatred of "Nolen and his niggers," he had no reason to lie about what he heard and what he observed. The most damaging recall Harris offered involved overhearing a conversation between two O-wing guards, R. A. Maddix and J. R. Dykes, who would later be involved in the yard murders. Dykes was one of the guards against whom Nolen had filed a suit. "If we could get him [Nolen] in a room for five minutes, we'd show him," Harris heard one guard say to the other. Harris said he overheard other things but refused to be specific. "In other words, they would whip on him," Harris summarized. "They felt they could?" Harris was asked. "Well," he answered, "they could have if they didn't think that he would file a writ on them."

After the Causey and Powell deaths, Harris and the rest of the Aryan Brotherhood prepared for the expected reopening of the outside yard with personal insults and racial challenges to the blacks. The blacks responded in kind. The whites believed, and rightly so, that the blacks wanted revenge for the killings, particularly for Causey. "There had been no retaliation for that kid," said Harris. "So they still had to show face, even though it's two years later. In your mind maybe it ain't right but that is neither here nor there. They had to do something as far as revenge for that because he was pretty well liked."

Sergeant R. A. Maddix, a stocky Southerner who carried his belly a few inches in front of his wide leather belt, was the program sergeant responsible for reopening the exercise yard. Although Maddix said he was aware of the "racial vendetta war" in O-wing, he stood by his decision that once the yard opened both blacks and whites would be placed in the yard to exercise together. The only way the staff was going to stop the racial war, he told a white trusty clerk named John Martin, was to put everyone on the yard, "and if there was trouble, kill a couple of those black bastards over there." As the opening of the yard approached, Maddix began talking about the officer who would man the gun tower. The gun guard selected was

Opie G. Miller, who, like other guards assigned to gun towers, had trouble getting along with almost any inmate, white or black."

On December 29, 1969, Maddix handed out mimeographed sheets to O-wing prisoners informing them about yard release procedures. The men would be allowed to exercise in groups of up to twenty-five. Each inmate would be allowed to carry a towel, since all the showering would be done in the newly installed yard showers. "When maximum yard is announced," Maddix had written, "each inmate who desires to go to the yard will remove his clothing and stand by with his clothes in his arms for release. *Failure to prepare for yard release,"* the directive continued in underlined type, *"will be considered refusal to exercise, and will result in the inmate's exercise for that period being cancelled."* Maddix's handout then directed the inmates to the O-wing sally port, a five-by-five-foot caged area, where the men would be given an unclothed body search. "So please cooperate," Maddix concluded, and signed his name.

When the prisoners considered the underlined sentence, mulling it over together with the almost constant exchanges of racial taunts and insults and the sly digs from Maddix and other guards, they concluded that "failure to prepare for yard release" was somehow equivalent to a lack of courage or simple fear. "It was like an insult," a black con told me. "They knew we was gonna get it on but they wanted to make sure so they slip this chickenshit thing in. But these guys don't have the tendency to be afraid. There'll be so much trouble every day, we lose the fear of death and things because we see it all the time. You could get killed anytime, you know, so we don't fear dying. We were mad because this tension had built up. So we didn't care about the fighting. It was more of a pride thing. No one is going to lay back in there and be scared to go up to the yard. If the yard opened, everyone would go out. Jug Miller, he said he felt like somebody was going to get killed. He had this feeling, you know. He's expressed that but still he went out. And everybody went out. When it came time, it was kind of quiet, though, going out."

■

The whites also had to summon courage to go into the yard, but most had agreed that if the gun guard started shooting, they had less to worry about than the blacks. "The guards wanted to get rid of some hard rocks at the prison, especially Nolen," said a white O-wing con named Howard ("Smiley") Hoyle. Hoyle, who constantly exemplified his nickname with blue eyes squinting under a tuft of blond hair, was doing five to life for burglary. He remembered that about a month before the exercise yard reopened, Nolen had argued with several of the guards about being fired from his porter's job. Black inmates said Nolen wanted to retain the job so he could keep an eye on the white tier tenders who were passing out the food trays, making certain they wouldn't put ground glass in the food or rub a little feces around the rim of a cup. Some hours after the argument, Nolen asked Officer Dykes (against whom he had filed a writ) if he could have the black culture and history books which had been left in Ed Whiteside's cell. Nolen told Dykes he had permission to read them while his comrade was in strip cell isolation. Dykes, who Nolen thought hated him, told him that he would pass the books out to whoever he felt should have them. The two continued to argue and finally Dykes opened Nolen's cell door slightly and ordered Nolen to put his hands out to be handcuffed. If Nolen was that smartass, he could do with a little time in isolation himself. Nolen refused to stick his hands out. Dykes, alone on the corridor with Nolen, called Nolen a motherfucker and yelled for help. Several guards came running and all jumped in to fight Nolen. Finally, one guard smashed Nolen over the head with a tear gas gun, knocking him unconscious. He was dragged off to a strip cell.

The other black inmates on max row protested. They did about the only thing that came to mind: they threw urine and fecal matter at Dykes whenever he walked by the cells. "We threw some liquid on the man," one black prisoner told me, smiling. "Next time he came by, we threw some more liquid on the man." After one toss, the guards concluded that some of the stuff was flying out of Hugo Pinell's cell. The officers came back down the corridor with tear gas guns and sprayed Pinell's cell and those on either side of him. "Come on out," the guards ordered. "I ain't comin out," Pinell answered. The guards fired more salvos of gas into his cell. "Come on out, take all your clothes off and back up to the door and let me put these handcuffs on you," a guard instructed. Pinell was trying to say that he'd had enough but he couldn't speak because he was choking on the gas. He waved a white towel. The guards put cuffs on Pinell, Thomas Meneweather and another black prisoner and dragged them to the strip cells, where they were locked in for fifteen days with R.D. —restricted diet—and total darkness.

(Within two years, Pinell would be charged with the stabbing death of a Soledad guard. Later, while on transfer to San Quentin to undergo neurological and psychiatric tests, Pinell was, among others, charged with the murder of three guards and two white inmates, and the attempted murder of three other guards, in the August 1971 incident in which George Jackson was shot and killed.)

At Soledad, "Yogi" Pinell, a twenty-eight-year-old Nicaraguan mulatto doing time for rape, was a close friend of Nolen's. He had been placed on max row for "assaultive behavior." Pinell said he had a premonition about the exercise yard. Days before it was reopened, he begged Nolen not to go out into the yard. "I'm tired," Nolen told Pinell. "I'm sick from the pressures. I've got to go out there."

Yogi was also disturbed by Sergeant Maddix's underlined sentence in the mimeographed handout. "This was the only underlined paragraph in the whole yard list," Pinell commented. "Can you imagine the effect it would have on an inmate of maximum security caliber, after reading that underlined paragraph? It sounds like a provocation. What was the result? Everyone went out. Common sense would indicate that after being segregated for so long, it would be reasonable to expect one or two fistfights." When the yard finally opened, Yogi wasn't even there. He had been taken to a court hearing.

The day before the yard opened, the men on max row were given chest x-rays by the Monterey County public health agency. Bob Hayward, a white con who was working on a fifteen-to-life sentence for robbery and attempted murder and was chairman of the Inmate Advisory Council, was helping with the checkups. As each Adjustment Center con stepped into the van for his x-ray, Hayward listened while a guard commented on each. When Nolen glared at the guard before stepping into the van, the guard said, "Now, there is an asshole who is never going to get out. Either somebody is going to kill him or we're going to."

Like Pinell, Alvin ("Jug") Miller had bad vibes about the yard. Miller, described as a follower of Nolen's, had been in his share of racial brawls in prison, during one of which he was stabbed in the back on an upstairs tier in the Adjustment Center. Transferred to San Quentin, he was returned to Soledad after about a year. Jug Miller, short and slight of build, was doing five to life for robbery, and his CDC "make-sheet" said he was "considered a racist and allies with Black Extremists." Five days before the yard opened, Miller wrote a letter to his parents in Los Angeles.

> My dear Mother & Dad,
> I received your letter today 1-8-70. It found me
> well and very proud to here from you and Dad as always.
> . . . Things have been sort of tence latley. Don't know
> what might happen but don't worry. I'm trying to stay
> out of trouble if I can but got to take care of myself
> also. I hope you understand. I wish I could talk to you
> and explain what the facts are about this hole I'm in
> but sence I can't, please believe me. I don't get in
> trouble unless it is necessary. Please understand. All
> I want to do is come home, thats all, but in a place
> like this I had to learn to accept it as it comes. So,
> Mother and Dad, please don't think I'm all bad because
> some things you just can't get away from. But please
> remember I'm trying to be good.

As long as I know my loving Mom and Dad are well and fine, I'm fine. So try not to worry too much because before I get into bed I say a prayer for you and Dad every night, hoping that my absences from home doesn't get you too upset, especially when I get into anything I can't help. . . .
Will close for now.

Love Always
Sweet Black Jug
Loving Mom and Dad

Jug Miller added a short postscript, using a code that varies from inmate to inmate: "P.S. the weather is pretty bad up now. Rain and earth quakes. I think it might be a storm. Smiles." Danger but optimism, his father thought when he read the postscript.

Jug's body arrived before his letter.

The O-wing exercise yard, a 40-by-150-foot concrete rectangle, was flanked on the west by O-wing's drab beige brick wall and on the east by the prison's hospital wing. Across the length of the yard, parallel to the hospital wing, ran a twelve-foot-high cyclone fence, topped with rolls of barbed wire. The north end of the yard was enclosed by a fifteen-foot-high wall of cinder blocks. The south end was closed off by a perpendicular continuation of the cyclone fence, separating the yard from the dental offices. On the southeast corner, extending into the yard from the medical area, was a concrete ramp that connected the yard with the hospital waiting room. Entrance to the hospital, if needed, was through two locked doors.

Along the O-wing wall prison officials had placed a heavy punching bag, a speed bag, a pull-up bar, a water fountain and an open-air shower platform. A basketball hoop and backstop stood at the center of the yard near the south end, while the north end wall served as a backstop for handball. Twenty feet over the yard, atop the dental wing on the south end, Soledad workmen had erected a wooden booth, the new gun tower for the yard. In the booth that January morning was Opie G. Miller, a retired Army man and a reputed expert with the .30 caliber semiautomatic which he held in his hands.

Miller, fifty-one, had joined the Soledad guard staff in August 1962, a year after he retired from the Army as a noncom with twenty years' service. A short, stocky man with an oval face and slightly receding cropped hair, Miller was a product of Woden, Texas, a small agricultural town that is excluded from most atlases. As a guard, Miller had a reputation among prisoners and staff of being sullen and severe. That was probably the reason he was often assigned to standing watches in gun towers, where he would have little, if any, direct contact with inmates. Two days before the opening of the yard, Miller was "checked out" in the use of the .30 caliber rifle. As in the past, he performed well.

On the morning of January 13, John Martin, the trusty, had just finished his clerical duties for the guards in O-wing. The young white inmate was sitting on a table in the officers' area when Sergeant Maddix picked up the intraprison telephone and called the gun booth where Opie Miller had been sitting since 7:55 A.M. Maddix said he was about to open the yard.

The release for yard exercise began at 8:45 A.M., when W. L. Nolen's cell door was opened by a switch in the officers' area. "Prepare for yard release," a guard yelled down the max row corridor. Nolen stepped out of his cell and walked down the corridor to the cagelike sally port. As directed by the mimeographed sheet handed out by Sergeant Maddix two weeks earlier, Nolen carried his clothing and a towel under his arms. Inside the sally port, he handed a guard the towel and his clothes, which consisted of coveralls, foam rubber shower shoes, a T-shirt, shorts and socks. While the clothes were being examined for shanks and razor blades by one guard, a second officer conducted a skin search, looking for concealed weapons in the prisoner's mouth, under his tongue, in his hair, in and behind his ears, under his armpits, between his toes, under his feet and in and around his rectum and genitals. The skin search is routine for all prisoners entering and leaving the maximum security cell area. "Spread 'em," a guard ordered. Nolen grabbed his buttocks and leaned forward. The other officer handed Nolen his clothing and the inmate dressed to enter the exercise yard.

Nolen was the first prisoner released into the yard. As he stepped onto the concrete pavement in the quiet gray moments of that Monterey winter's morning, he could look back over his right shoulder and see the armed guard, Opie Miller, above and behind him some thirty feet way. Nolen walked away from the gun, stepping across the thin puddles of rain water toward the handball area at the north end.

Two white inmates—a lanky, lean-faced Chicano named Joseph ("Colorado") Ariaz and Smiley Hoyle—entered the yard after Nolen. The make-sheet on Ariaz described him as "assaultive" and noted that the Chicano "boasts about disliking niggers and considers them less than human." According to prison records, Hoyle himself was a racist. Just months earlier, he had stabbed a black prisoner in another wing of the prison. That's what landed Hoyle in the A/C in the first place. Ariaz and Hoyle ambled over to the fence near the concrete ramp leading to the hospital wing and joked with a homosexual who was leaning from an upstairs hospital window.

Minutes later, Richard ("Cactus") Ferguson, "Hawaiian John" Fanene and Billie ("Buzzard") Harris joined the two near the hospital fence. Ferguson, twenty-two, was doing three to life. Guards said he enjoyed playing a "tough guy" role and was the "leader" in several "riotous situations in the Adjustment Center." Fanene, twenty-four, was of Samoan ancestry. Soledad officials said he was "not necessarily a racist, but identified with whites." They described his behavior as "assaultive," placed him on max row for spitting on guards and burning prison property. Harris was, as mentioned, a white supremacist.

By the time the white trio joined their comrades at the hospital fence, three other black inmates—Earl Satcher, Ed Whiteside and John Randolph—were in the yard and had joined Nolen at the far north end. Satcher, twenty-eight, a tall, powerfully built Black Panther from Long Beach, California, was serving five to life for robbery and auto theft. A prolific poet, Satcher was, according to prison officials, "a black racist" and "known for his Black Nationalist activities." When he entered the yard, Opie Miller motioned Satcher to proceed to the farther end. Satcher walked over to Nolen and they slapped hands and talked.

John Randolph, twenty-five, was also a Black Panther. Although Randolph was serving a relatively brief sentence, six months to five years for manslaughter by automobile, the O-wing program administrator, E. A. Petersen, said Randolph "demonstrated racial agitation in all [prison] facilities" he had been in before coming to Soledad. Associate Warden Clem Swagerty (whom prisoners described as a white racist) said Randolph was an "extreme racist that has been found with flammatory literature, fire setting devices and threats to the President." The associate warden noted that Randolph had "numerous transfers due to racial problems and appears to be an adjustment center case until his discharge."

Ed Whiteside, twenty-six, had been transferred to Soledad from Folsom because of his participation in racial fights there. Doing one to life for second degree robbery, Whiteside, said Soledad officials, "has demonstrated extreme hostility towards the staff." Whiteside and Randolph joined Nolen and Satcher and the four men took a few steps to the center of the handball court and began warming up, slapping the handball against the cinderblock backstop. Nolen and Randolph played for a while but the ball sailed over the fence and they stopped. When someone threw the ball back over the high fence, Whiteside took Nolen's place. Satcher, both hands hanging onto the ends of a white towel around his neck, laughed and joked and acted as a sort of greeter to other black prisoners as they entered the yard.

Raymond Guerrero, twenty-nine, a white inmate doing six months to ten years for narcotics possession, was another veteran of racial brawls. Soledad officials said Guerrero had, just two months before this date, been in a fight in which a black was badly beaten. Guerrero was the eleventh man into the yard. While he was joining the whites at the south end, Hawaiian John Fanene left the group, walked to the heavy punching bag along the O-wing wall and began pounding it. Between jabbing combinations, Fanene looked toward the gun tower. He said Miller, the gun guard, held the rifle "poised," as if ready to fire. This worried Fanene because he had been wounded in the yard at San Quentin and still carried the scars. Fanene stopped working on the heavy bag and moved over to the speed-punching bag, where he kept watching the tower as he punched.

When Thomas Meneweather entered the yard, he "automatically" glanced up toward the gun tower and found himself "looking into the muzzle of O. G.'s carbine." Meneweather, Soledad officials said, had a "serious disciplinary record." He made zip guns and bombs and furnished them to other blacks on max row. When he entered the yard, Miller motioned him to the north end with a wave of the gun barrel. Meneweather challenged Randolph to a game of handball.

While Fanene punched the speed bag and glanced nervously at the gun tower, another white racist was cleared for yard exercise. Noted for "extreme assaultiveness" and as a man who "hates blacks," Ronnie Dean ("Harpo") Harper was twenty-one years old and serving a life sentence without possibility of parole for kidnapping for purposes of robbery. Worse for this day, Harpo was a close friend of the whites responsible for Clarence Causey's death, thus having earned a special hatred from the blacks, who wanted to "tattoo some knuckles onto the man's face." Harpo Harper joined the whites near the hospital fence.

The last two blacks to enter the yard were Cleveland Edwards and Alvin ("Jug") Miller. Edwards, twenty, was doing a relatively lengthy six months to ten years for struggling with a police officer. Soledad officials didn't like Edwards because he had a "negative attitude towards authority." Petersen, the O-wing administrator who ordered the opening of the exercise yard, knew that Edwards had "attacked Harpo Harper while both were serving isolation sentences and beat him severely." Twenty-three-year-old Jug Miller, who would die within minutes, was serving five to life for robbery.

The last inmate to enter the yard before the shooting began was Robert ("Chuko") Wendekier, twenty-one, a white con who was doing six months to five years for possession of a weapon. According to prison records, Wendekier was noted for "riotous behavior" and had "assaulted a number of inmates." Prison officials said that Wendekier, a Hawaiian, "goes with whites when trouble starts."

By now, fifteen men had entered the yard. Each had been skin-searched for weapons. Almost all were considered "racist" by prison officials. Almost all had a prison record of racial fighting. All were aware of the racial score to be settled for the Causey killing. Since they were unarmed, no one expected to get killed, but a free-swinging, knee-jabbing, foot-stomping melee was anticipated as guards, inmates and prison staff awaited the beginning spark. It was like placing scorpions and black widow spiders in a shoebox. O-wing administrator Petersen knew that Billie Harris, whom Petersen described as a "racial agitator," would be placed in the yard with Ed Whiteside and Eugene Grady, two blacks who had just fought with Harris in a racial battle at Folsom, a fight in which seven men were wounded. Worse, Petersen knew that Harris was a good friend of a white con named Tommy Kendrick, whom Petersen said was involved in the killing of Clarence Causey. Worse still, as Petersen admitted in a confidential memo to Warden Fitzharris, "Most of the men [in the yard] have been to the other lock-ups [prisons] at one time or another and know most of the inmates in the other lock-ups. The hate or alliances go deep and many are of long years standing, i.e., a friend of mine was stabbed by a friend of yours, so I'm going to have to stab you."

Eight whites and seven blacks were in the yard when the shooting started. They had been released for yard exercise in the following order:

W. L. Nolen	Black
Joseph ("Colorado") Ariaz	White
Howard L. ("Smiley") Hoyle	White

Earl Satcher	Black
Richard A. ("Cactus") Ferguson	White
Edward Whiteside	Black
Eric ("Hawaiian John") Fanene	White
John Randolph	Black
Billie D. ("Buzzard") Harris	White
Thomas Lopez Meneweather	Black
Raymond Rodriguez Guerrero	White
Ronnie D. ("Harpo") Harper	White
Cleveland Edwards	Black
Alvin ("Jug") Miller	Black
Robert ("Chuko") Wendekier	White

An eighth black, Eugene Grady, was also scheduled for exercise. Grady, rotund and soft-spoken, had just completed the skin search and was putting on his shorts when the first shot was fired.

The carnage began shortly after Chuko Wendekier entered the yard. Wendekier walked under the basketball hoop in the center of the yard and ambled over to the fence, where he began talking with Harper, Harris and Fanene, who had just stopped punching the speed bag. The four men laughed and joked about the "niggers" playing handball, about getting out on the yard for the first time in more than a year, about the anticipated fistfight and about the gun guard pointing the rifle around.

When Fanene left the speed bag, W. L. Nolen began punching it. Nolen called to Meneweather, who had been helping Nolen with his court petitions against the prison, and suggested that they punch the heavy bag. Nolen worked with the heavy bag while Meneweather held it and watched. Meneweather had also been anxious about the gun tower. He noticed that the gun guard had his aim on them as they approached the bag and kept the rifle leveled at them while Nolen punched it.

Nolen, who had won most of the boxing matches he fought in prison tournaments, had just given the heavy bag a few combinations when Wendekier approached the drinking fountain along the O-wing wall. As Chuko passed near him, Nolen yelled at him and threw a quick right, slamming his knuckles into the white con's forehead. Wendekier returned three punches, then decided that Nolen, with his boxing experience, was too big and too fast to square off against. Chuko dove for Nolen's legs, grabbing his blue denim trouser legs, trying to pull Nolen down. Meanwhile, Fanene, who had walked up with Wendekier, was standing slightly behind Chuko. Fanene threw a few punches at Nolen, punches that whizzed past Wendekier's ear, but he missed. Fanene, his mind flashing quickly on the scar he still bore from the San Quentin yard, turned once more to look at the gun guard. He watched as Opie G. Miller aimed and fired.

The first bullet tore into Nolen's chest, piercing his body just to the right of the breastbone. A white witness saw Nolen sag to his knees, clap his hands behind his head, elbows shaking, and fall forward, his forehead slamming into the concrete. Wendekier said he kicked Nolen a few times, unaware that Nolen was bleeding to death. Meneweather, who had let go of the bag he was holding for Nolen, started for Chuko to stop him from kicking his black friend. He didn't reach Wendekier because Billie Harris and Harpo Harper jumped him first.

"Watch out," Cleveland Edwards yelled at Meneweather.

Meneweather, a powerfully built man and a judo expert, turned to meet Harris and Harper. He caught Harris in midair, letting the white con's momentum carry him, and threw Harris to the pavement. Edwards called that he would look after Nolen but as he ran toward the fallen black leader the gun guard squeezed off another shot. Edwards grabbed his stomach and fell on his face. The shot went through Edwards and smashed into Meneweather's left hand.

John Randolph and Ed Whiteside were playing handball when they heard the rifle shots. They spun around and saw Edwards fall to the concrete, holding his stomach. Randolph started running, zigzagging toward the fence near the hospital, then back toward the shower stalls. He heard another shot. The bullet hit Jug Miller in the gut as Miller was running along the O-wing wall toward the fight scene. Randolph, who was just a few steps away, tried to grab Jug

Miller to stop him from falling but he couldn't. Miller was dead weight. He fell near the pull-up bar and speed bag as Randolph let go and turned to face Billie Harris, who had got up from Meneweather's judo throw. Randolph and Harris glared briefly at each other. Then, glancing at the carnage around him, Harris decided to stop fighting. He walked a few steps, paused, and felt a burning sensation in his groin. He had been shot in the testicles.

Satcher, who had been pacing back and forth in the northwest corner of the yard, also had headed for the fight. By the time he got to the middle of the yard, at least three shots had been fired. Satcher squared off against Cactus Ferguson, each feinting with left jabs and threatening rights, but neither landed a punch. When the fourth bullet was fired and both men noticed that inmates had actually been shot, they put their hands down. Two of the wounded blacks moaned. Harris, a testicle shot off, sat on the concrete pavement, loudly cursing the blacks and the gun guard. Satcher cupped his hands to his mouth and yelled, "It's all over with."

"Well, it better be all over with," Opie Miller, the gun guard, yelled back.

The four surviving black prisoners first tried to figure out who was the most seriously wounded. Satcher and Randolph, kneeling over Nolen, asked how badly he was hit. "I'm probably hit in the leg," said Nolen, but his shirt showed bleeding in the chest and back. The men decided to move Jug Miller.

"Everyone was now waiting for the doctor," said a witness, "but after about ten minutes nothing happened. We then began hollering to the gunman in the tower to open up the emergency gate to the hospital, but he refused and just stood there with his rifle aimed at us." After fifteen minutes passed, Meneweather decided to try to take Jug Miller off the yard. He kneeled down so two other black cons could place Miller across his back and shoulders. "I started to walk toward the door through which we had entered the yard," said Meneweather, "but the tower guard pointed the gun at me and shook his head. Then I started forward with tears in my eyes, expecting to be shot down every second, but the tower guard told me, 'That's far enough.' "

"If you take another step, it'll be your last," Opie Miller shouted from the tower. "Nobody leaves the yard until I get an official O.K."

John Randolph and Ed Whiteside carried W. L. Nolen up the hospital ramp but they were stopped by a guard who pointed a tear gas gun in their faces. "I started cussing and inching forward," said Randolph, "until the gunman in the tower told me to stop and pointed his rifle at us. So we stopped."

By this time, Nolen had drifted into shock and was trying to swallow his tongue. Randolph slapped Nolen's face and the wounded man calmed down. But a minute later Nolen's eyes rolled up to the top of his head and he started biting his tongue. "I began slapping his face again," said Randolph, "but to no avail."

While the blacks were arguing with the guards about taking the wounded off the yard, two white prisoners—Ariaz and Guerrero—moved to the north end of the yard and played handball. They played for about ten minutes.

Finally, three guards and two MTAs (civilian medical technical assistants) appeared at the O-wing sally port and walked onto the yard. The guards were carrying tear gas guns. An MTA stopped by each of the wounded black prisoners and mutely shook his head three times. The guards said the wounded could be brought in off the yard but that the men would enter through O-wing instead of directly up the hospital ramp to the emergency rooms. This meant a long circuitous route to the hospital, through the series of O-wing doors, down part of the prison's main-line corridor and through the hospital security doors. Both the blacks and the whites protested, arguing that the hospital gate, whose ramp jutted out into the yard barely twenty feet from the wounded men, should be opened. They knew that prison laundry was taken in through there almost every day. The guards refused.

There was more trouble as the men were carried in. Once inside the officers' area, Ed Whiteside slugged Cactus Ferguson, who was helping Wendekier carry Billie Harris into the wing. That blow started a second fight and the guards joined in. Harris, who sat crumpled on the floor with his groin wound, said he watched while three guards battered Whiteside and Randolph with billy clubs.

The bullets that ripped into Nolen, Edwards and Miller did not kill the men outright. According to witnesses, all three men lay bleeding in the yard for fifteen to twenty minutes before officials would unlock any gates to take them off the yard. The guards never did unlock the two doors which led directly to the prison hospital.

A "corrected copy" of the highly confidential report of the chief medical officer at Soledad, Dr. Daniel W. Boone, stated that Nolen "was brought to the hospital in a moribund condition . . . from a circular 4 mm. wound in the right 4th interspace just to the right of the sternum." The bullet was about as close to the middle of a man's chest as a shot can be placed.

Jug Miller, the doctor said, was brought to surgery in a "near moribund state." Miller had a four-millimeter circular wound in the "epigastrium just below the xyphoid process." In layman's terms that means just below the middle chest, slightly above dead center on the stomach.

Cleveland Edwards was carried into the prison hospital "bleeding profusely from the left femoral area," a large artery in the groin. Boone reported that he tried to expose the severed vessels to control the hemorrhaging but by then the "subject had already succumbed."

Billie ("Buzzard") Harris lost a testicle.

After the other prisoners were returned to their cells, a guard walked along the tier to check on other wounds. Meneweather pointed to a bullet wound in his hand. Randolph complained of a bleeding head wound. An hour after the shooting, an MTA went through max row, stopping by the cell of each inmate who had complained of a wound or an abrasion to ask whether he wanted medical attention.

"No, I don't need anything," Randolph answered, "but how are the wounded? How's Nolen?"

"Fine," the MTA answered.

"And Edwards and Miller?"

"Fine." The MTA laughed. "They're just fine."

Before that medical check was made, even before the water from the high-powered hoses washed the blood from the cement yard, word of the killings flashed among the 2,700 inmates in the other wings. The blood on the yard, witnesses said, would have shown four victims at four different locations. Prison officials, explaining that four shots were fired into a single mob, would dispute that later. When state investigators arrived, the yard was clean.

"They called here," said W. L.'s father, O. C. Nolen. "When the first guard called up, it had just happened. 'Mr. Nolen,' he says, 'afraid your boy got hurt. Fact,' he said, 'I think he's killed.' So I said, 'Wait a minute. You mean to say W. L.?' 'Yeah,' he says. So he got a little nervous. So I said, 'Calm yourself down and tell me how it happened.' " The guard had trouble explaining to the elder Nolen what had happened. "I can't understand what you're talking about," Nolen complained to the guard. "Make yourself clear." The guard turned the telephone over to Warden Fitzharris.

"Fitzharris," said Nolen, "was the one who explained to me that W. L. had got killed. He said W. L. and two other black boys had got killed. Well, he said it was an accident. So I said, 'Accident?' He said, 'Well, they got shot accidentally.' It was about 10:30 or 11:00 A.M. [The three were killed about 9:15 A.M.] They didn't make no explanation. I think he said they got shot accidentally. I'm almost sure those were the words he used. Then I called back to try to get other information, which wasn't too much. There was three black boys had got killed and one Caucasian had got shot accidentally."

"They changed the story all the way down the line," Addie Nolen added. "We have some of them stories. We didn't keep up with it but I know it was a different story every day. Then W. L. come home. They released it [the body] that Thursday."

"Well," said Mr. Nolen, "the mortuary never did bring up anything about the gunshot wounds."

"We didn't ask," said Mrs. Nolen, " 'cause they was trying to let it go as light as they could, you know. They was trying to do it as quick as possible with us."

In the days that followed, Soledad officials issued several versions of the incident. Immediately after the shootings, Ellsworth Ferguson, a prison spokesman, said a fight broke out among sixteen inmates who were brought to the yard for exercise. A guard yelled and whistled for the men to stop fighting, but the men wouldn't stop. Then, said Ferguson, "fearing that some of them would be injured," the guard "fired four times at the edge of the crowd." Later that day, Warden Fitzharris said the guard believed that the attackers were beating their victims to death and fired only to save the victims. He did not mention race.

That evening, the prison leaked a more incredible report, stating that a group of black prisoners were trying to castrate a white inmate but the guard fired into a crowd to break it up. There was no mention of what weapon might have been used in the castration attempt. There was no mention of the fact that each prisoner on the yard had been skin-searched. No one suggested that fights are common in prison or the fact that the killing of the antagonists was unprecedented. It was strange, however, that the white prisoner whom the gun guard was trying to save from castration was shot in the groin by that very same guard.

Even Billie Harris, the white leader and presumed castration victim, complained of the shooting. "They had no right to shoot those hammers. Hell, it was just a fistfight." Besides, Harris added, the guards expected a fistfight. It was like "Cassius Clay and Joe Frazier." In fact, said Harris, many guards wanted "ringside seats."

Some time after the yard tragedy, Billie Harris submitted to a deposition on the events at Soledad. The deposition, a stenographed question-and-answer session, occurred because the families of the three slain black cons, represented by San Francisco attorney Melvin Belli and his associate John Hill, filed suits against the CDC and Soledad Prison. In the following exchange, Harris is questioned by Charles Kirk, a deputy attorney general, who was representing the prison in the legal suit.

Q: Were any of the men there on max row known as racists?
A: Sure.
Q: Who?
A: Me, for one. . . .
Q: Was there any talk among the inmates about who was going to be the gun in the tower?
A: Yes, there was a lot of talk about who was going to be up there.
Q: What was the talk about?
A: Heard that he was a dog, but I don't know.
Q: What do you mean by a "dog"?
A: Not a [real] dog, but you know, he didn't like too many people.
Q: Did they say he was a racist?
A: Yeah, I heard that. . . .
Q: Were you looking forward to the opening of the yard?
A: What forward do you mean?
Q: Well, were you looking forward to a chance to exercise?
A: We knew there wasn't going to be no exercise.
Q: What was it going to be?
A: Go out there and fight a while and then maybe after everybody is off isolation, we might go out there and exercise now and then.
Q: You thought there would be a fight at first?
A: Everybody knew that. There was no thinking.

To the public and the press, Soledad officials refrained from using the word "race" or even alluding to racial problems at the prison in their early versions of what happened. Within the week, however, Warden Fitzharris admitted that "a whole bunch of pent-up animosities, mostly along racial lines," set up the fight. He announced that there would be two investigations, one by the CDC and one by the Monterey County district attorney's office. Fitzharris said sixteen prisoners were involved, that most of the prisoners on the yard were beating up on two others and that the guard fired into a "milling mass of prisoners after they ignored his shouts and whistles warning them to stop. . . . It was thought," Fitzharris added, "that the gun would keep them from fighting."

What Fitzharris and his aides told the press differed substantially from what they were telling their CDC superiors in Sacramento. But even CDC director Raymond Procunier and his staff were not getting the full truth from Soledad.

The first secret incident report to reach Procunier was drafted by Soledad associate warden Clem Swagerty, a lean blond Southerner. It was an intriguing four-page document, whose title—"Racial Gang Fight on O-wing Yard, Sixteen (16) inmates involved, Four shots fired and four men wounded and removed from the yard"—was comparable in length to the eyewitness accounts submitted by the guards. Only when the reader reached the final words of the twenty-line synopsis did he learn that anyone had died from the shooting.

Here is Swagerty's narrative of what happened:

On January 13, 1970, at approximately 9:15 A.M., it was necessary to fire four shots in order to stop a gang fight in the O-wing yard. Release to the yard had been almost completed, lacking only one inmate to go to the yard when a gang fight erupted, involving blacks against whites. There were eight Negroes on the yard, four Caucasians, two Mexicans, one Samoan and one Hawaiian. From the Gun Officer's observations it appeared that the blacks were pressing the fight when the white inmates made a stand and they were attack [sic]. It appeared that Nolen A-77268 (Deceased) and Satcher A-70893 were leading the black attack. All inmates became involved in the fight and when the Officer's whistle was ignored, it appeared that several negro's [sic] had one white man down and were severely beating him. The Officer, at that time, fired two shots with no effect as the group continued to press the fight. Two more shots were fired and at that time Satcher stood waving his arms to the group and the Gun Officer calling for truce. The two groups then ceased fighting and went to different sections of the yard based on ethnic groups. The hospital was called for medical assistance and gurneys, and they responded immediately. Additional staff was called into the unit to facilitate moving the wounded and the lock-up of the remaining inmates on the yard. Inmate Satcher assisted in carrying one of the wounded inmates into the first floor of O-wing.

Inmates Wendekier B-12961 and Ferguson B-3785 assisted in carrying inmate Harris into the first floor of O-wing. After they had placed Harris on a table and were in the process of a lock-up, inmate Randolph B-3841 attempted to attack them and had to be physically subdued and handcuffed before he was locked up. Apparently the only personnel injured in the incident was Captain [Charles] Moody who suffered a bite on the hand from Randolph.

After the men were locked up, Swagerty said they were charged with violation of Director's Rule D-1201, Inmate Behavior, and all were found guilty of the charge. The whites were sentenced to twenty days of in-cell status, no exercise; the blacks were sentenced to twenty-nine days. No explanations were offered as to why the blacks were confined to cell isolation for an extra nine days.

Also on the CDC director's desk was the official but secret eyewitness account of Opie Miller, the gun guard. His full report read as follows:

At approximately 9:10 A.M., this date, I was on duty as O-wing Yard Tower Officer while the Maximum Security Row inmates were being released for yard exercise for the first time, with a total of sixteen (16) inmates on the yard (eight [8] white and eight [8] negro.) The Negro inmates, with a signal, led by inmates Nolen A-77268; Satcher A-70893 and Miller B-16243, converged on the group of white inmates and attack [Opie Miller has exactly the same spelling problem as the associate warden; one wonders if the same person wrote both reports] the group of whites against the wall in the shower area. I immediately blew my whistle loudly several times, then fired at the legs of two inmates assaulting inmates who were down against the wall. I could not determine whether they had weapons or not. It was apparent to me that they meant to kill as many of each other as possible and did not mind if they were killed in the process. As soon as the blacks saw that several of their group were wounded and were outnumbered, they broke off this attack and inmate Satcher started yelling for a truce, saying "It is all over. Let's quit this and get those that are hurt out." The fighting stopped and they started yelling to get the wounded out. The yard was cleared of inmates two at a time, the inmates segregated themselves and obeyed all orders and the evacuation of the yard went without further incident.

Respectfully submitted,
O. G. Miller, Correctional Officer

The gun guard's account, brief as it is, seems to be less than accurate. Opie Miller must have known the men were unarmed. He knew they had each completed a thorough skin search. He knew that the yard itself had been "shaken down" for weapons just prior to the yard opening. He knew that wire mesh windows prevented other prisoners from throwing weapons into the yard. He knew that Satcher didn't lead the fight. Even the white inmates in the yard, men who called Satcher "chicken," asserted that he didn't approach the center of the yard until the end of the brawl. And, of course, if the blacks didn't "mind" how many of them were killed "in the process," why did they stop? The inmates said they heard no whistles but again, in the heat of a fight who listens for a whistle? Later, Opie Miller would change his story, claiming that he actually shot at the cement pavement and that ricochets killed the men.

Supporting statements from twelve other guards and officials did not reach Sacramento until after January 20, more than a week following the incident. The supporting statements were included in Swagerty's "first supplement" to the earlier incident report. All of the guards' statements, however, were dated January 13. The accounts, some as short as nine lines, were sparse in facts. One "fact" which was repeated in eleven of the twelve accounts was that one or more whistle blasts preceded the gunfire.

Leonard Dart, a second-watch civilian MTA, had written the one report that did not mention a whistle. He said he was in the MTA office dispensing medication when he heard the first rifle shot. He walked out of the office to the physiotherapy room so that he could look into the O-wing yard. By the time he reached the window, he heard a second shot. He saw a small group of inmates "fighting among themselves." He also observed two "colored inmates" and a white inmate "lying on the concrete." "Another shot was fired," Dart wrote in his report, and "another colored inmate fell to the concrete." Then there was a fourth shot and Dart saw Billie Harris walk several yards and drop to the concrete. "The fighting then stopped," Dart reported.

Guard M. W. Crisp was about to release Eugene Grady into the O-wing yard when he heard a "police type whistle blow . . . followed by a gunshot." Crisp immediately ordered Grady to his cell, locked the black inmate in and walked over to the O-wing window to look into the exercise yard. From his position, he could see the entire center of the yard. Crisp said Nolen was lying on his back, about in the middle of the shower platform, his feet stretched toward the O-wing wall. Edwards, the guard said, was lying parallel to the shower platform. The wounded black was on his left side facing O-wing, with his head directed south, toward the gun booth.

Except for Crisp's reporting on the placement of the bodies, no other guard seemed to have witnessed anything at all, except Opie Miller. Windows line the entire length of the O-wing corridor and each has a clear view of the yard. Knowing that a fight would erupt, knowing that they would have to break it up, admitting that they called in extra men to stop any fight if one developed, it is curious that no guard, *except the gun guard,* watched the yard in case a fight did take place. Of course many guards must have been watching. They simply left that out of their reports to CDC director Procunier. The most noteworthy admission in Crisp's confidential statement is that he could recognize the dying blacks and identify them by name. Opie Miller probably recognized them too but he isn't saying so.

Two weeks after the yard killings, a Monterey County grand jury met to hear two days of secret testimony to decide whether charges should be brought against Opie Miller. It was a *pro forma* affair. After twenty minutes of deliberation, the jurors concluded that Opie Miller took the only reasonable course open to him when he fired the shots that killed Nolen, Miller and Edwards.

The grand jury may not have heard the truth either but no one knows what they heard since the testimony was never released. The

Monterey County assistant district attorney, Ed Barnes, told reporters that though he would have liked to release the testimony, he was not able to because the investigation was secret and because no indictment was forthcoming from the deliberations. However, Barnes did say that the testimony took fourteen hours and was provided by twelve survivors of the fight and seventeen nonprisoners. Acknowledging that there were substantial discrepancies in the witnesses' accounts, Barnes pointed out that they ranged from inmate accusations of "deliberate murder" to one inmate who corroborated the gun guard's account of the incident, even though the prisoner "admitted" hating Opie Miller's guts.

According to what Barnes said about the testimony, at least one of the four shots fired by Miller was a ricochet shot which did not hit anyone. A second bullet appeared to have been fired at the concrete deck of the yard. David Buard, a ballistics expert from the state's Department of Justice, told the grand jurors that all three deaths and the groin wound may actually have been inflicted by only two bullets.

Opie Miller testified that although he fired no warning shot, he whistled and shouted for the men to stop fighting. The assistant district attorney supported Miller's testimony by pointing out that two other factors mitigated against a warning shot fired into the air. Noise and ricochet from a ground bullet would have been greater, thus attracting more attention. And such a shot fired into the air might have gone into the North Facility yard, where other inmates were exercising. The grand jurors took his word for that. They were never taken to the yard or they would have seen that it would have been next to impossible to fire into the North Facility; that a shot fired into the air would have gone toward a range of uninhabited mountains. If they had been taken to the gun booth, they would have seen that the shooting range from the booth to the victims was a bare seventy-five-foot down-angle range, about the distance one would fire when plunking ducks in a shooting gallery.

Then there was the testimony about Opie Miller himself. His associates testified that Opie was a "very calm deliberate person, the best they could select" to deal with a situation that called for cool judgment. The assistant district attorney minimized the racial aspects of the conflict. He said these prisoners were just "hell bent on fighting." And, as a personal aside to reporters, Barnes confided that Opie Miller—far from being a deliberate killer—had been "greatly upset by the killing."

IV

January 16: Revenge

In the quiet early hours of that Monterey winter's morning on January 13, the twins Gary Alden Branson and Larry Allen Branson, Caucasians, were marking time in Soledad's Y-wing for a burglary conviction. Native Californians, they consider themselves "proud Okies" because their parents migrated west to the Sacramento area in 1942. Their father was a stern alcoholic who often beat his twelve children; he was simultaneously fathering and raising another family elsewhere. Their mother, a strict disciple of the Pentecostal Church, raised her children in the fundamentalism of the faith.

The twins' criminal history is minor but lengthy. The charges read: "littering . . . runaway . . . runaway juvenile home . . . malicious mischief . . . no operator's license in possession . . . and [shades of *Alice's Restaurant*] illegal dumping." Like shuffled papers, the twins were moved from juvenile hall to juvenile hall, from one boys' home to another, and finally—after a drunken burglary of an empty residence ("We thought it was a good idea at the time")—to Soledad Prison for a term of six months to fifteen years.

Except for the two maximum security wings, O and X, Y-wing is the roughest and toughest in the joint. It is located almost directly across the main-line corridor from O-wing. The Bransons had been assigned to the wing about three months before. Having accepted working assignments in the industrial shop area, the twins on this particular morning were preparing to go to work, "just standing around as usual, milling around and bullshitting as usual and all of a sudden the officers started running everywheres." Red lights started flashing off and on. A cacophony of sirens, alarm bells and whistles shattered the morning calm. Guards quickly locked the corridor doors to Y-wing and the Bransons could hear four shots being fired, two and then two with about three-second intervals. The four shots were being fired while the red emergency lights were flashing.

Within minutes, every inmate in the prison was locked into special security status. Word passed by mouth that three blacks had been killed on the yard. "I didn't think too much about it at the time," said Gary Branson. "I went to school." In the afternoon school sessions, however, Branson sat a bit uncomfortably while black inmates and white teachers argued heatedly about the yard killings. The blacks were calling it murder. They were saying that the guards had deliberately slaughtered their brothers because they hated them.

Within the next few days, the blacks went on hunger strikes, burned prison furniture and dispatched a voluminous amount of mail to their families and attorneys and to state officials, demanding an investigation. Fistfights erupted in numerous housing wings. White and black cons alike walked around with magazines stuffed in their shirts to blunt knife attacks. For three days, the heat increased. Dozens of cons—blacks, whites and Chicanos—were being slashed and cut.

By the evening of the third day, Friday, January 16, there were rumors that the Monterey County district attorney's office had almost finished its investigation and had already reached a conclusion about the yard slayings. The blacks were wondering what would happen to the white guard who shot three of their comrades. The Bransons and other white inmates were wondering the same thing. "It was hot as hell," said Gary Branson, "like a firecracker fixin' to explode. Everybody said watch your back. Watch everything. The blacks is kill-crazy."

Continuing their hunger strike, the blacks didn't go to chow that evening. When the white cons of Y-wing returned from dinner, they found the blacks heavily congregated in the wing's ground floor television room. The Bransons asked a white friend what was going on. "Well," he told them, "the cons are waiting for the news. They want to find out what they're going to do, whether the pigs are going to hang that officer or not."

The whites were afraid to go into the TV room. Amid sporadic outbursts of angry epithets alternating with hushed moments, the black prisoners heard the Monterey County district attorney tell the press that, in his personal opinion, his investigation of the shooting deaths of the three black inmates showed "probable justifiable homicide by a public officer in the performance of his duty." The DA said he would continue the investigation and would present his evidence to a grand jury for consideration. The blacks were enraged. The white cons worried most for themselves. They figured the guards should be able to take care of themselves. They also knew that it might take years but prison scales of retribution and revenge always seem to seek a balance of their own.

Like other wings on the Soledad main line, Y-wing branched off from the quarter-mile corridor of movement and prison activity. The wing's three stories of tiers wrapped around the building in an elongated U shape, the cells backing against the outside walls. A walkway and railing fronted each tier. The center of the wing was open from ceiling to floor. That Friday, John V. Mills, twenty-six, was the lone relief guard on the evening shift for Y-wing. He was a "fish bull"—a rookie. Short of stature, Officer Mills had to use a chair to get a set of dominoes from a high shelf for the Bransons.

John Mills probably never knew any of the truth about the killings on January 13. Even though he had been working there for nearly a year, the young guard continued to pull odd-hour shifts and assignments in various wings and units of the prison. The quiet-spoken officer had not yet found his niche in the prison. He was not particularly hated by inmates. In fact, the inmates judge that some guards, like Mills, are doing time in a lousy job. The guards who are despised and vilified are those who go out of their way to give a convict a hard time. Maybe Mills wasn't hated because he hadn't been there long enough. Maybe he wasn't hated because he didn't hassle people. The inmates who remember Mills at all describe him as a docile little guy who rarely spoke with prisoners.

The prison was preparing to lock down for another night. No one was out on the main line. Even the guards who were supposed to be manning the corridor were off in Control, chatting with their mates in the little bay window behind which switches can be pulled to shut off the corridor into three sections and release the tear gas vents beneath the floor. In the individual wings, convicts with enough "good time" had their own keys to their "houses" or cells. All the cells would be locked with a single bar switch at lock-up time but until then an inmate decided for himself whether his door was locked or open.

As relief officer, Mills simply had to be present and keep an eye out for trouble. It was a boring job, generally. Much of his time would be spent talking with a few inmates, getting out some games, settling a minor dispute or leaning back against the square-paned glass that looks out of the wing to the beige-colored main-line corridor. Like the other housing units, Y-wing smelled of concrete and wax, layers and layers of Lysol and strong green soap over layers and layers of wax. It was a heavy dull odor that got into everything, including the food and clothes. At night, the inmates would be showering, playing cards, dominoes or checkers or just leaning against a friend's cell door, rapping away another day of their time.

Around 6:30 P.M. Mills was grabbed from behind and slugged insensible. He had a whistle which he could have blown but he was unable to reach it. There was little noise as Mills was dragged up the iron stairs in a corner of the wing to the third tier, and most of the inmates in the wing probably did not notice that he was gone from the first floor. There was blood on the ceiling of the second-floor stairwell, blood on both upper landings, on the handrails leading to the third tier and on the walls. On the third tier, the only sound was a fleshy thunk of fists pounding Mills's face and body and later the whapping sound of the guard being beaten with his own flashlight. Mills's body was edged over the railing of the catwalk, lifted slightly higher and shoved over the edge.

The Branson brothers were playing dominoes when a glass bottle shattered against the wall behind them. The twins jumped up from the table and flattened themselves against their cell doors. Just then, the second bottle hit. They looked up toward the second tier and saw a black inmate grinning and laughing as he threw bottles. Then, angling their view upward, the Bransons saw Officer Mills "come flyin' through the air and hit the deck."

"You could hear the keys dangling as he fell," said Gary. "As he came down, the body leveled out, kind of turning, and hit at a sideways angle right beside one of the tables. He hit the deck in such a way that it looked like he tried to stand back up real quick and then he fell again and lay still. Another friend of mine was playing dominoes but he didn't move, even when the body hit near him. He stayed out there even when the bulls come into the wing.

"After the body hit, everybody started clapping. Then everybody started climbing the railings, jumping over the railings, unlocking their doors, running over the stairs and locking themselves in. People were yelling, 'Hit the doors. They got the pig. They got the pig. They got the officer.' After Officer Mills hit the deck, it wasn't a minute and a half and everybody was in and quiet. Boy, were they quiet. Nobody wanted to stay out there. They might come in there and start shooting in the wing. Prison's full of little holes where they shot in the past. I said, 'Shit, they're sure going to do us in now.'"

When a main-line guard became suspicious because he couldn't see Mills through the glass-paned door, he walked into the wing and found the guard's body, sprawled and bloodied, off to a side of the concrete floor. Near Mills's body the guard found a note. It read: "One down, two to go."

Officer Mills died about forty-five minutes after he was found, never having regained consciousness. He was the first guard to be killed at Soledad.

Minutes after Mills's body was found, Soledad officials began the investigative task of shaking down all the cells in the wing. The inmates were ordered out of their cells, walking backward, naked, hands over their heads, and were taken into interrogation rooms one by one. While one group of guards interrogated, another group searched the cells. Each of the wing's 138 prisoners was interrogated several times about the killing and held incommunicado from the outside, from friends, family and attorneys. Except for answering investigators' questions, the prisoners spent their time in their cells in constant lock-up. The incommunicado process continued for two weeks.

An inmate named Thomas York described Mills's attackers as three blacks. He identified them as George Jackson, Fleeta Drumgo and John Clutchette. York claimed that Jackson and Drumgo took turns hitting the guard but that Clutchette was merely standing nearby. York, a Jamaican, added that perhaps his testimony would enable him to get out of Soledad and return to Jamaica.

Larry Eskew, a white inmate, told investigators that Jackson, Drumgo and Clutchette attacked Mills, then he changed his mind and deleted Clutchette from the list. Eskew said Jackson was the man who was hitting Mills in the face with a flashlight. A third prisoner, William Worzella, reported that he saw Jackson and Clutchette standing over the body of a "white man." He said he didn't see Clutchette do anything but he saw Jackson hit what he, Worzella, would describe as a "white" body.

At the trial, York, Eskew and Worzella kept quiet about the prison's interrogation procedures. An all-white jury refused to believe their testimony.

The Branson twins were also witnesses. They told the prison interrogators that one of the attackers looked like Jackson but they couldn't be sure. They were certain, however, that they could not identify anyone else. Yet the Bransons were supposed to testify at the trial because they responded well to the cajoling and coercion techniques which prison officials and investigators brought to bear.

The prosecution, as it developed, had good reason not to call the Bransons to the witness stand. The twin brothers would have told a stunned courtroom how they were threatened and coaxed into testifying for the state. They would have explained how, after they had agreed to become "snitches," their eyewitness accounts were altered at various blackboard coaching sessions conducted by the stocky militaristic guard captain, Charles Moody, and the prosecuting assistant district attorney, Ed Barnes, a gangly, kind-looking old man. They tell it here under interview stipulations that the statements not be attributed to either twin directly. They say they still fear for their lives. They're afraid Moody will either kill them or contract to kill them.

When the Bransons were interrogated the first night, they told their inquisitors that they had been asleep. The guards nodded their heads sympathetically and returned them to their cells. By the second night, however, Moody and his guards kept telling the Bransons that everyone knew they were witnesses and that the twins' lives were in danger. "Your name is out on the line," Captain Moody told one of the brothers. "You're going to get killed if you stay here. We can't protect you in an open wing like that."

"Captain Moody came off heavy with me," said the other Branson. "I walked in and he said, 'Hello, Branson.' I said hello. He said, 'I'm Charles Moody, captain of Soledad Training Facility. Listen,' he said, 'I know you and your brother. I know what happened up there. A lot of people are telling me you was standing by your cell and they know you seen it. You've been implicated in this,' he says. 'I've been looking at your record. You're due to go to [parole] board pretty soon. The funny thing about them boards is if they think somebody

is holding back some information, especially something like this . . .'
He was using all kinds of psychological tricks. He says, 'I can't tell
you you won't go home but I can tell you I'm positive you won't.'

" 'You might be young right now, but you're not going to be young
always. I had this gray in my hair then too.' And he fingered with some
hair on his head. Then he looked down at me and says, 'You've got a
little gray already. But then you may not live to get much grayer. From
what I've heard from these other guys that know you, they're really
heavy after you.

" 'Those niggers out there want you,' he said. Just like that. He
even said 'nigger.' 'You know, of course, it's not going to be easy to
protect you. The only way I know of is with those six little cells
down there in the dungeon. They're called solitary confinement. The
best we could do is just keep you locked up, you know, year round.
There's no telling when you'll go home 'cause it's unlikely that the
board will let you, 'cause they'll know you're holding something back.

" 'But God damn,' he says, 'I'd hate to rot in there and I know you
would too. And nobody knows for sure whether they'd get you or not.
You know how these dudes work. Fire in people's cells. Cut and
stab on the line.

" 'On the other hand,' he says, 'we could put you in a place that's
safe. We can't promise you anything, of course, but it would be
easier.' Winks and all that shit. 'And you'll get out a lot faster. You
can figure it out from there. You're not dumb. You know we can't
make no promises or anything but I know that if it was me and I told
the people what they wanted to know, I'd know they'd treat me
right.' "

During their third session with Moody, the Bransons decided to
testify for the prosecution. The twins felt it was a "matter of stay
there and die or get out and die." They opted to "die outside."
Before they would tell what they saw, the Bransons insisted that they
be transferred out of Soledad. Moody saw to it, ordering the twins
transferred to the California Men's Colony at San Luis Obispo that

same day. And no sooner had the Bransons stepped off the bus than Moody was there, ready to talk.

"I valued myself as never being a snitch," one Branson said. "I valued that with pride. Even to myself, I always thought it was an honor to die rather than to give up anybody else. But I like girls and I like wine and I like beer and I like dancing and romancing and what have you, see. And I didn't like the idea of being stabbed forty-seven times, like I seen some people get it in there. So I decided to go ahead and give it up under the psychological pressures they were using.

"But the funny thing was when they questioned us, they wanted us to say certain things. Even though you would tell them the real truth about what you saw, they wanted certain things down there. The major differences between what we saw and what they wanted was they was trying to put it down in a different area than where it took place and they put it down that three guys were up there on the tier instead of one or two and they wanted it started in the shower room because they said that's where Officer Mills screamed from."

While the inmate witnesses gathered at the San Luis Obispo CMC in minimum, comfortable security, Soledad officials began preparations for having them returned to Soledad for the long but delicate process of pampering and coaching. Since the men were "snitches," their lives would have been endangered if they were placed among the general inmate population. There was, however, one area where the witnesses—there were nine of them—could be housed. For more than two decades, South Facility or South Barracks had been the dormlike minimum security area for convicts who were about to be paroled. Complete with its own gymnasium, kitchen facility, baseball diamond and lounge area, South Barracks seemed more like an easy stint at summer camp for the nine witnesses than time at a state prison.

The men were allowed to doff their prison blues whenever they had a visitor. This was particularly encouraged when defense attorneys for the three Soledad Brothers—as Jackson, Drumgo and Clutchette would come to be called—appeared. They were even allowed to drive cars to meet the defense attorneys. Moody told one of the witnesses that this was to "put the lawyers out of phase," to make them think that the inmate witnesses were out and free already. "Moody said to drink their coffee and smoke their cigarettes and tell them nothing," one Branson said. " 'Tell them you'll say your shit in court. They got a court order to see you guys but you don't have to talk to them,' " Moody admonished.

"One big fun house was what it was," said Branson. "Some guys even managed to get laid. It was easy to get anybody that came in for a visit. The witnesses would have been there forever if they'd had their wives or girl friends. That's how good prison really was." While they waited for the trial to begin, the men went hunting with Captain Moody, chasing rabbits along the foothills of the Gabilan Mountains. In contrast to the rigid food rationing in Soledad proper, the witnesses could have all they wanted to eat. "I was getting fat," said one of the Bransons. "A man could drink a gallon of milk a day and they said nothing. A man could eat twenty-four, thirty-five sweet rolls and they said nothing. If you wanted six eggs for breakfast you could have six eggs for breakfast. We had snacks two or three times a day. Sometimes Captain Moody made pizzas for us. Went over and bought the stuff outside and brought them back.

"The guards brought us anything we needed. Toothpaste. Cigarettes. Hair oil. Combs. Brushes. Everything. They ripped it all off the other inmates on the main line and brought it to us. They was illegally stealing it more or less." Words failed, said the Bransons, in trying to describe what a "fine time" they had those last few months at Soledad. Sometimes the guards hunkered down and played poker through the night with the young witnesses, gambling for the "ducats" which served as official prison money and for cigarettes. It was "friendly gambling," one Branson said. Prison rules and regulations would call it something else. Captain Moody, everyone agreed, was an excellent poker player.

Occasionally, their idyllic days in South Facility were interrupted with more coercive doses of fear and intimidation, which the "snitches" felt was generated by the guards themselves. "For starters," said a Branson, "they tried to tell us that the Black Panthers were going to kill us. They played the hell out of that. They said we could call the guards any minute and they'd come running with guns." For their part, the guards provided their charges, felons all, with a variety of weapons, ranging from billy clubs and baseball bats to tear gas guns.

"I don't remember the day or anything," said one Branson. "The guard said somebody was there in our facility and that he had on a jacket with Levi's. The guard told us to arm ourselves with our baseball bats and clubs. And there come Captain Moody in Bermuda shorts. So we're all chasing around with these baseball bats. 'If you see somebody,' they told us, 'lay it on him. Beat him. Kill him.' He emphasized it: 'Kill him.' Now, if we had seen somebody in there we'd 'a' killed him. Beat him to death. I thought to myself while we was running around down there with those baseball bats, 'This is some kind of insanity.'

"They scared hell out of a courtroom in Pixley [California] with this Panther talk. One of our witnesses, Green [Manuel Green, who later testified in the Soledad Brothers case], was in jail in Pixley and he's got a court appearance and so they put some pressure on him. They told him the Panthers might try to kill him. So they got to protect him. Green, who's frightened out of his wits, tells the sheriff. So the sheriff says he's never had an important prisoner in this tiny town before. And the sheriff's got all these visions of the Black Panthers coming in on chartered buses, I guess, to assassinate Green. So they got the courthouse ringed with bailiffs and in the courtroom they got all these jackassed deputies with these nine-millimeter pistols that nobody knows how to use. So Green is on the witness stand and this one deputy that doesn't know how to use the pistol cocks the damn thing, puts it in his pocket, rear pocket, sits down and the damn thing goes off. Green stands up and hollers, 'I've been shot,' and falls to the floor. The judge jumps down onto the floor and crawls out of the room. The clerk runs into the wall and pisses in his pants. Meanwhile, they've all got their guns out on each other and it turns out the deputy's got a bullet in his ass."

The Bransons also had more serious reflections. "Sometimes they'd come over and sit down and have coffee and doughnuts and they'd put everything up on the blackboard and worked it out to where every inmate was and who was doing what. And one witness would be asked such and such about what color was the shirt, or was there a turban on Jackson's head or did he have a T-shirt on over his head? What color was it? If one said it was green and the other said it was blue, well, they make it to where both of them got it blue or both of them got it green. Whichever way they wanted it. Kenneth Carter got coached a lot. Well, they coached Bob Langley a lot too because he was older and they figured he was con-wise and wouldn't be able to remember and everything. Then Gordon Prop got all his information from Langley. And Langley didn't know that much about what really happened.

"Mr. Barnes said something like this happened so quickly that it's easy for everybody's story to be partly different. But the blackboard sessions was run so they wouldn't be different. Captain Moody ran the sessions. He was number one. Barnes was second. Third was a guard named Sarge and Tony Rodriguez from the prosecutor's office. They wanted us to say certain things. They wanted three guys up there. And they wanted it started in the shower room instead of where it really happened. 'But aren't you sure it was down on this end right here, Branson? Down right here, huh? And you'll be sure, right?' And I said, 'Yeah, right.' "

The Bransons figured they were never called to testify because they were more certain than the others about what they had witnessed. At the request of prison officials they had twice submitted to a lie detector test. The Bransons were in an uncomfortable predicament. Their first choices were simple. If they testified, radical blacks would try to kill them. If they did not, Moody and his men might try. At first, they feared Moody more than they feared the blacks. Later, they feared the outside and the blacks more. In the interim, their seeming sense of fair play rebelled against the pat hand which prison officials and prosecutors were dealing themselves in preparation for the jury trial. The Bransons began to whisper their discontent, telling another witness that if they ever got to court, they might just "drop a bomb on Moody." The man they told, Thomas York, informed Moody and the Bransons were never called to the witness stand.

The Bransons were released from prison when the Soledad Brothers trial started late in 1971. At the time, Captain Moody had not heard of the Branson "bomb." Just before they went up before the parole board, Moody told the Bransons that whatever he said to the board would determine whether the twins would be released almost immediately or be held in custody until after the conclusion of the trial. The brothers said they believed Moody well enough to "play his game." The parole board asked the twins how they were treated. They said O.K. The board asked if the Bransons were going to be witnesses in the then forthcoming trial and the brothers answered yes. The Bransons were asked what they thought their "crime problem" was and one twin talked about his "emotional attitude" and how he "failed to use my better judgment." The brothers were released.

Captain Moody had kept his implied word. Still, the Bransons are not fond of him. "Captain Moody," a twin said, "hated every convict there was and hated blacks worse than everything else. He even hated the witnesses but he had to pamper us. He had a job to do."

The Bransons said they themselves have never been prejudiced against any minority groups. Having grown up with "Mexicans and niggers," they believe "everyone's got a right to live." They feel an affinity for blacks and Chicanos because, as poor whites, they are part of the oppressed.

"See," said one of the brothers, "all poor folk are oppressed. That's why Jackson was a revolutionary person. I talked to Jackson. There's a lot of times he talked to you he gritted his teeth. A lot of times you talked to him and he smiled like anyone else. He told me several times, he said, 'Ten years now I've been here for a little old chicken-shit robbery at a gas station.' He said, 'They don't want me out because they know that when I get out I'm going to write about this place."

V

Salinas Justice

One afternoon late in January 1970, the telephone rang in the
suburban Pasadena home of Mrs. Georgia Jackson. The caller, a
black Monterey County public defender named Phrasel Shelton,
wanted to know why Mrs. Jackson had not gone to Soledad Prison
to visit her son George. "If you want to try to save your son from
going to the gas chamber, you better come up here and see about
him," the public defender told Mrs. Jackson. "What do you mean?"
she asked. "Well," Shelton explained, "didn't you know that he's been
charged with killing a guard here in Soledad? They say he's been
going to court. This is his third court appearance since the charge."
And the public defender added, "I wondered what happened to you
and I wondered if you knew about it." "No," Jackson's mother
replied.

At about the same time, Mrs. Doris Maxwell received a note
from her son, John Clutchette. The note said: "Mother— Help!
Won't let letters get out. Send lawyer. Might not let you come in. Life
is in danger. Hurry, Speedy." Mrs. Maxwell was surprised that her

son was in trouble. Speedy had already got his date: he was supposed to be paroled in three months.

Inez Williams, Fleeta Drumgo's mother, had been calling the prison for days, ever since she read that a guard had been killed in Y-wing. A prison official told her Fleeta was fine and that there was nothing she should be concerned about.

Throughout the investigation and the interrogation period, the prison neglected to notify the families of the suspects that their sons were in trouble. Indeed, after receiving Clutchette's letter, Mrs. Maxwell was told by one prison official that her son, now a suspect, needed no attorney and that she shouldn't inconvenience herself and attend the arraignment. When Mrs. Williams finally learned that Drumgo was a suspect, she called again, only to be told, "It's just routine. Nothing to worry about." The prisoners themselves knew what to worry about. John Clutchette told of his own fears in a letter he wrote during the investigation. Soledad officials refused to mail the letter because it was "detrimental" to the prison. Unless such a letter is addressed to the governor, a state official or an attorney, such "detrimental" letters can be stopped, and routinely are.

January 18, 1970

Shirley:

Just these few lines to say hello and get you up
on the latest. You've probably heard about the three
Blacks that were murdered last Tuesday. Well, a police
was killed Friday and they have me and I don't know
how many other Blacks locked down for investigation—
which really means suspicion of murder. The only crime
I'm guilty of is being Black and the friend of someone
they don't like. The one who is guilty is the police
who created the circumstances which worked some emotions
to the point where people felt they had to strike out.
    Maybe this will bring the problem into sharper
focus. It's not a matter of Black or White being on
trial, but rather Justice being on trial. It took them
three days to come to the verdict of justifiable homicide.
I wonder how long they are going to keep me in here on

a speculation. The only thing I'm concerned with is whether this will cause me to lose my [parole] date.

Get in touch with mom and tell her I believe they
have cut all visiting off so try and get some type of
lawyer for the people, even the NAACP or anyone, because
they probably won't let her in. They don't like the public
to know what's going on unless it's in their favor. The
District Attorney was here an hour after the happenings
and nobody else knows anything because they have everyone
locked up.

I wrote you and my mother before but they kept
sending the letters back.

Speedy

Prison operations remained at a standstill for eleven days. Educational and vocational classes were canceled, the industry shops closed.
In the Soledad Central Facility, all of the fifteen hundred inmates
remained locked in their cells. Small groups were released at meal-
time. They single-filed to chow under the nervous scrutiny of a guard
force that was doubled almost overnight. "We have a very tense, very
critical situation," an associate warden told the press. "We're trying
to play it cool and play it safe."

They played it cool and safe until January 27, when Assistant
District Attorney Barnes began a public relations crusade against the
three black defendants. Because the dead guard had been badly
beaten, Barnes went to some length to point out that the three suspects
were athletes. Jackson, Barnes said, was known around the prison as
"Karate Jackson" because he was an expert in that Oriental art.
Soledad guards took the cue. Thereafter, whenever Jackson's name
was mentioned, it came out "Karate Jackson." It didn't really matter
to them that Jackson's real nickname was "Comrade." Whenever
Jackson was escorted from O-wing to the Soledad visiting room now,
main-line corridor officers guarding the O-wing door would bellow,
"Clear the area. Karate Jackson's coming out. Clear the area. Look
out for Karate Jackson."

John Clutchette, at six feet one inch and 220 pounds, was an inch taller than Jackson and thirty-five pounds heavier. Barnes, in announcing the indictments, said Clutchette was a weight lifter. That image sunk in. Maybe Clutchette lifted Officer Mills up and threw him over the railing. Although Fleeta Drumgo was only five feet eight and weighed 145 pounds, Barnes noted that the lithe, quick black "likes to play basketball."

The assistant district attorney wanted to steer clear of a revenge motive, however. Tying in Mills's death with the January 13 killings would have meant an intense investigatory and legal discovery process into those deaths. Barnes stated blandly that Mills was simply "picked because he was available. There was nothing personal against Mills." It was just that on the night of January 16 Mills had the misfortune to be a "white man, a guard and the only one in the wing." Barnes added that his investigation was continuing and that there was a possibility of more arrests later. None were made.

Three days after his indictment and two weeks after the isolation of Y-wing prisoners, George Jackson wrote to an attorney. Not knowing what attorneys in nearby Salinas might take his case, he wrote to the California Rural Legal Assistance. The CRLA turned down the case because criminal proceedings are not accepted by the organization. Jackson, Drumgo and Clutchette appeared in court without attorneys.

The Monterey County Courthouse in Salinas is an imposing structure. A massive square of sandy beige concrete and cement, trimmed with turquoise green, the building sits on land that was once a vast mustard pasture for roving cattle. Architecturally, it might be considered 1930 California modern, with a touch of Spanish in its carefully rounded archways, a dash of early American frugality in its clean, sparse lines.

Salinas had been a rural boom town, a transportation center that mushroomed around a major California crossroads where stage-coaches from Monterey and San Juan Bautista intersected with the more heavily traveled north-south roads between Los Angeles and San Francisco. As a city, it was laid out just after the Civil War, when two men, standing on two sides of a wooden fence, walked and marked off the city limits by driving wooden stakes into the ground. They decided to call it Salinas, combining syllables from the names of the Spanish land grants, the old Sausal and Nacional ranchos.

The town grew rapidly. Settlers soon discovered that the Salinas Valley, which took its name from the town, was an extremely fertile farming area. One early family found, for example, that they grew enough grain in one harvest to pay off a seven-year lease on their property. Eventually, the main tracks of the north-south run of the Southern Pacific Railroad were laid through the center of the town and by 1873 Salinas had become the county seat. It grew so fast in the next fifty years that by 1924, Salinas—with more than $8.4 million in its banks—could lay claim to being "the wealthiest community per capita in the United States." It could claim other superlatives too, such as the largest beet sugar factory in the world, the largest strawberry farm, the largest freesia bulb ranch, the most expensive high school, the world's only goat milk condensery and California's first college. The population then was five thousand. Now fifty-five thousand people live in Salinas and times have changed.

Today, to hold on to its special identity, Salinas turns to other claims, such as "Salad Bowl of America." The town remains a hub of vegetable transport, producing about eighty million dollars' worth of vegetables, mostly lettuce, carrots and artichokes. But there have been other changes and these have bothered many of the townsfolk. Along with the intensified agriculture have come the migrant farm workers, mostly Chicanos, and along with the increased industrialization and post–World War II population movements have come the blacks. That was all right at first, but recently militant Chicanos such as Cesar Chavez have been organizing the farm workers, and blacks and Chicanos together have been protesting housing discrimination. In the city's schools, where many of the teachers are elderly Okie women who settled there in the 1930s and 1940s, there is a growing conflict between their educational philosophy and that of the younger Chicano students.

A half century ago, its residents called Salinas a "veritable paradise," a "landmark of human progress" where "at every corner can be found beautiful buildings." The first person to chronicle the isolation strip cell. The charges, she said, were "unbelievable." John, Steinbeck, who wrote eloquently of the hardships of the Okie migrants, the antilabor and antiworkingmen mood among the older residents, the chilling swift justice of the vigilante committees.

About the only Salinas characteristic that hasn't changed in the past few decades is the annual state rodeo, the largest in California. For four days each June, some eighteen thousand cowboys and more than one hundred thousand short-sleeved spectators jam the city's streets and cram into the California Rodeo Grounds just north of town. In fact, civic-minded folk and active chamber of commerce types were in the midst of plans for the 1970 celebration when the pretrial hearings began in Salinas. "We don't want that bullshit going on during the rodeo," one businessman commented. "They can't get that trial over soon enough to suit me," said another. And it seemed that everyone involved, from the district attorney's office to the prison administration to the courts, was doing all he possibly could to help. In fact, everything was moving along fairly smoothly.

The Monterey County district attorney's office did not follow the usual procedures in seeking indictments against the three black inmates. Barnes could have gone through the municipal court in a preliminary hearing and got the indictments but he chose the grand jury route instead. Grand jury procedures made his job easier. It meant that he skirted a court hearing in which defense counsel would have been allowed to cross-examine witnesses and have access to "discovery," that is, view and challenge whatever evidence the prosecutors would present. In grand jury deliberations, except for questions raised by the grand jurors themselves, there is no challenge of evidence or cross-examination of witnesses. Indeed, the state picks whatever witnesses it wants on the stand. Although Opie Miller testified at his own grand jury proceedings, the three black inmates who would be charged did not appear at theirs.

What was probably most unusual in this particular instance was that Barnes had begun the indictment in the municipal court. However, a day before the preliminary hearing was scheduled to be held, Barnes got the grand jury to hear his witnesses and came away from the jury room with his indictments. After the indictments were handed down, a Soledad Prison official telephoned Clutchette's mother in Los Angeles to tell her that the preliminary hearing had been canceled. Instead, her son would be arraigned in superior court the next morning. "That's tomorrow," the Soledad official added, "so you don't have to come."

Mrs. Maxwell was frantic. She had not secured an attorney for her son and she was surprised that the hearing was moved up. In desperation, she called Fay Stender, a white, radical attorney whose name her son had mentioned, and asked if she could appear with him in court. Mrs. Stender calmed the black woman, told her not to worry; she would see to it that Clutchette was represented. Catching the midnight flight out of Los Angeles, Mrs. Maxwell stayed with friends in San Francisco and made the two-hour drive to Salinas the next dawn.

Fay Stender was in a quandary. She had thought she would be representing George Jackson because one of her clients, Black Panther leader Huey Newton, had already asked her to speak with Jackson about her representing him. In addition, Mrs. Stender had talked about representing Jackson with a black state senator, Mervyn Dymally. Dymally, who held a powerful senate post as chairman of the Senate Democratic Caucus, had visited with Jackson at the request of Newton. Dymally was shaken by his visit with Jackson. The senator said Jackson was brought to him shackled and chained. "He was trembling so," said Dymally, "that he was unable to light his own cigarette and was obviously terrified. Conversation was extremely difficult. This visit disturbed me very much."

There was one complication for Mrs. Stender, however. Jackson was already represented by the public defender, Phrasel Shelton, who had been court appointed. Where Mrs. Stender stood in all this was unclear, even to herself. Unaware that the grand jury indictments had already been handed down, she felt uneasy about appearing at the preliminary hearing on behalf of Drumgo or Clutchette because she might have to change clients. It was clear that she wanted to represent Jackson and a change would have been awkward. She telephoned the Monterey law offices of Heisler and Stewart, a firm that was "of counsel" to hers, and asked Rich Silver to stand in for one of the defendants. She also asked Silver to provide another attorney to appear for the third defendant, leaving it up to the attorneys themselves to decide who would represent whom. Silver agreed to represent Drumgo. He asked Floyd Silliman, who had been his law school roommate, to appear for Clutchette. Silliman assented and the two hurried over to talk with the district attorney, to prepare themselves for the preliminary hearing.

The DA had a surprise for them. Due to the indictments from the grand jury, there would be no preliminary hearing. There would be no cross-examination of witnesses and there would be no presentation of any physical evidence either—until the trial. Anything the attorneys wanted to read or see would have to be got piecemeal and only through a court order.

While they awaited the arraignment, the attorneys established their representation of the three defendants. Shelton felt slighted and withdrew from the case. Mrs. Stender, anxious to provide more experienced representation for Jackson during the trial itself, joined Jackson in asking John Thorne, a bearded, heavy-set, radical attorney from San Jose, to join in the defense. Thorne agreed.

When Mrs. Georgia Jackson arrived at the courthouse, they were dragging in her son in chains. She had gone to the courthouse to meet the attorneys so they could drive to the prison together. She had no sooner arrived than "suddenly we saw George and they were dragging him in, out of a car. You should have seen his face when he looked up and saw us. You never saw a face like that in your life. When he looked and saw us, that head snapped up like that and he put on that grin and from then the fight started. I saw his face transformed when he looked up and saw us. I said, 'Well, this is going to be a battle.' "

John Clutchette's mother, Doris Maxwell, was in a different frame of mind when she watched the Monterey County deputies shove and half-drag her son into court. "Why are they doing my baby like that?" she wailed, and yelled at the deputies to be more careful in handling her son. Mrs. Maxwell had been allowed to talk with John during the court appearance and when she met reporters afterward she proclaimed his innocence and complained about the conditions in his isolation strip cell. The charges, she said, were "unbelievable." John, she explained, wiping away a constant stream of tears, was the eldest and "mildest-mannered" of her six children. He had had some "trouble with the law" but certainly "nothing like this." It was just plain crazy. And the craziest part was that Clutchette already had received his parole date from the Adult Authority. She was expecting him home on April 20. "It just doesn't make sense," she cried, sobbing. "He was coming home. Why would he jeopardize that?"

Anyway, she added, her son never hit anybody first in his life. "I used to have to scream at him just to get him to fight back." She was also angry at the district attorney for describing Clutchette as a 220-pound weight lifter. Her son weighed 205, she said, and had given up pushing iron a long time ago. With no prompting she offered that John had been a close friend of Alvin ("Jug") Miller, one of the blacks slain in the O-wing yard, but declared, "It's a long, long step from grieving for a brother to actually taking retribution." She also worried about the conditions in the strip cell where her son was kept while waiting for the trial. He had complained to her that he had to sleep on a thin pallet in a freezing cell. "Black as he is, his fingers were blue this morning," she said.

While one group of reporters stood on the courthouse steps talking to Mrs. Maxwell and covering the arraignment, another group was inside Soledad Prison, called there to witness a solemn ceremony. Prison officials wanted the press to see that several hundred inmates had signed a "scroll of sympathy" for the widow of the slain guard and had collected two hundred dollars. Both the check and the scroll were presented to Bernadette Mills while flashbulbs popped and television cameras rolled. "I want you to know," a white con told Mrs. Mills, "that John was a personal friend of mine, even though he was a staff member and an officer, and not only of mine, but of most of the inmates he came in contact with." Prison officials added that the institution's credit union had begun a trust fund for the guard's son. Mrs. Mills and some friends wept.

"This is case CR-2406," Superior Court Judge Gordon Campbell intoned in an almost empty courtroom. "The people of the state of California versus George Lester Jackson, Fleeta Drumgo and John Wesley Clutchette." Judge Campbell had entered from the front left corner of the courtroom and peered about the empty space, turning his balding head slowly from side to side. He was a small man, slightly shorter than medium height, but he seemed very fit, athletic even in his sixties. He swam at the Salinas YMCA every day. His fondness for Chinese food accounted for his nickname, Chinese Gordon.

All of the defense attorneys—Silliman, Silver, Thorne and Stender —were present when Judge Campbell gaveled the arraignment proceedings to begin this February 24. So was Jackson. The two other defendants were nowhere to be seen. Because they were not present, Thorne quickly objected. "Your Honor, I would—" Thorne began but he was cut off by Judge Campbell. "This is an arraignment as to the defendant Jackson," Campbell said. Thorne said he realized that but wanted to make an objection. Judge Campbell refused to hear any. The judge said he wanted to "complete the arraignment before you have a right to make your objection." Thorne objected several more times but the judge pressed ahead. Legally, it's unclear whether Campbell could have refused to hear an objection. There were no legal precedents on the subject simply because it hadn't happened before. Nevertheless, Thorne planned to challenge Campbell on that point, charging judicial error.

Judge Campbell had a widespread reputation for being tyrannical about what he considered proper courtroom etiquette and the pace of judicial proceedings. There had been occasions in which the judge interrupted an attorney to remind counsel to button his coat or to refrain from leaning on the courtroom furniture. He had also stopped sessions to order a bailiff to see that spectators did not lean back or put their elbows on the top edge of the benches. He turned down many objections because they hampered the smooth flow of justice.

The judge turned toward the husky blue-denimed black prisoner seated in chains at the defense table. "Your name is George Lester Jackson?" he asked.

"Uh-huh," the prisoner acknowledged.

"You have been indicted, Mr. Jackson, by the 1970 Monterey County Grand Jury for the crimes of, in the first count, of violation of Section 4500 of the California Penal Code. It's claimed that you on or about January 16, 1970, in the County of Monterey, California, while serving a life sentence in the state prison, that is the Correctional Training Facility at Soledad, did with malice aforethought, commit an assault upon the person of another, John V. Mills, who is other than an inmate, by means of force likely to produce great bodily injury and that as a result of such assault it's claimed, and as proximate result thereof, that John V. Mills died January 16, 1970. That is count one. Count Two. You are charged along with Fleeta Drumgo and John Wesley Clutchette with murder of one John V. Mills, claimed to have taken place on or about January 16, 1970, in Monterey County, California. Do you understand what you are charged with?"

Jackson said yes.

The court clerk tried to ask Jackson how he pleaded to count one but the question was not answered that day because of a number of defense objections which Campbell heard and denied. The attorneys objected, first of all, to the fact that two codefendants were not present in the courtroom for the arraignment. Campbell had insisted on processing each defendant at the exclusion of the other two through each of the arraignment proceedings.

Clutchette's attorney, Floyd Silliman, had been practicing law in Salinas for several years. He pointed out to the judge that he had "never known a case to have taken place in these courts where the codefendants were not present at all court proceedings involving their fellow codefendants." Campbell denied Silliman's point, stating that since Silliman's client was not in the courtroom to identify Silliman as his attorney, counsel "would be better to take up the matter when that person is here in court."

Thorne had one further objection, one that would be repeated throughout numerous courtroom sessions. He asked the court to remove the handcuffs, shackles, chains and leg irons which were wrapped around his client's neck, waist and crotch, and to allow Jackson to appear in civilian clothes instead of prison garb. Campbell parried the motion the first time it was brought up by asking whether the defendant was an inmate at a state prison. Yes, Mrs. Stender answered, Jackson was serving a sentence in which he might have been released in six months to life on a second degree robbery conviction "in which he was induced to plead guilty ten years ago."

Well, his lips aren't shackled, the judge observed, and claimed that the shackles and chains were necessary for security reasons. Similar motions to remove the chains were denied in the future—at least until a higher court overruled Campbell's decisions on appeal. Mrs. Stender tried to point out that only in court cases where the defendant had provoked some security problem or tried to escape or threatened to escape had shackles and chains been required. She offered to produce testimony that her defendant had never tried to escape, that he had never caused a commotion in a courtroom, and to cite specific cases, but Campbell interrupted and said he was familiar with those cases. The judge went on to insist that this was not a trial "in the presence of jurors or others that would be casting upon his guilt." Besides, the judge added, that's the way it's done in Monterey County.

"We have a prison system in this county and these things happen every week and sometimes a number of times a week.

"Proceed with the arraignment," said Campbell.

Defense attorneys told the judge that one of the major obstacles in their counsel with their clients was that they had not been able to interview them privately. Thorne offered to put Fay Stender on the stand and have her testify under oath that she had been unable to discuss with Jackson any of the "facts, matters and problems" surrounding the charge except for a brief period when guards stood by a door and overheard all that was said.

The assistant district attorney objected to that. He said prison officials were concerned about the safety of the attorneys. That's why prison interviews were brief and that's why the doors were open and a guard stood nearby, in case an inmate attacked his attorney. However, Barnes added, prison officials are "concerned about the safety of persons and I think they would want a specific waiver from the attorneys for any untoward incident that might occur in such a situation." In other words, Barnes wanted the defense attorneys to sign waivers that would release the prison from any blame in case their black clients were involved in an incident in which the attorneys might be injured. "I strenuously object to that statement of Mr. Barnes," Thorne shot back, "and suggest that that is one of the most racist kind of statements I have ever heard in a courtroom of the United States."

"I don't think it's necessary to bring race into the courtroom," Judge Campbell admonished, and went on to order that all future interviews "be outside the hearing of any public officials."

Floyd Silliman asked that defense investigators be allowed to inspect Y-wing, particularly the area in which the crime was alleged to have been committed. Barnes did not object but the judge was disturbed by his silence on the matter. "Well," the judge asked Barnes, "does the district attorney's office have any observations to make on this request?" Oh yes, said Barnes. The request is very "broad and ambiguous. I think he should make it specific." Very well, said Campbell, and instructed Silliman to submit a written motion. The court would then hold a hearing on the request. Weeks later, by the time attorneys were allowed to inspect Y-wing, the area had been changed. The corner stairway up which the assailants dragged Officer Mills had been sealed with cement and a new stairway had been constructed in the middle of the wing. Months later, defense attorneys would have possession of photographs which purportedly showed blood on the stairwell and walls but the pictures would be inconclusive. The question of the location of the struggle would be compounded by the Bransons' allegation that prison officials and the district attorney's office wanted the struggle to have taken place in a different location from where it actually occurred. This, both the Bransons and the defense attorneys charged, better enabled the state to select which defendants they wanted.

The initial arraignment hearing concluded with the judge ordering all parties not to "release to any news media information or opinion concerning the trial or any issue likely to be involved, other than the date and place of trial, the names of the defendants and attorneys, the contents of the indictment and the pleas of the defendants." This ruling brought a quick complaint from the defense. They charged that they were being intimidated and noted that the district attorney's office had already fired its salvos to the press, releasing such erroneous information as Jackson's nickname of "Karate" or Clutchette's weight-lifting ability. Judge Campbell rejoined that violation of his publicity order would be followed by "swift" punishment for contempt.

Ordinarily, complaints of excessive pretrial publicity are issues raised by defense attorneys. The notion that defense would object to the publicity gag was highly unusual. The defense attorneys renewed their efforts to remove the gag rule a week later. In a written motion, they stated that the ruling was "overbroad and invades the defendants' right of free speech and their constitutional right to educate the community as to the general issues posed by the prosecution." They also noted that the right to a fair trial was not imperiled because all the publicity had been issued by the prosecution and law enforcement agencies and it was all detrimental to the defense. The effect of the ruling was not to prohibit publicity but to prohibit the defense from talking with the press.

Judge Campbell heard arguments on the written motion the following day, March 5, and rather than reverse his publicity order, he did the exact opposite. He tightened the gag rule by ordering that all motions bearing on the publicity order be sealed until he had a chance to read and release them himself. In a move for which veteran Monterey County courthouse reporters could recall no precedent, Campbell cleared the court of press and spectators three times during the hearing while defense attorneys pleaded for a rescinding of the publicity order. Complaints by counsel that their clients were being denied a public trial were unavailing.

Defense attorneys then asked for copies of witness statements, to inspect any evidence in the possession of the prosecution and to visit the prison wing so they could better advise their clients prior to entering a plea in the case. Campbell denied the request for "lack of any showing or citation of authorities," even after Fay Stender cited two cases in which discovery was allowed before pleas were entered. Thorne offered to cite the U.S. Constitution and the Constitution of the state of California. Too late, the judge said. "The court has ruled on discovery and inspection."

Then, fearing additional adverse publicity, Fay Stender asked that the grand jury transcript be suppressed from release on grounds that the material, based on "psychological coercion and tainted evidence," was "illegal, unconstitutional and prejudicial." "That motion is denied," said Campbell. Stender asked that the transcript not be released until the attorneys could have an appellate ruling. "That motion is denied," said the judge. "The court," he added, "took good care of the defense in precluding the release of it so they would have time to take care of any prejudicial matter in it."

"That," Thorne angrily told Campbell, "is the most savage favoritism that I have ever heard in the courtroom. You're saying that I'll make special orders so the district attorney won't be in contempt when he releases material that is totally adverse, totally illegal, totally improper, in our belief, and certainly adverse to the opportunity of a fair trial for this defendant, but you turn right around and say to us we can't even have our motions that are filed in this court made available to the public."

When Clutchette's turn came, Silliman approached the bench. "All right," said Judge Campbell. "With respect to the motion for pretrial discovery as to the defendant Clutchette, do you wish to make any observations?"

"Before proceeding to that, Your Honor," Silliman responded, "I would like to have the court's ruling as to my preliminary motion to have the other—"

"Oh," said Campbell before Silliman could even identify his motion. "That motion is denied."

Like Stender, Silliman asked for suppression of the grand jury transcript. However, he surprised the court by filing a written motion on the spot and by offering to present one of the three inmate witnesses who had appeared before the grand jury. The inmate witness, Tom York, said Silliman, is "close at hand to offer testimony that he was psychologically intimidated and coerced to give the testimony that he did give" to the grand jury. "On that basis, we would certainly have a very strong motion to quash the grand jury indictment, and to release the testimony of a tainted witness before the grand jury would certainly prejudice this trial." York, Silliman added, was at that moment confined in the county jail, about two hundred yards away from the courtroom.

The judge, not hearing any objection from the assistant district attorney, asked if he had any comment. Barnes said that he thought it was "merely a matter of discretion" of the court. Campbell decided not to rule on the motion, in effect denying it. By the time the court convened again, weeks later, Thomas York had been transferred to a jail in southern California, near Los Angeles.

Judge Campbell was impatient throughout the proceedings. He continually fretted that too much time was being taken up by these arguments, though it had been his decision—and a highly irregular one—to have each of the defendants appear separately, thus forcing each of the attorneys to make the same motions over and over again. One morning during the first hearing, the judge looked at the clock and announced that it was ten o'clock and that the defendant had had more than a fair share of the court's time. During the second hearing, Campbell cut short Silliman's presentation by stating, "I have indicated you have had far, far more than a fair share of the court's time. Mr. Silliman, the court is through on this phase of the case now." Toward the end of the afternoon, the judge looked once more at the clock. "It's four o'clock in the afternoon," he observed. "We started at ten o'clock this morning. The court feels it has talked a good deal about the matter [of pretrial publicity]."

"We were perfectly willing," Silver reminded the judge, "to handle this all at one time."

"Wait a minute," said Campbell. "Are you going to talk about the order of publicity?"

"I'm willing," said Silver, "to talk about what the court is willing to talk about."

"I'll listen to what you have to say," said Campbell, "but not in such a way that it will defeat the court's ruling." The attorneys could not suppress a guffaw.

Later, the court, by its own volition, made procedures even more difficult for the defendants. Campbell declared that all motions filed by the defendants' attorneys would have to be filed separately. Thus, if the defendants wanted to interview witnesses, each attorney would have to draw up his own brief and file it. Thorne said he knew of "no rule of court . . . no law in the books," that gave the court that power. The ruling was imposing an undue burden on the defendants, especially since all previous practice indicated that joint motions could be filed, with each of the defense attorneys signing the same document. Even the assistant district attorney failed to comprehend the judge's ruling and suggested that it was merely a misunderstanding, that Campbell meant there could be joint motions if all participated in the drafting and signing of the document. The judge said no, separate papers had to be filed.

By mid-March, the case was receiving a great deal of local publicity. The next hearing, unlike the previous ones, was not heard in an empty courtroom. Now the room was crammed with more than a hundred townsfolk, blacks, Chicanos, law students and other spectators. More than fifty were turned away because the seats were filled. Eying the crowd, the bailiff offered a warning about proper behavior. "This judge may be a little bit more sensitive than others," he said to the crowd. He suggested that they not chew gum or react to the proceedings in any way. A group of law students who arrived late asked a deputy if extra chairs could be placed in the wide aisles. "The judge will have to decide that," he answered. "It's his courtroom."

The spectators abruptly stopped whispering when the three black prisoners shuffled in, dripping with chains. It was the first time that all three were allowed in the same superior courtroom. Their hands were cuffed and chained to chains around their waists. These iron knots linked with more chains which wrapped around their crotches. Their legs were manacled and chained together and padlocks swung as they stepped forward. Nine uniformed guards, most of them wearing sidearms, accompanied the prisoners. The three defendants wore neat starched blue denims. They looked cheerful.

"All rise," the bailiff intoned.

Judge Campbell looked around the audience and rapped his gavel. He was speaking to "those in the audience," he said, "as a matter of courtesy. The court doesn't want to have anybody embarrassed by being visited by the bailiff. It expects you to sit comfortably and properly, not the way you might sit or act at a barbecue table or the local corner pool hall." The spectators were stunned. They had been silent all along, but now they began whispering about what the judge had just said. He gaveled them to silence.

"He looks like Julie," one law student whispered. The student was referring to Federal Court Judge Julius Hoffman, who presided over the Chicago Conspiracy Trial. As this observation was passed down the rows, some of the spectators looked carefully at Judge Campbell. Indeed, Judge Campbell did resemble the Illinois jurist.

To cut off an expected defense motion for removal of the chains, Judge Campbell pointed out that this particular hearing was "not a trial on the merits. There's no jury in the jury box to see the defendants in chains," he said, but added, "and in some situations, why, that might be a possibility too whether they are chained or not chained when there's a jury in the courtroom." John Thorne disagreed with the judge's assessment. "There's now a definite change of circumstances in this courtroom," he said. "There's a courtroom filled with citizens and those citizens are obviously individuals who might well appear on any jury that is selected." "The court denies the motion," Campbell said firmly, again pointing out that Jackson was a "lifer."

Fay Stender asked to correct the record on the judge's misstatement. "With respect to what?" Campbell asked. "Your Honor said Mr. Jackson is serving a life sentence. That is not true. Mr. Jackson is serving an indeterminate sentence of one to life. He is eligible for parole from that sentence. That's different than saying a life sentence. I think the record should reflect that." "That is quite true," Campbell said. "It's a distinction without too much of a difference." Hearing murmurs from the spectators, Campbell again banged his gavel.

As the lawyers presented other motions, Campbell often rustled a few papers, leaned back in his chair, averted his face. His fingers played at his mouth. He leaned forward and came to life only when ruling on a motion or when pressing the proceedings forward. He did take notice, however, when defense attorneys submitted a motion to dismiss the indictment because of the unconstitutionality of the grand jury proceedings and on the basis of the makeup of the panel. Judge Campbell, as the presiding judge in the superior court, had been in charge of selecting that panel, a blue-ribbon group of jurors composed almost entirely of acquaintances of the judges in the district.

The defense argued that the process of selection of jurors systematically excluded the poor, blacks, Chicanos and the young. Despite the best of intentions, they said, a middle-class white is not able to understand cases involving people and situations so removed from his own experience. They weren't arguing that the entire panel should be made up of poor people, blacks, or Chicanos, merely that they be represented.

Judge Campbell noted that he himself had directed the selection of names for the grand jury and distinctly remembered that one of the thirty names submitted was a name of Spanish or Mexican ancestry. "I think it was Rodriguez or Gonzales or something," he said. Unfortunately, this particular Mexican was not picked. However, the judge added, there were two "Americans of nigra ancestry" on the current grand jury. What did the defense have to say to that?

Defense offered to show that no blacks had served on a Monterey County grand jury for a number of years, that the two blacks selected for the 1970 panel were middle-class blacks who served as token representation because of recent criticism and that, in any case, those blacks did not represent blacks like their clients and neither did the grand jury represent the people of the county. They asked for a separate hearing on the grand jury motion.

Judge Campbell hadn't been listening too closely. "I have it here. It's in writing. It's not just recollection," he said, referring to the Spanish surname of the prospective grand juror who was never selected. He didn't tell them, however, which name it was, Gonzales or Rodriguez or an entirely different one. Then he denied defense motions for a separate hearing, "there being no showing made to justify an evidentiary hearing." And added, "Should any appellate court, on the basis of the record in this matter, order what the defendants demand, that is, of course, its prerogative."

Defense then renewed their motions for discovery, access to Soledad's Y-wing, interviews with all eyewitnesses and access to all other physical evidence held by the district attorney or prison authorities, so they could advise their clients as to plea. Such rights of discovery, it should be noted, are matters of routine in cases of suspects arrested on the street, in their homes, or anywhere outside prison.

But this case seemed different, particularly when Clutchette's attorney, Floyd Silliman, informed the court that the area in Y-wing where the alleged crime took place had been changed. The judge rapped his gavel at the murmuring spectators. "The court," he said, "would be interested in what you have to say as to that." Silliman told the court that the stairwell up which someone was supposed to have dragged the guard had been changed, that a new stairway had been built in the center of the wing, that the railings around the third-tier catwalk, from which the guard was allegedly thrown, had been removed and replaced. Judge Campbell asked defense counsel if the sketches and diagrams provided by prison officials weren't enough. Campbell also asked if there were any photographs available "from previous times," addressing his question to Silliman, who had, along with other defense attorneys, been denied access to Y-wing. The defense had five photographs of Y-wing which prison officials had given them several days previous to the hearing.

What Silliman wanted to know, however, was how, in view of the reconstruction, either they or a jury could view the scene as it was on the day of the alleged crime. "By the time they get through," Silliman said, "it may end up looking like a country club." "The inmates who were in Y-wing," Campbell suggested, "they would be able to testify to its condition before, would they not?" "How would I know?" Silliman answered. "I haven't been allowed to ask them."

Campbell asked the assistant district attorney for comment and Barnes replied that he had understood there had been "some modifications in all the wings," reconstruction to center stairways, and that the reconstruction would be "prison-wide."

"I would go so far," Silliman concluded, "as to allege conspiracy against these defendants in this case because either they made these changes after the incident in question and as a result thereof, or if it was an institution-wide idea that they were going to put a center staircase in all of the wings, then it would be very interesting to find out why they started with Y-wing. Couldn't they have saved it for last, knowing that we would be wanting to get in there?"

The attorneys renewed their motion for discovery—physical access to the scene of the alleged crime—but Campbell denied the motion, stating he would not rule on the request until other pending matters had been disposed of—including the defendants' entry of a plea.

Despite the denial, Rich Silver pressed the point of the need for discovery prior to the submission of pleas. "I know of no case," Silver said, "that says a person does not have a right to discovery before entrance of plea. . . . This court has denied us that [discovery] and in so doing is denying these defendants a right to a fair trial, the right to any trial in denying us the right to effectively represent them."

He was merely following the law, Campbell countered, observing that "there are lots of laws that the court doesn't agree with but the court has to follow."

For the first time in the hearings, Judge Campbell smiled. He had removed what he thought was the last obstacle and now was the time for the prisoners to enter a plea. "The court will now take up the pleas of the defendants," he said, and then read the indictments against Jackson. "How do you plead?" he asked the black prisoner.

Mrs. Stender quickly filed a demurrer. Judge Campbell declared a recess.

The demurrer, another motion to quash the indictment, was based on a challenge to the constitutionality of Section 4500 of the California Penal Code, which provides a mandatory death penalty for a life term prisoner who assaults a guard.

After a fifteen-minute recess, the court resumed. The judge said that he was not surprised by the demurrer. He had prepared himself for such an eventuality and thus he was able to rule on it without delay. The demurrer was overruled on all grounds.

Mrs. Stender asked for a separate trial. "Denied," said Campbell. The judge managed another smile. "Now, with respect to the defendant Jackson . . ." he began again, rereading the charges and concluding with, "Now, Mr. Jackson, how do you plead?"

Jackson stood mute.

"The defendant Jackson," the judge said, "is within the immediate presence and hearing of the court and stands mute and therefore the court enters a plea of not guilty."

He asked Fleeta Drumgo the same question. "Mr. Drumgo," Silver answered, "believes that the proceedings so far have not been in the interest of justice and, in fact, a sham and a farce and for this reason he elects to stand mute."

Campbell entered a not guilty plea.

He turned to Clutchette. "I have instructed him to remain mute," said Silliman.

Campbell entered a third not guilty plea and set the trial for June 15. The defense quickly objected to the short time span. "I think five months is plenty of time to prepare for trial," stated Campbell.

"We're not talking about five months," said Stender.

"Four months or three months." The judge shrugged.

Actually it was slightly less than three months, but the judge eased up and extended the date to June 22, a week later. Now, said Campbell, he was prepared to reopen the motion on discovery. Barnes objected to the release of the names of witnesses until just before trial for "security reasons." Right, said Campbell; there might be a "possible retaliation."

John Thorne was angry. "Where is there any evidence anywhere in this record," he asked, "that any witnesses are going to be subjected to any retaliation? The district attorney hasn't said it. Certainly we haven't said it. I never heard that term before in this courtroom until Your Honor raised it."

"I thought that is what the district attorney said," Campbell replied.

"I meant to," said Barnes.

Fay Stender, fearing that the state, in the intervening two and a half months, could intimidate even more witnesses, made "an offer of proof" that "80 percent of the inmates there now can be coerced to give any statement they want at all. We are entitled to this now," she said of the list of witnesses, "before they really put the screws on."

That's not it at all, said Campbell. "There are certain persons that are called snitches and informers and so forth and it isn't always the healthiest thing in the world to be in that category in a prison."

Barnes agreed. To support the judge's statement, he mentioned an incident that had happened the previous day at Soledad, in which two guards were held as hostages. Barnes pointed out, of course, that the real purpose of the attack on the guards was not to harm them but to get at a certain prisoner. That's why, Barnes said, release of the names of witnesses would be dangerous. This was a fine stroke on Barnes's part since it would not be until more than four months later that a jury would strike that guard story down and believe the inmates' version, which was that the guards had fabricated the incident.

Judge Campbell asked Barnes how much time he wanted before releasing the names.

"Three weeks before trial," the assistant district attorney replied.

"It's the order of the court," said Campbell.

After the day's hearing, while driving back to San Jose with his brother's attorney John Thorne, Jonathan Jackson wondered how his brother George could possibly get a fair trial.

"Every motion, every motion," Jonathan said. "Denied."

He also anguished over the ten years that his brother had spent in jail and the chains that dripped from George's body. "Good God," Jonathan cried. "Isn't there some way to get those damned chains off him?"

He was silent for a while, then began talking about high school in Pasadena. He found it more difficult to study these days, he said, and was again silent.

"Ten years," he said later. "This is the way the pigs have been treating my brother for ten years and all because he refused to lick the jailer's boots. All this because he stood up like a man."

A pretrial hearing on March 27 began with arguments over defense rights to names and statements of prospective witnesses, names which Judge Campbell had ruled, at the district attorney's urging, would not be released until three weeks before trial. Judge Campbell, however, was on vacation and Superior Court Judge Stanley Lawson was presiding.

At the outset, Lawson asked Barnes for comment on the release of names of witnesses. Barnes replied, "We resist that motion vigorously." "Well," Lawson came back, "don't you think the defendants are entitled to know the names of those witnesses?" Yes, Barnes said, but he had already offered to produce the names three weeks prior to the trial itself. "Why not now?" the judge asked. Barnes explained, as Judge Campbell had previously, that release of the names would create a difficult security problem for the prison. The men would be subject to retaliation. Well, Lawson observed, those men would be subject to assault within the three weeks before the trial and, of course, after the trial.

Barnes retrenched. He pointed out that defense attorneys had been granted permission to interview all of the 130 or 140 inmates in Y-wing. During the course of the interviews they would surely talk to the less than twelve men whom he wanted as witnesses. "I think that is needlessly burdensome," said Lawson, and granted the defense request for names.

"Do I understand the court," Barnes asked, a bit incredulously, "that we have to disclose the statements of all witnesses?"

"Yes. Why not?" said Lawson.

"At the present time?" Barnes asked again.

"Why not?" asked Lawson.

Barnes shrugged. He asked the judge to recall *People* v. *Lopez,* a case that broached the question of defendants' discovery rights when possible intimidation existed. The judge said he was aware of the case. "I feel this way," he said, a touch of finality in his voice. "I am not going to require these people to go down and interview a hundred and thirty witnesses."

Defense attorneys then asked for investigative results on the January 13 killing of the three black inmates on the grounds that prosecution might use that as a motive, pointing out that Barnes already had "strongly intimated" the connection of the two, and that the killing of Mills was revenge.

"I may have said on one occasion that some of the inmates indicated that such might have been a motive, but I do not know. . . . This matter of the January 13 incident is strictly irrelevant."

Silliman asked if Barnes would stipulate that he would not later use revenge as a motive in court. "I don't know what the motive is to this," Barnes answered, "but I would certainly not want the court to tie my hands if anything might come up at a later time." Then, to Silliman: "If counsel wishes to tie my hands he should tie his also and make a statement right now as to his intention in the matter."

"I have," said Silliman.

"Yes, he has," said the judge.

Lawrence Mansir, a deputy attorney general representing the interests of the Department of Corrections, quickly offered Barnes some support.

"I think it is not relevant," Mansir said, "what actually happened and whether it was justifiable or not or whether the grand jury reached the correct conclusion or not; the only thing relevant to motive is what the defendants knew and what they thought."

Judge Lawson said Mansir was correct. This court would not be retrying what the grand jury had already considered. Barnes said producing the grand jury transcript would be more difficult than imagined since it was not transcribed. Lawson denied the defense motion.

When defense counsel asked for a copy of the Department of Corrections' Manual of Procedure for prison rules on guard assignments and medical treatment, the judge didn't even wait for Barnes to speak up. "I take it you object to that," Lawson said to Barnes. "Yes, Your Honor," said Barnes. "Sustained," said Lawson.

Later, Barnes produced Warden Fitzharris, who was sworn in to testify on the difficulties of providing security for the three defense counsels during their interviews. It would be best, the two men agreed, that defense counsel interview the 130 or so witnesses in the order that the prison suggested. Fay Stender objected to that procedure. She would consent only to an alphabetical order. "No big sweat," was Fitzharris's only comment to that.

Comparisons between the Campbell court and the Lawson court are intriguing. On the surface, there seemed to be major differences, particularly in style and mood. Where Campbell referred to "Americans of nigra ancestry," Lawson spoke of blacks. Where Campbell was strict and oppressive in his applications of the rules of etiquette, Lawson seemed more relaxed and informal. Where Campbell rustled papers and seemed to ignore many defense arguments, Lawson paid close attention. Where Campbell was brusque and often interrupted defense attorneys, Lawson was polite and presided over what seemed like an open forum. And yet, except for the release of names of witnesses, Lawson did not permit defense access to all of the information it needed. He would not overrule any of the restrictive orders that Campbell had laid down. Nor would he extend the short and impossible deadlines which Campbell had insisted upon. In the end, defense counsel had little to show for their efforts.

Judge Campbell returned from his brief vacation in time to preside over the next two hearings.

Judge Campbell had been watching the crowds swell from one pretrial hearing to the next. It was a curiously mixed affair: businessmen from the county, young students from Santa Cruz, housewives from Salinas and San Jose, militant blacks from Oakland, radical whites from Berkeley, and large numbers of Chicanos from San Francisco and the Salinas Valley. He could see some from the window of his chambers, long-haired and blue-denimed, marching around the courthouse, fists raised and clenched, shouting Black Panther slogans, demanding freedom for the Soledad Brothers. And inside the courtroom, where they jammed the benches, it was clear what side they were on.

Judge Campbell was troubled. He did not want "the foreign influence," as he put it, to affect the court or the proceedings. He knew that he could maintain order in the courtroom, even clear it of all spectators if it came to that. The problem was what to do about the demonstrators outside. He decided to write a law.

The letter he wrote to the Salinas city council was carefully drafted. In order to preserve a fair trial, he suggested an "emergency city ordinance." To provide what help he could, the judge enclosed a Louisiana statute which the U.S. Supreme Court had "expressly found constitutional."

May 7, 1970

To the Honorable
The City Council of Salinas, California
Salinas, California 93901
   Re: Trial of People v. Jackson et al.
     No. CR-2406, set for June 22, 1970
Gentlemen:
  As presiding judge of the Superior Court of California for Monterey County for the year 1970, it is one of my duties to preserve a fair trial atmosphere for all persons connected with any trial, including the above case.

  I have been informed through reliable sources, and from seeing copies of publications, that demonstrations are planned for the above mentioned trial, which could improperly influence the conduct thereof, and which could result in danger to persons and property.

  It seems only prudent in the exercise of reasonable foresight that an emergency city ordinance be passed to aid in the prevention of any improper activities.

All Superior Court judges are in full accord
with this request.

A law on the subject that was expressly found
constitutional by the Supreme Court of the United
States is attached hereto as a model.

We request your immediate consideration of
this matter.

Sincerely,
/s/ Gordon Campbell
Judge of the Superior Court

Attachment

Photocopies: City Council
              City Manager
              City Attorney
              Chief of Police

EXCERPT FROM
B. ELTON COX, Appellant
v.
STATE OF LOUISIANA

. . . Whoever, with the intent of interfering
with, obstructing, or impeding the administration
of justice, or with the intent of influencing any
judge, juror, witness, or court officer, in the discharge of his duty, pickets or parades in or near a
building housing a court of the State of Louisiana
. . . shall be fined not more than five thousand
dollars or imprisoned not more than one year, or
both.

Salinas city councilmen said they didn't know what to do with the
judge's proposed law and handed the matter over to their city attorney, Warren Lynch. The following week Lynch noted that there
"is a serious question" whether a city had jurisdiction to legislate on
a matter relating to the "atmosphere" surrounding a state court trial.
But, he added, he could report fully on the judge's request at the next
scheduled city council meeting.

Word of the Salinas city council's foot-dragging quickly reached the state capital. The day after the city attorney made his remarks to the press, State Senator Donald R. Grunsky, a conservative Republican from Watsonville, a vegetable shipping and packing center twenty-five miles north of Salinas, offered an "urgency statute" whose wording was exactly like the one Campbell suggested.

The bill did not pass in the state legislature.

It also failed in the Salinas city council. On May 17, the Salinas city attorney reported to the council that Salinas had no jurisdiction. The Louisiana state case which was upheld by the Supreme Court and which Judge Campbell offered as a model was described as not relevant. "It is my opinion that the conduct and control of trials in state courts . . . are matters which fall within the realm of state control." This, he added, also included "conditions in public areas of streets, sidewalks, courthouse grounds, parking lots and courthouse buildings, as well as the conditions in the courtroom itself."

At the May 14 hearing, Judge Campbell began reversing and modifying some of the discovery rights which his colleague Judge Lawson had granted seven weeks earlier.

The day began with Fay Stender asking the court to order Soledad officials to provide a recording made by Warden Fitzharris or Deputy Warden Black, telling the entire Soledad population that black prisoners attacked whites in the yard, that black inmates had been the cause of most of the recent troubles at the prison. Campbell said that had no relevance to the proceedings. Stender reminded the court that defense counsel already had a recording in which Black stated that the murder of the guard Mills was a reprisal for the death of the three blacks. She had, she said, another recording by Black, in which the deputy warden said black inmates attacked the whites and that was why the black prisoners were killed. "Your Honor," she concluded, "don't you believe, in this case, that something concerning the state of mind of all the black inmates in the prison—"

Campbell interrupted. "What I'm saying is let's suppose that the victim was—although I understand he was one of the most popular guards there—let's suppose he was one of the most hated—" Stender,

Thorne and Silliman objected immediately. "I'd like to ask the court," said Silliman, "from where you derive your information that the person alleged to have been killed was one of the most popular guards at the prison."

"Well," Campbell answered, "the court doesn't have to do that but the court will and the court states that it came from the news—various newspaper stories about it long ago." He denied the discovery motion for the third recording.

He also modified the order from Judge Lawson on the release of witness names. He told the defense attorneys that they could not use these names in their interviews with other witnesses, a ruling that would cause immense difficulties to the defense. What the ruling implied was that defense attorneys would have access to all witness statements in the hands of the prosecution and could use the statement in their interviews but not divulge who said it. For example, Thorne could show a witness statement to his client, Jackson, and Jackson might say, "That's not true. Who said that?" Thorne, under the new ruling, would have to say, "I can't tell you." If Thorne could have used the name and replied, "Well, John Doe says that," then Jackson might respond, "That's impossible. John Doe was in the hospital." Then Thorne would subpoena the hospital records and prove Doe a liar. Judge Campbell did not agree with Thorne's argument and stuck to his modification: defense counsel could not identify witness names to anyone, not even to the men on trial.

Thorne turned to another matter. He asked Campbell to explain why he sent the "emergency ordinance" letter to the Salinas city council. "I would request Your Honor to be sworn as a witness, as an adverse witness under the law and in accordance with the Evidence Code so we might question Your Honor concerning the letter."

Campbell was angry. "The court will state that the source of the information was the sheriff and the chief of police." Thorne asked that they be called to testify to the judge's allusion, in his May 7 letter, that demonstrations were anticipated "which could result in danger to persons and property." Request denied, said Campbell.

However, Campbell added, he would have the documents, his letter and page one of the Salinas *Californian* sealed. "The horse is gone," said Thorne. "If you want to lock the barn door now, that's fine."

On the contrary, said Campbell. It was Thorne who raised the question of His Honor's letter in the first place. "These things would never have come out if you hadn't asked what prompted the letter."

It had been a long day and Campbell was still angry. He recessed the court. Thorne asked if transcripts would be made available to defense counsel free of cost. "I said motions are denied."

The last week in May, defense attorneys moved to disqualify Judge Campbell for cause. Peremptory disqualifications in which judges are removed from trials at the outset with no cause stated are not uncommon in Monterey County. Disqualifications for cause are.

The defendants contended that Campbell was prejudiced against them and had been consistently inconsiderate toward them; they charged that the judge had made up his mind how to rule on some motions even before they were argued and that Campbell had violated his own rigorous ban on pretrial publicity.

It was now up to Campbell to answer the motion by admitting or denying the charges or simply to consent to the disqualification. If he admitted the truth of the allegation or consented to the disqualification, the case would be reassigned to another judge. If he denied the charges, another judge would conduct a hearing to determine whether he should be disqualified.

Campbell consented to disqualification three days later and assigned Anthony Brazil, another superior court judge, to hear the case. By consenting, Campbell avoided an open court confrontation on the defense allegations.

The first hearing before Judge Brazil began on an awkward note for the judge. The courtroom was again packed. Brazil had barely opened the proceedings when defense attorneys asked the first question. "Where are the defendants?" said Thorne. Oh, said Brazil, he had thought that their presence was not legally necessary and he "so instructed the sheriff."

The defense objected and refused to proceed in the absence of their clients.

Judge Brazil said he would adjourn the proceedings until the defendants could be brought to court in the afternoon. Before adjournment could be called, however, an argument developed on the seating of spectators.

Judge Brazil's third-floor courtroom in the old courthouse building generally has a seating capacity for legal personnel and an audience of eighty. When spectators began to file in, however, sheriff's deputies advised them and defense attorneys that the courtroom had been rechecked a week ago by the Salinas fire chief and he had restricted the total capacity to fifty.

Rich Silver, Drumgo's attorney, said he wanted to add the restricted seating arrangement to his reasons for seeking a change of venue, as "part and parcel of attempts by county officials to deny these defendants a fair trial." He also told the court the sheriff had called him recently, expressing concern for public security at this trial. The sheriff asked Silver for fingerprints and photographs of the defendants' relatives.

Debate on these and other motions proceeded until Silver asked Judge Brazil to disqualify himself for cause. "I could not possibly do that," the judge answered. "For me to say that I was prejudiced in any way would not be telling the truth."

To Silver's criticism of the seating capacity, Judge Brazil said simply, "I can't understand why you want a crowd of people." He recessed the court until 1 P.M. and ordered that the defendants be brought to court at that time. A short, slender man, Brazil arched out of his deep black leather chair and strode into his chambers.

He returned quite unexpectedly, however, and reconvened the court into session. He said he was "inclined to grant" a change of venue. The spectators began to smile. Brazil paused a moment, perhaps trying to phrase what he would say next, perhaps savoring a climactic moment. Then, tilting his head to a slight angle, Brazil announced that he would, in fact, grant the change of venue to San Francisco.

The courtroom erupted into cheers and applause. After the noise abated, Judge Brazil appeared on the verge of explaining his reason for the decision, then broke off abruptly.

"What good does it do to talk?" he said quietly. "It serves no useful purpose."

VI

Orchestrating a Movement: The Soledad Brothers

George Lester Jackson was born on September 23, 1941, in one of Chicago's oldest sections, the west side. Part ghetto and part factory slum, the area had seen its waves of immigrants: Jews, Poles, and then, in the years prior to World War II, the blacks. Lake Street near Racine, where the Jackson family first lived, was a montage of workingmen and their labors. The floorboards of the Jackson flat vibrated with the cacophony of drills, hammers, car horns and revving engines from the garage below. Across the street and down the block, factories clanged, banged and whirred into early evening. An elevated train clattered a few yards away from the Jackson front window and screeched to a halt not far away. "I felt," Jackson said, "right in the middle of things."

The first impression Jackson had of the white world was given him by Superman. He wasn't really disturbed by the fact that Superman was white; he merely felt that if there was a counterpart, the entity would be Supernigger and that would be he, George Jackson. He once tried to prove this to himself by tying a tablecloth around his neck, climbing to the roof of his apartment house, edging up over the rusted iron fence that bordered the roof and, having made other final adjustments for flying, preparing to leap. He would have jumped to an early death had not his sister Delora grabbed him and pulled him from the edge.

Jackson's second impression from the white world came in school. "Seeing the white boys up close in kindergarten," he recalls in his autobiography, "was a traumatic event. I *must* have seen some before in magazines or books but never in the flesh." When he saw his first white youth, George, in his curiosity, felt his hair, scratched his cheek; the white boy responded by hitting George in the head with a baseball bat, knocking him out. The event so disturbed Mrs. Jackson that she decided to send her son to a church school, Saint Malachy's.

Young George soon learned that Saint Malachy's was actually two schools situated across the street from each other. The white kids went to one; the blacks attended the other. He recalls that all his classmates walked to school, fought and played on sidewalk pavements while "they," the white kids, rode to school in large private buses and romped and ran on large tree-studded lawns surrounded by an eight-foot-high wrought-iron fence.

In 1949, after the birth of two more children, Frances and Penelope, the Jacksons moved to a larger apartment. Pay raises in the post office have never been very significant, and the Jacksons ended up moving to a tougher, more violence-prone ghetto area in exchange for more space. "The neighborhood around the place was so vicious that my mother never, never *allowed* me to go out of the house," Jackson said, adding that the only way he managed was to throw his coat out a window and offer to take down the garbage.

To protect George from the hot idle summer in the Chicago ghetto, Mrs. Jackson sent him to Harrisburg, in southern Illinois, her hometown, where he could live with her own mother, Irene, and her sister Juanita. Until prison days, the summers were periods for learning, fishing, hunting, identification of edible vegetation, and theft. "My mother and father will never admit it now, I'm sure, but I was hungry and so were we all," he wrote. His "activities went from stolen food to other things"—gloves for winter, marbles and games for amusement, ammunition for small game in and around Harrisburg. Occasionally, his mother would catch him with something that was stolen and scold him severely but, for the most part, George managed to live two lives, "the one with my mama and sisters, and the thing on the street."

Jonathan was born in 1951. At about that time the family, now numbering five children, moved to the Troop Street projects and George began having run-ins with the law. Although they caught him for mugging a couple of times, the police never took him in, relying instead on a kind of instant "oak-stick" justice, a few raps behind the ear. He made love to the "very loose and lovely girls" who frequented the project's stairwells, the hangout at the time, and he stopped attending school for a while. He ran away from home "a thousand times," vowing never to return.

"Jonathan, my new comrade, just a baby then, was the only reason that I would come home at all," he wrote months before Jonathan died at the Marin County Courthouse. At last, he had "a brother to help me plunder the white world."

After a series of bookings "on suspicion of" one thing after another, Lester Jackson decided to move his son out of the Chicago ghetto environment. He secured a transfer to the Los Angeles post office and in 1956 packed George into a secondhand Hudson heading west for Watts.

The move didn't change matters. George's problems began the first day he and his father arrived. The 1949 Hudson was the first car the Jacksons had owned and George wanted to drive it. He knew nothing about cars, but when his father went to visit a cousin and left him with the car, the baggage and the ignition keys, George turned a corner, streaked down one block, paused for a traffic light, turned a second corner and drove through the plate-glass window of a Watts barbershop. "Those cats in the shop had become so immune to excitement," George recalled, "that no one looked up. I tried to apologize. The brother that owned the shop allowed my father to do the repair work himself. No pigs were called to settle this affair between brothers." His father bought the necessary materials and repaired the damage.

The first entry on Jackson's rap sheet is dated January 5, 1957. Still only fifteen but already a six-footer and weighing nearly two hundred pounds, he was arrested for stealing a motorbike. When police stopped him, Jackson said he had just purchased the bike, reached into his pocket and produced a yellow sheet of paper which was signed by a Roy Ward. The paper was a bill of sale for the vehicle. Police who checked out the address on the sheet said the residence was a vacant lot. They felt that Jackson was trying to bamboozle them and hauled him in. George appeared in court accompanied by his parents who by this time were in L.A. The judge made him a ward of Juvenile Court but released him to the custody of his parents. Jonathan, then four years old, was also in court that day. "You be a good boy," the judge admonished George, "and you'll go far." The judge made a point about how light-skinned the Jacksons are. "Look at your little brother, how cute and nice he is," he said, pointing to Jonathan. "And your mother is a nice-looking woman. You know that families like this go farther than the real dark families and the real black people. People take all that into consideration."

Within two weeks, Jackson was in trouble again. Police said he dropped through a skylight and stole a crash helmet and other motorcycle equipment. Officials didn't explain how they caught up with him, but they ordered his mother to produce him at the old Georgia Street Juvenile Station and she complied. Jackson, according to police, eventually admitted to the theft, saying that he wanted to run away from home. What became more serious, however, was a juvenile officer's charge that Jackson pummeled him when he tried to search the youth as part of the booking procedure. As Russell M. Traphagen, now retired, tells it, Jackson knocked him down and kicked a woman associate when she tried to jump to his aid. The woman ran across the hall to the detective bureau for help. When help came, Jackson reportedly had Traphagen bent over a desk and was slowly forcing him toward a long steel spike sitting atop a blotter. "This guy would have put that spike through my back," Traphagen told a *Los Angeles Times* reporter. The juvenile officer said his narrow escape led to a new station house regulation that all desk spikes thereafter be blunted and bent into a reverse L shape.

That year, Jackson spent several months in juvenile detention in Paso Robles on charges of breaking into a department store and attempted hijack. During the hijack, one policeman started firing point-blank at Jackson, who was holding his hands up. George charged as the policeman kept firing. During the struggle, George's two partners managed to escape. "He had only wounded me twice by the time I closed on him," George said. One bullet went through his forearm. Another grazed his leg. In the police car, hospital treatment was offered as a reward for cooperation. Jackson didn't cooperate so it was two full hours before the cops drove him to a clinic near the police station. Then he was sent to Youth Authority Corrections in Paso Robles.

"The very first time, it was like dying," said Jackson of his Paso Robles experience. "Just to exist at all in the cage calls for some heavy psychic readjustments. . . . I never adjusted. I haven't adjusted even yet, with half my life already spent in prison. . . . Capture, imprisonment, is the closest to being dead that one is likely to experience in this life."

Jackson would later recall that he was never beaten at the reform school, that the food was good and adequate, and that he spent most of his time reading. The young Jackson made average grades at Paso Robles, completing the tenth grade, and was adjudged by his counselor to be of "high average intelligence." He was out in December 1957, after serving seven months. He enrolled in Manual Arts High School in Los Angeles and completed the eleventh grade.

In the spring and summer of 1958, Jackson went to work. For a time he was employed as a mixer and truck loader for a Hollywood beverage company, while he worked part-time at an East L.A. drugstore. Both jobs paid a dollar an hour, and within a few weeks he had saved enough to pay seventy-five dollars for a 1948 Mercury. In June, following an argument with his father, Jackson drove off to Bakersfield, where he rented a small apartment and secured work from a labor contractor. Because the contractor angered Jackson by his comments about blacks, Jackson slashed the seats of the man's bus with a knife. Jackson was arrested and spent ten days in jail. He met a woman who "felt almost as unimpressed with life" as he did, lived with her briefly, made a few friends. Soon he was broke, and he and two comrades borrowed a car. Before a week had passed, all three were in Kern County jail, charged with a $105 gas station robbery. To keep the three men separate, the jailers put George's two partners in the "felony tank" in different cells and placed Jackson in the milder "time tank," which was used for drunks and vagrants. Two months later, Jackson escaped.

It was a simple escape plan, one that worked because Jackson counted on his white jailers' inability to distinguish between one black and another. Kern County police had put a drunk in the time tank with Jackson to serve two days. On the morning of the second day, Jackson took the sheets off his bed and walked back to where the other black was sleeping. Jackson woke the man up and asked him if he would help in an escape attempt. No, the man answered, and dismissed Jackson with "one of those looks and a wave of the hand." Jackson sat down and began tearing a sheet into long strips. "What are you doin' with that sheet?" the man asked. "I'm tearing it into these strips," Jackson answered. "Why you doin' that?" the man asked again. "I'm making a rope," said Jackson. "Watchew gonna do with that rope?" came the question. "I'm going to tie you up with it," Jackson finally explained, and when the jailers called for the other black to be released that morning, Jackson appeared at the tank door and walked out. He was seventeen.

Jackson made his way to Harrisburg, Illinois, where he had spent much of his youth. There, in November, according to Kern County Deputy Sheriff Robert P. Johnson, Jackson "got involved in some type of cutting and they traced him to us through his prints." Deputy

Sheriff Johnson was dispatched to Illinois to bring Jackson back. He did, shackling the youth and accompanying him across the country on a train. Johnson, who hated Jackson, described the youth as "arrogant" and a "braggart." A month later, Jackson escaped once again from the Kern County jail. He had been involved in a fight with inmates in the felony tank and was taken to Kern County General Hospital for treatment of some minor injuries. While waiting, handcuffed, in the crowded emergency room, he and another inmate dashed down a hallway and fled from the hospital. He was recaptured the following morning on a golf course, where he reportedly broke into the pro shop and was trying to file off his handcuffs. Recommitted to the Youth Authority, he again served as a juvenile offender until paroled in June 1960.

Out on the streets again, Jackson went to work. He had been trained as a butcher during the most recent incarceration and found work with a meat-packing firm in Los Angeles. When business slowed down he was laid off. He found a second job, but was laid off again. With what little money he had saved, Jackson bought an old Chevrolet and in early September 1960, he and a friend took off for Tijuana to have some fun. They returned on the eighteenth, five days before Jackson's nineteenth birthday.

It was Jackson's last day of freedom. That night, Jackson and his friend went cruising, "looking for some chicks." The friend asked Jackson to stop at a filling station, went inside, held up an attendant for seventy-one dollars and came out to tell George to "get going." Jackson did, but one of the filling station attendants had jotted down the license number when they fled. Police checked the registration and went to Jackson's Pasadena residence, where they were told he was in Los Angeles visiting a friend. When confronted by the police, Jackson readily admitted that his car had been in the filling station at the time of the holdup but he said he had merely gone there for gasoline and been forced at gunpoint to drive a bandit away from the scene. Later, police said, Jackson told them he had been a passive participant, declaring that his companion, high on reds purchased in

Tijuana, had suddenly pulled a gun when they stopped for gas and committed the crime himself. The companion, however, told police a different story. He claimed that the holdup was Jackson's idea and added that Jackson had supplied the gun.

The police didn't know whom to believe, but the case was solved when both pleaded guilty. The public defender, burdened with a heavy caseload and caring little to go to trial, had pointed out that if Jackson fought the conviction, his previous record at Paso Robles and Kern County would hurt him more than if he pleaded guilty and threw himself on the mercy of the court. For doing so and sparing Los Angeles County the court costs, he would be given a light sentence in the county jail. It didn't work out that way at all. When the sentence was handed down, Jackson was given one year to life imprisonment in state prison. He would never come out. He was eighteen when arrested on the last charge, nineteen when he entered Soledad Prison, and thirty when he was shot to death on the San Quentin yard.

In prison, Jackson made some new friends. It was there, he said, that he "met" Marx, Engels, Lenin, Trotsky, Mao and Fanon, and they "redeemed" him. "I'm supposed to be a criminal. I'm supposed to have a criminal mentality," he told me during one of our interviews. "Why, I was robbing people when I was twelve, with a great big ol' gun. But always, always, my whole slant in plundering things was in solidarity with other blacks against the white world." Jackson viewed crime and criminality much as the early American black rebellion leader and minister Nat Turner did. When Nat Turner was asked to confess to a series of murders and other crimes before he was hanged in Virginia in 1831, the black rebel turned the question around: "I've been asked to confess . . . to *what???* I simply don't feel *guilty.* I have ventured my life for the deliverance of my kind. I am a willing sacrifice to their cause. I have failed, and if you gentlemen would render me a favor you would take me out and hang me immediately."

Jackson quoted the Nat Turner statement several times. He believed it. For Jackson, the relationship between blacks and whites in America hadn't changed since the days of slavery. Blacks haven't been a part of white American society. They've been captives, rebelling and resisting unjust bonds, political, economic and social suppression, organized racial injustice. For Jackson, criminality in America, as defined by the white power structure, is a "very small knot of men and women" who are protecting their constitutional right to own and control the resources, the labor and the minds of the people who live on this continent and, by a logical capitalist/ imperialistic extension, the world. Laws are formulated by this small group so that it can maintain its elite ownership and management condition, thereby controlling the masses of minorities and poor whites. For Jackson it is a "society above society," and the only response of the people "will take some form of violence." Like Marx, Jackson does not call this individual or collective violence a crime: it is simply an antithesis to the capitalist thesis.

Jackson met like-minded black revolutionaries in prison, revolutionaries such as Bill Christmas, James Carr and W. L. Nolen. Christmas, who was alive when Jackson first wrote about him, was shot to death during the attempt to take hostages in the Marin County Courthouse shooting. James Carr, Jackson's closest friend in prison, was gunned down in front of his San Jose home about eight months after Jackson was killed in San Quentin. Carr, who was assassinated by contracted killers, was a controversial figure both before and after Jackson's death. Police said he was trying to help Jackson escape from San Quentin. Conversely, there were some unsubstantiated rumors stirring among West Coast radicals that Carr was an agent for the police. One version had it that he was going to be a surprise witness for the state in the Angela Davis trial. He was shot and killed in front of his San Jose home during the trial.

Jackson met W. L. Nolen in 1966. A year earlier, Jackson had been caught with some escape tools in San Quentin and confined to maximum security isolation. When he was returned to the general prison population in March, his work assignment was the prison hospital. Soon after, Nolen was brought to the San Quentin hospital with a bleeding stab wound in his back. The blacks who helped sneak Nolen into the hospital told Jackson that Nolen had been attacked by a gang of white racists. Nolen asked Jackson to keep the matter to himself. He planned to get even. "I fed him morphine tablets," Jackson later wrote, "gave him a tetanus injection and sewed the hole in his back as best I could." After the two became friends, Jackson and Nolen formed a clandestine Marxist-Fanonist study group, both men supporting each other in lectures and group discussions which took the cloak of ethnic awareness meetings. Nolen, the boxer, and Jackson, the karate expert, also took turns teaching their black comrades how to defend themselves. Eventually, before both men were transferred to Soledad, they managed to politicize the Capone gang, the toughest group of blacks at Quentin.

"We tried," said Jackson, "to transform the black criminal mentality into a black revolutionary mentality." He was immensely successful. Indeed, the politicization of black prisoners in the California prison system—even coming as it did after the civil rights movement, Malcolm X, Martin Luther King, Eldridge Cleaver and the Black Panther party—owes its energies and direction to Jackson more than anyone else. He was, as he put it once, the "focomotor."

Of course, his beliefs and his energies earned him the lasting hatred of prison guards and various prison administrations. Between 1962 and 1970, Jackson was cited forty-seven times for disciplinary infractions. He was denied parole ten times, even though his crime partner in the gas station robbery had been released years before. Prison officials say his first disciplinaries were for minor matters— playing poker, grabbing more food from the chow line when he was hungry. But they claim that the infractions became more serious.

In March 1962, after a black was stabbed in a racial fight, Jackson and several other brothers tried to "punish the assailant." They were stopped by guards, who shot at them, then gassed and chained them and transferred them to San Quentin. In December 1962, he was re-

leased from maximum and sent to the San Quentin general population, where he quickly saw that black inmates were being "misused,
abused, assaulted, and murdered." He and five other inmates formed
a general staff for the defense of black inmates. A year later, he was
again sent to maximum security for "paramilitary group" activities.

In April 1965, he was accused of stabbing a white prisoner. In
September 1966, a white inmate claimed that Jackson tried to stab
him. In January 1967, he was involved in a prison work strike which
turned into a "riot." Some white strikebreakers, taking matters into
their own hands, tried to lynch one of the striking blacks. Jackson and
his friends jumped in and broke it up. He was charged with assault.
A month later, Jackson said he attacked a Mexican inmate "for race
talk on the tier." In June 1967, a San Quentin guard nearly broke
Jackson's kneecap when Jackson tried to protect a white prisoner
from a beating. The white con had testified on behalf of some blacks
in a court case, and he was being worked over by other white
prisoners. In January 1969, he was transferred back to Soledad.
Within a month he had started another Marxist study group and had
taken over leadership of the martial arts class. In October of that
year, he was sent to isolation for possession of a "simulated weapon."
"I actually had a bent clothes hanger with some tape around it for
our karate class," Jackson explained. And three months later, in
January 1970, he was charged with murder and assault, the killing
of Officer Mills.

In June 1970, Jackson told me, "I've probably forgotten half the
stuff. The years run together on me and I don't see it as a train of
events any longer. I have always been a 'bad' con. Since the pigs have
never been able to break me through isolation, they have been forced
to frame me and set me up for the final kill."

A probation report prepared after Jackson's conviction for the
seventy-one-dollar robbery noted that although Jackson was "rather
young," he was not ready for professional treatment. "Other than
when he is placed within an institutional setting, he seems to have
very little capacity to accept reality restrictions. At the present time,

he is not anxious nor much aware of the serious nature of his anti-social behavior."

Ten years later, others offered their evaluation. In September 1969, four months before Jackson would be charged with killing the guard, a Soledad official named R. D. Cain wrote that Jackson had "good work habits" and was making "satisfactory progress." Two months later, J. Carpenter, another Soledad counselor, reversed that assessment. He wrote, "Subject has been doing less than satisfactory."

"Subject," Carpenter's report went on to note, "has been involved in a karate group and on 10/17/69 was found in possession of a simulated gun which he claims was used in the karate group practice. As we are trying to make room for South Facility inmates, subject should be considered expendable on basis of his record here and the circumstances of his transfer." Then, clearly in someone else's handwriting, eight more words were added to the report: "Failed industries assignment. But has many, many enemies."

Other disciplinary write-ups came quickly. On December 20, Jackson was charged with "stealing or dealing" and "offensive language." He was found "guilty" and given five days of strip cell isolation. Less than a month later, Officer Mills was found dead, and Jackson was written up for "inmate behavior" and sentenced to twenty-nine days of isolation in preparation for the murder indictment.

George Jackson, at thirty, had spent nearly half his life in prison. He had been denied parole as many times as the years he has been imprisoned for a seventy-one-dollar second degree robbery charge. The gray "jacket," his prison folder, is thick with disciplinary write-ups and accusations that describe a man who, in the beginning, was a sentient individualist. Ten years later, when a parole board leafed through his folder, groping for the "key" to George Jackson under the line "basic personality pattern," they found one word: "anti-social."

In February 1961, when George Jackson entered state prison at age nineteen, he was asked, as all newcomers are, to describe himself in a mimeographed questionnaire. "My name is George Lester Jackson," he wrote in a firm penciled longhand. "Direct descendant of Lester and Georgia Jackson. One member of the human race."

That questionnaire has never been made public. The young Jackson also answered some other questions on the forms. In one part the new prisoner was asked to complete a series of statements. He wrote as follows:

"I would make enemies if . . . *I conducted myself in an antisocial manner.*"

"I would get better if . . . *I had a proper education.*"

"I like to make love . . . *when it rains.*"

"A husband has a right to . . . *some freedom.*"

Of all the questions asked, Jackson left only one blank. He did not complete a sentence that began, "I am scared when . . ."

He was also given space to fill in his "goals in life." "To be a successful writer," he wrote, "and to take a normal place in society." He was also asked to state, simply, his philosophy. "I am of stoic nature. I believe in live and let live. I try to be easy to get along with and I try to get along with others. I don't make friends easily but I accept others as they are."

Like Jackson, Fleeta Drumgo and John Clutchette had been in and out of juvenile detention and state prison most of their young adulthood. Drumgo, now twenty-six, had spent eleven of the last twelve years in custody, and Clutchette, at twenty-nine, had been in and out since he was fourteen. Both were serving indeterminate sentences for second degree burglary when charged with killing Soledad guard John Mills.

Clutchette, however, had been a model prisoner since he had entered prison on the second degree burglary charge in 1966, and was expected to be paroled on April 20, 1970. In fact, as a matter of CDC procedure to prepare an inmate for release, Clutchette should have been transferred to Chino, a minimum security reception center. Generally, when inmates are given parole dates, they withdraw. They avoid any participation in petty disputes, gang or clique arguments, fights, or even disagreements with guards. They know that the smallest infraction could rescind any chances for "making the date." It seemed unusual that Clutchette would take part in killing a guard.

The Clutchette family moved from Houston, Texas, to the Los Angeles Watts ghetto in May 1943, so that the elder Clutchette, whom John is named after, could work in the wartime airplane industry. Clutchette, in the spring of 1972, described those years as "awfully dull," enlivened by gang activity and street fights, blacks against blacks, east side against west side.

"I was gettin' into a lot of trouble when I was livin' in Watts," he said with a slow, deep drawl. "You know, goin' back and forth to jail, just a little petty theft, gang fightin' and stuff like that." When he turned sixteen, the family moved to Compton, an adjacent neighborhood which was part black and part white. They were the only black family on the block, something that "sure was way out to me," Clutchette said, because the family had never "seen" integration.

The new neighborhood didn't keep him out of jail. In prison when the family first moved there, he came home and enrolled in junior high school for a while, then returned to jail. When he got out he entered high school. Then came a parole violation and he was in jail again; this time the imprisonment was spent at the Deuel Vocational Institute at Tracy and completed at Soledad's North Facility. He was paroled at nineteen and stayed out for almost five years before returning on his current charge, second degree burglary.

He still maintains his innocence of that crime. "They found out I was livin' with this woman," Clutchette explained, "and they came in the house and every damn thing in there was stolen, you know. She was on welfare and everything. She had five kids and the only thing they could trace down was this television set. I wasn't there at the time. I was at work. At this time, I was kinda squared up. I was workin' out there at North American Aviation, drawin' decent enough pay and makin' my own way."

The police came during lunch hour. They asked him to get into the patrol car. "For what?" Clutchette asked. "We'll find something," the officer answered. The cops found a couple of unpaid traffic tickets, added that to the charge of burglary or receiving stolen goods, and that was enough to lock Clutchette up until trial. Meanwhile, his mother, Doris Maxwell, who had remarried, had traced down the man who sold the TV set to Clutchette and his woman, but the man refused to testify and fled the state. "So I just rode the beef, man, you know, to keep anything from happening to her and the kids and stuff."

Clutchette feels that he should have been charged with receiving stolen goods. His attorney, however, advised him to plead guilty to the second degree burglary charge, pointing out that Clutchette had been working steadily since he'd been out and that the judge would take that into consideration. Clutchette agreed to his suggestion. But then the judge started mentioning his past record and handed down a sentence of six months to fifteen years. "I even did a little crawl for the government man and they still sent me to the penitentiary for that TV set."

Fleeta Drumgo, like Clutchette, was born in the South, in Shreveport, Louisiana, moving west with his family in his early childhood. He barely remembers his father because his parents separated when he was very young. He was only eight years old when his juvenile probation record began. The list of charges was similar to that of other black youths in Watts and other ghettos—fighting, petty theft. He remembers that his aunt took him away from Los Angeles for four years, until he was twelve, but when he returned, life still seemed to be a matter of exits and entrances to juvenile hall. At fifteen, he was sentenced to eighteen months for possession of barbiturates. Four months after he was released from this charge, he was recommitted for assault with intent to commit murder.

The latter charge, however, did not exactly fit the crime. In fact, Drumgo's mother, Inez Williams, is sorry now that she even called the police. Drumgo had never got along with his stepfather, and during one heated argument in November 1963, he picked up a

gun and fired several shots into the ceiling. Mrs. Williams called the
Los Angeles Police Department and signed the complaint. Drumgo
spent two and a half years at Tracy. But even there he had run-ins with
the staff. He was suspected of participating in Tracy's riots, and he
spent most of his time in isolation. Transferred to Soledad for the
remainder of his time, Drumgo served eleven months before being
paroled.

He had been out twenty days when he was arrested for burglary
at his partner's house. He was forced to confess at gunpoint, he said,
and was returned to Soledad in 1967. By 1970, he was hoping for
a parole date. Indeed, on the basis of his time served and the average
penalty time for other inmates on the same offense, he might have
been paroled a year before. But he had tacked up political posters
of his heroes, Rap Brown and Stokely Carmichael, on his wall, kept
some "black books" on his shelves, and was reported for it. When
Officer Mills was killed, Drumgo was about to have a parole hearing.
He had kept his discipline record clean and therefore he had expected
a release fairly soon.

The indictment of the three changed all that. Drumgo never was
granted that parole hearing. Clutchette's parole date was rescinded,
although he is out now, after having been acquitted. Jackson simply
refused to appear for two parole hearings which were scheduled. He
knew it was a waste of time.

I first met George Jackson on June 18, 1970, when he was being
brought out of Soledad's O-wing for a meeting with his attorney
John Thorne. At the time, I was part of a three-man team which
had been appointed by the state's black lawmakers to investigate the
prison. The three of us were standing in the main-line corridor
outside the massive red door which led to O-wing. Jackson was
coming out. As in court, he was dripping chains. "Stand clear," an
O-wing guard yelled at us. "Stand clear. Karate Jackson is coming
out." The guard cupped his hands to his mouth and barked twice

more, turning his head toward the east and west ends of the main-line corridor. "Karate Jackson is coming out. Stand clear. Karate Jackson is coming out."

Shoulders back, a brown folder crammed with papers under his left arm, Jackson walked a half pace in front of the two guards who accompanied him. He didn't know us but he managed a shy smile, looked toward the guard, then raised his right arm as far as the chains would allow, giving us the black power salute. At the urging of prison officials, we agreed not to interview Jackson or his codefendants, Fleeta Drumgo and John Clutchette.

What prompted the prison investigation was the number of telephone calls and letters that state senators and assemblymen were receiving in their district offices and in Sacramento. Most of the complaints and requests for an investigation were channeled to California's six black lawmakers, five of whom were assemblymen. The sixth, State Senator Mervyn Dymally, from Los Angeles, was one of the ranking Democrats in the upper house. Most of his constituents were black. Dymally was chairman of the Senate's Democratic Caucus, a member of the committee on Criminal Punishment and Parole Practices of the Senate Judiciary Committee, and the state's only black senator.

The Democratic leader in the lower house was John J. Miller, a lanky black assemblyman from Berkeley. In addition to his leadership role in the party, Miller served on two legislative bodies that affected the Department of Corrections. He was vice-chairman of the Criminal Procedure Committee and a member of the California Penal Code Revision Commission. Dymally and Miller, along with San Francisco assemblyman Willie Brown, wanted a state investigation into the numerous charges of prison abuse which parents, relatives, wives, inmates and others had brought to their attention. In fact, Dymally had wanted such an investigation ever since he visited George Jackson earlier in the year. The lawmakers decided not to hold a press conference at which to publicize the charges found in the letters and telephone calls. Dymally felt that a more effective tactic would be to meet quietly with CDC director Raymond Procunier, and ask him about the allegations and listen to his comments.

Procunier met with the legislators in May. Dymally invited Fay Stender to join the meeting. Procunier listened to allegations that black prisoners were given contaminated food; that ground glass, urine and fecal matter had been occasionally mixed in with their food; that the inmates suffered threats on their lives; that the January 13 killings were not "justifiable homicide" but, at best, negligence and, at worst, murder; that blacks suffered racial harassment from guards who addressed them as "niggers," "hammers" and the like. The group asked for a biracial investigative commission to look into the charges.

That is not necessary, Procunier said. He denied that any of those conditions existed at Soledad, and commented that he did not see the need for a biracial investigative commission. Instead, he proposed that the legislators or their representatives visit the prison unannounced on June 1 to see the institution in operation at first hand. When the Black Caucus arrived at Soledad, they learned that Procunier had modified his original proposal. It was not to be an unannounced visit. Not only that, but Procunier himself was there to welcome the group and announced that he would join in the tour. Procunier's team included Warden Fitzharris, associate wardens Black and Swagerty, O-wing program administrator E. A. Petersen and two members of the CDC Sacramento staff, a pleasant, straightforward public information officer named Phil Guthrie, and Frank Powell, a pudgy, round-faced, cigar-chomping young black who advised the director on "ethnic matters."

After a front-office briefing, the group proceeded to O-wing, where they spent two hours interviewing black and white prisoners. The prisoners repeated the charges made in the letters: food contamination, racial slurs from guards, the murder of three black inmates on January 13. However, other charges were made. Various guards, some inmates declared, were setting up racial fights at three-to-one and six-to-one ratios by leaving certain cells unlocked. The inmates added that a few guards smuggled weapons to favored white inmates. Eugene Grady, the black prisoner who would have been the sixteenth man to enter the yard on January 13, complained specifically that he had received no medical attention for a severe ulcer which caused him to spit blood.

In addition to hearing confirmation of the charges mentioned in inmate letters, the visitors met convicts who had no idea why they had been removed from the general prison population, the main line, and locked up in O-wing. Some said they thought they were there "for investigation" only, although they had been there for some weeks. An illiterate Chicano inmate was unable to read a letter he recently received from his attorney and complained that no one would read it to him.

Afterward, in Fitzharris's office, Procunier commented on the charges. The reports of contaminated food and coffee, he said, were "beyond belief." When pressed about the reason so many O-wing prisoners had given similar reports, Procunier replied, "I don't know what I can say. You either have faith in the system or you don't." He then turned to the Soledad administrators who sat to his left and right. Had any prison inmate placed urine in another's coffee in the last six months? he asked Fitzharris, Swagerty, Black and Petersen. They categorically denied that any such thing could have taken place.

When one group member asked about Grady's bleeding ulcer, Fitzharris said, "We have to have a lot of blood before we give an x-ray. Otherwise, everyone would want one." He added that he would have someone look into Grady's case. Next to be raised was the problem of inmates being locked in O-wing without knowing the reason for their isolation and maximum security status. Procunier stated, with the agreement of Fitzharris, that all inmates of O-wing had been told why they were there. Fitzharris readily agreed to have his staff inform them once again.

A week after this visit, the black legislators learned that seven more black inmates had been confined in O-wing and were, in fact, in the wing on the day of the tour. They were sentenced there as punishment for soliciting donations from inmates for the Soledad Brothers Defense Fund. Prisoners could legitimately collect money for the deceased guard, Soledad officials had decided, and they even arranged a press conference to announce the event. However, collecting money for the legal defense of the suspected assailants, who proclaimed their innocence, was, as one official put it, "a horse of a different color."

At the conclusion of the June 1 visit, Dymally and Procunier agreed that two staff members of the Black Caucus would be permitted to spend "an extended period of time" in the prison during the summer to further investigate the inmates' allegations. The period of time was later shortened to a few days. That is where I came in—quite by accident. Once the time allowed for investigation had been narrowed, various members of the legislative group wanted to send in a six-man team: three administrative assistants or staff consultants—Dan Visnich, Jim Turner and Martin Fassler (a University of California–Berkeley law student); and three reporters— Tim Findley of the *San Francisco Chronicle,* Bill Marmon of *Time* and me, representing *Newsweek* at the time. Several of the lawmakers, however, balked at sending three reporters. After some discussion, they evidently decided to send one reporter. Fassler and I were "hired" as legislative interns and I took a vacation from *Newsweek.*

We drove down to Soledad on a hot, muggy June night and met Frank Powell, the CDC's ranking "ethnic-relations" man, at the prison gates the following morning. Powell's presence, as our escort officer, produced untold difficulties in the interviews, since some of the inmates recognized him as "that cigar-chomping dandy from Sacramento" and quickly passed the word to others. Powell insisted that we "stick together" for "security reasons." He leaned against a nearby wall or an adjacent cell while we interviewed. When we said we could work more efficiently without his presence, he seemed hurt by the suggestion. These are dangerous, violent men, he reminded us. They might want to kill us. Besides, one tour was easier to conduct than three. A few inmates—the ones who thought Powell was "just another bull"—refused to talk with us, pointing out that since we were "running around" with Powell they'd just as soon talk with Fitzharris because that, they said, was "about all the good it'd do."

Despite suspicions, most of the prisoners were candid in their complaints. "We have nothing to hide," a white prisoner from Los Angeles told us in the prison dining hall. "They do. You won't be able to do anything about this place but it's nice you came. This is the first time I've ever had barbecued chicken in this joint, and I've been here three years."

We made some disturbing discoveries. The men were given physical examinations when they entered prison, none in the years thereafter. One prison psychiatrist was assigned to handle the needs of 2,787 men. The men were "disciplined," with consequences ranging from twenty-nine days in the "hole" to a life term, without due-process procedural safeguards; it was the guard's word against the inmate's. When we looked at the roster boards in each wing, we noticed the letters W, N, M beside different names. The M stood for Mexican. We were told that there was equality in the vocational training and shop courses, but found a white predominance in the more desirable trade classes, such as printing, dentistry, hospital and maintenance shops. We asked that the CDC investigate the prison hospital to find out whether the blacks assigned there were in actual training or, as we were told, sweeping floors. In each program, we discovered that there was a "foreman" or "lead man" position, filled by a white. The elderly Catholic chaplain told us he was afraid to enter the cells to talk with prisoners. He didn't trust the inmates; they didn't trust him.

The prison went to extremes to maintain racial fairness, we were told. They gave us an example. The prison, as a whole, is divided statistically into four racial categories: white, Negro, Mexican-American and other. Whites make up 48 percent of the population; the "coloreds" the other 52 percent (27 percent black, 23 percent Chicano and 2 percent other). The fairness, the officials pointed out, comes in the sense that this ratio is maintained not only in each wing, but on each of the three tiers within each wing. Such a balance presents a problem from the inmates' point of view because the tiers are rated on a discipline/reward system. First-tier inmates on the main line are required to lock up in their cells at 7:30 P.M. Second-tier inmates go to bed at nine-thirty; third tier at eleven P.M. The problem comes in "promoting" a man from one tier to the next. A white, we were told, cannot be promoted to a cell that was formerly occupied by a "colored" and, conversely, a "colored" cannot be promoted to the cell of a former white inmate. We asked an A-wing guard about promotion of Mexican-Americans and the fifty or so "other" races. "In tier grading," the guard answered, "we make no difference between the whites and the Mexicans." He added that "Chinamen and Japs can also go in those cells." Nearly all the inmates disliked being lodged on Grade I status, the first tier. Up on Grade III, the prisoners can go to bed early, undisturbed by the games, conversations and television noise on tier I, the ground floor.

Inmates also complained about the lack of "meaningful" academic and educational programs. "I'm tired of Dick Tracy comics," said an O-wing member of the Aryan Brotherhood. "If my family sends a book in, the people here won't let it through. We have nothing creative to work with." Officials do scrutinize books entering the prisons and a number of books and magazines are not allowed in. Underground newspapers or magazines such as *Ramparts* may be contraband at one prison but not at another. George Jackson's book of prison letters, *Soledad Brother,* was not allowed in Soledad. The discretion is the warden's. The trend is toward more restrictions; a new regulation requires books to be mailed directly to the inmate from the publisher.

As in earlier and later interviews, blacks charged that the guards were still calling them "niggers" and "hammers." White inmates, even members of the Aryan Brotherhood, agreed that this was so. Inmates of all races told of the fomentation of racial hostilities by guards and other correctional personnel. They reported incidents which ranged from set-up killings to more subtle maneuvers such as writing a disciplinary report on a white inmate for having long hair while overlooking a black prisoner who obviously had longer hair. "We're getting hip to that," a white inmate commented, "so it doesn't bother us so much anymore. But you just know they can always find some dummy who'll waste a guy for fifty bucks and a transfer."

After the interviews, we met with Fitzharris, Black, Swagerty and Petersen. We reported inmate grievances and offered a list of sixteen recommendations which included the establishment of an inmate grievance board, hearings for prisoners facing punishment, ethnic and racial educational programs for guards, the employment of psychiatric therapists, and yearly physical examinations for prisoners. The warden and his deputies were unenthusiastic. The recommendations did not reflect the real conditions at Soledad. "Things are running real smooth here," Fitzharris told us. "We just don't have those problems."

We asked about the recreation equipment, particularly the weight-lifting apparatus, which was color coded to indicate usage according to race. The older, more worn, barbell equipment, marked with distinctive red dots, was reserved for black inmates, we were told. When we asked the administrators about it, we were informed that this was "traditional." To make changes in this area could be "very volatile."

A black member of our group asked whether it would not be wise to transfer the O-wing program sergeant, R. A. Maddix, pointing out to Fitzharris that it was Maddix whom prisoners accused of spitting on them, beating them and calling blacks "niggers" and "hammers." Jim Turner, the black legislative aide, mentioned that Maddix had been exceedingly racist toward him. "If that happens to me," Turner asked, "what do you think happens to the inmates when the doors are closed and he's left in charge?" Deputy Warden Black answered. "Officer Maddix is very custodial-conscious," he said. "We've investigated his procedures to make certain that they are humane. At times I have questioned Officer Maddix's abruptness and gruffness

and he's worked on it on occasion but, dammit, the man gets results."
When we asked about racial coding on cells whereby blacks could not advance in grade to cells formerly occupied by whites, and vice versa, we were told that the "inmates wouldn't stand for an open cell-grading system." We pointed out that it was the inmates who suggested it, but Black said such a system would be "unrealistic." Other improvements—annual physical examinations for inmates, psychiatric exams for guard applicants and additional psychiatric therapists to administer to inmates—would be "too expensive."

"We've been through all this before," Fitzharris said with an air of finality. "Most of what you suggest has been covered before. And we've found that it won't work." Point by point, he refuted each suggestion or recommendation with one of two comments: the cost was too great; the prisoners would not agree to change. Our reiterations that the inmates had suggested the changes were brushed aside.

Recommendations were made that O-wing prisoners be given greater access to the prison library and group counseling sessions; that the exercise period be extended beyond the daily half hour, that more food and a more varied diet be provided; that the medical officer spend more than ten minutes a week in a wing which housed about a hundred men; that men who had no toothbrushes be given them; that inmates be allowed to exercise in the outdoor recreation yard even if only in segregated groups: all these were brushed aside as "too burdensome" to effect immediately. They said they would "look into the matter." Within two months, O-wing prisoners went on two hunger strikes and a mattress-and-clothing "burn-in" to make the same demands.

There was little left for our group to do but put our recommendations on paper. As the prisoners themselves predicted, it was another one of those studies to be filed and forgotten. Once the investigative report was approved by the lawmakers, Dymally made the decision to present it quietly to CDC director Procunier and wait for a response. This, Dymally thought, might do more good toward improving conditions for the men. Taking the report to the press might prove self-defeating amid all the anticipated bickering between the legislators and the CDC. Procunier did not reply.

While the report shuffled around CDC offices, a second guard was killed at Soledad. Forty-year-old William C. Shull was found stabbed to death in a recreation shack on the yard of North Facility. The guard's tall, husky frame bore the marks of forty-two stab wounds. What shocked Soledad officials most was the manner in which they learned of the murder. An anonymous caller, telephoning from somewhere within the prison, told them that Shull was dead, that they could find him in the rec shack. The shack functioned as a recreational equipment storage area and any inmate on "unstructured" or free time on the North main line could have access to the area to sign out sports gear.

Fitzharris said he knew of no motive for the slaying. There was absolutely no indication that it was in retaliation for the killing of the three blacks in January, he said. "There is little connection between the inmates in North and Central Facilities and I don't believe that the connection that exists is firm enough so that the North group would be involved in a Central Facility grievance," Fitzharris said. Besides, he added, "Shull was not disliked by the inmates of North Facility. He has shown he had the ability to handle men and was a master sergeant in the Army, a position he could not hold unless he was able to get along with men. There was no motive that we can see," the warden concluded. "It doesn't make sense. There seems to be no inmate racial tension or problems of any kind that the staff can observe—here or at Central Facility."

Sergeant John Hartz, president of the California Correctional Officers Association, disagreed with Fitzharris. He speculated that the guard's death was yet another retribution for the January 13 slayings. "Now we have another killing. Was that retaliation?" Hartz asked, then answered, "You know the remark made after Mills, 'one down, two to go.' " Hartz lamented the plight of the guards. They must take the brunt of "so much stuff" within the prison system, he pointed out, and are the ones who "must do all the work but get less money than a welfare recipient."

Asked about Hartz's comments, Fitzharris said with his usual aplomb, "I'd be very surprised to learn this killing had anything to do with the other one."

In Sacramento, Governor Ronald Reagan told a press conference that he and his cabinet were actively concerned about the tension and violence at Soledad. "What is happening," he said, "what you are seeing reflected inside the institution is a reflection of what is taking place outside. The growth of prison violence merely reflects the fact that a greater percentage of men in California prisons today are hard core criminals."

On July 30, the Department of Corrections announced that it would grant a request from Soledad guards that the custodial force be increased. The CDC said it would add nineteen new officers to the force. This would allow the guards to work in pairs, a prison spokesman said, since the two guards killed had been alone when they were attacked. The prison also made arrangements to transfer 275 men to other institutions in the state. The transfers came after a fight on July 31 involving forty prisoners, Chicanos and whites, in the North Facility recreation yard.

Ellsworth Ferguson, an elderly black man who is listed as an administrative assistant at the prison, gave reporters an account of the fight. It began, he said, when a white inmate struck a Chicano from behind with his fist. A guard on duty in the yard blew his whistle and gave orders to disperse. Two shots were fired into the air by the gun guard in the tower and the men stopped fighting. After they calmed down, they were returned to their cells. No injuries that required hospitalization were reported.

Ferguson declined to comment on comparisons and contrasts between the January 13 and the July 31 fights. The numbers involved were certainly greater in July. There was more of a chance that the men were armed, since they were on the main line and had not been skin-searched. And why, this time, did the guard choose to shoot in the air?

CDC director Procunier assumed the traditional ostrich position. There were many reasons for this. His subordinates, guards and prison officials alike, were so complaining about their own lot that any kind of wavering toward the demands of inmates and radical reformers would have weakened Procunier's position within the CDC. At least, that was the way he felt about it. The director privately agreed to changes within the system, a new "liberalization" as he put it, but the timing would have to be very discreet. The guards were threatening strikes, revolts and mass resignations. Wardens, deputy wardens and other prison administrators in various state facilities were standing squarely behind the guard force. After all, in their eyes it was these prisoners who wanted reform who were killing their brother guards. And it was those "dilettante bullshit radical attorneys" who defended these "killers" who were also pressing for reform.

The counterthrust from the CDC was threefold: increase the guard force, strengthen existing security procedures, and work to eliminate aggression from the minds of violent inmates through drug therapy.

Because Procunier did not reply to the Black Caucus's report, the California lawmakers released their findings on August 3, during the opening ceremonies of the new offices of the Soledad Brothers Defense Committee. "Soledad is the worst hellhole in America," black Assemblyman Willie Brown declared as he handed out copies of the report to the press. He apologized for the brief twenty-six-page document, stating that it was "a meager one," but added that "what it does say is that the situation cries out for immediate attention."

The report drew three basic conclusions and listed thirteen recommendations. The most emphatic conclusion was that if even a small fraction of what the inmates charged was true, as the investigators and lawmakers believed, then that was enough to amount to "a strong indictment of the prison's employees (on all levels) as cruel, vindictive, dangerous men who should not be permitted to control the lives of the 2,800 men in Soledad."

Secondly, the report urged an "independent, thorough and immediate investigation of Soledad prison with special emphasis on the treatment accorded inmates by employees." Thirdly, the Black Caucus asked the state legislature to create an organization independent of the CDC to conduct this investigation and be responsible for follow-up work, suggesting that the body include persons nominated by the state bar association, psychological and psychiatric associations, the various public defenders' offices, and groups of "concerned, involved laymen" like those working in privately operated halfway houses and the American Friends Service Committee.

Most important among the specific recommendations was the suggestion that the state legislature create a permanent full-time salaried board of overseers for the state prisons. Made up of persons nominated by the organizations listed previously, the board would be responsible for evaluating allegations made by inmates, their families, friends and attorneys against prison employees charged with acting inhumanely, illegally or unreasonably. Admittedly, such safeguard functions could be covered by the CDC itself or by petitions and suits filed in federal and state courts. However, the CDC was hog-tied by personal loyalties and bureaucratic/budgetary problems and it certainly did not lust to redress inmate grievances, fearing a revolt from the correctional staff. The courts, meanwhile, simply weren't hearing petitions which alleged cruel and inhumane treatment.

The Black Caucus Report suggested that the board of overseers meet regularly at each prison, much as the parole board does, to hold hearings at which inmates and staff might testify. The board would have the authority to discipline prison employees for violations of prison conduct regulations and to recommend criminal prosecution for criminal acts. The recommendation was made because conversations with inmates showed a compelling need for such a body.

Within the jurisdiction of the CDC, inmates have no avenue to seek redress for breaches of morality or violations of law by prison employees. The guards are answerable only to their superiors, and their superiors are former guards who rose to positions of authority through the system.

"In a world where many crimes are punished by indeterminate sentences, where the parole-granting authority acts in secrecy and with vast discretion—and gives heavy weight to accusations by prison employees against inmates," said the report, "the prisoners feel trapped unless they are willing to abandon their desire to be independent men. A Board of Overseers, independent of the Department of Corrections, would serve to right, if only slightly, the absolute absence of 'civilian' control over prison employees, an absence which allows all manner of informal (sometimes corporal) punishment to go unchecked."

The investigators assumed that the CDC already had rules against guard harassment of inmates, but they nevertheless urged that such intentional intimidation be ceased. The Black Caucus said it was "convinced" that such intimidation was being practiced because "too many inmates, regardless of race, told of personal indignities and frequent harassment from correctional officers. Naturally, prison officials are quick to deny any intentional wrongdoing, but the charges from both witnesses and subjects of intimidation are so widespread that we are inclined to believe that such intimidation exists and must be either overlooked or condoned by officials at the institution."

The investigators were aware that many parole requests had been turned down because the inmates had not done "clean time," but in fact many infractions had been provoked by prison officers. It is the guard who writes the report which is then inserted in the inmate's prison file, and prison guards rarely include the names of any witnesses who have offered testimony on the prisoner's behalf. And even on the rare occasions when alternative testimony is recorded, the parole board hardly ever takes the time to summon the witness.

Aware that whenever an inmate was charged with a serious misconduct he was thrown into the "hole," the investigators suggested that prison rules be changed to mete out punishment only after a hearing with full procedural safeguards, including the right of the inmate to counsel, the right to confront his accuser and, if any reasonable doubt of the prisoner's guilt exists, the possibility of acquittal. The report charged that current practices are "honored only in the most totalitarian societies," commenting that "institutions of correction and rehabilitation in a free society should mirror our finest traditions, not our worst."

The report noted that about half of the state's prisoners are either blacks or Chicanos, often sensitive to racial insults, ethnic slurs or other insensitive and demeaning treatment. Prisoners who already have deviated from society's behavioral standards may well be deviant in other respects which require understanding and compassion rather than punishment. Therefore, correctional officers should be chosen who have some understanding of psychological problems. The report recommended that psychiatric examinations, designed to test a person's ability to deal with the stresses of prison life and with the personal and emotional needs of inmates, be required of all applicants for positions with regular inmate contact. For existing staff, the report urged the establishment of an in-service program to educate staff members on ethnic and racial issues.

Warden Fitzharris publicly described the report as "unfair." He said he had been superintendent of Soledad for six and a half years and had the "total backing" of CDC director Procunier. To the specific charges in the report, Fitzharris conceded that incidents such as allowing favored white inmates to put urine or ground glass in coffee for black prisoners could have occurred. Nevertheless, he insisted, "I'm certain it was not with our approbation or approval." The warden went on to point out that racial problems had been "blown up out of all proportion by the news media" and he added that Soledad was not "racially torn" as "has been often charged." "I don't think it's so bad here," he concluded.

The following day, Lieutenant Governor Ed Reinecke discounted the Black Caucus Report. He did not go into a point-by-point refutation of the charges or even bother to comment on the recommendations. He suggested that, "If the present violence [at Soledad] is clearly attributable to uncontrolled inter-group racialism, then it would seem that some consideration would have to be given to segregation of the races." He called reporters a day later to say he had been misquoted. He said "separation" of the races. "Segregation," he reminded the writers, "carries overtones that imply more than physical separation. All I meant was that if you have one or more prisoners who are going to fight, it is the responsibility of prison officials to separate them."

Governor Reagan struck the same chord at his press conference that day. Racial separation of Soledad prisoners might become necessary as a temporary measure, the governor said, although "none of us are committed to the idea of segregation"—permanently. "If you've got two gangs of people that are getting into fights, whether it is in a street or in an institution, the most common-sense thing to do is to separate them." He said the Black Caucus Report was fanning the flames of trouble at Soledad. "I don't think that inflammatory type statements" help solve the problem.

Two state legislators, both from the Salinas Valley, picked up where Reagan left off. One of the men was State Senator Donald Grunsky, the Watsonville Republican who had submitted Judge Campbell's antidemonstration law as a bill in the senate. Assemblyman Bob Wood, a conservative Republican from Greenfield, made a hurried overnight trip to Sacramento to meet with prison officials and CDC staff representatives. Wood huddled with Fitzharris, guard Sergeant Moe Comacho, president of the Soledad chapter of the California Correctional Officers Association, and two officials from the California State Employees Association, Clyde Woodward, president of the Soledad chapter, and James Cummins, the regional director. The men emerged from the meeting calling for a broadly based task force investigation to "clear the air of misunderstandings and misinformation about the Soledad situation."

"Contrary to some published reports," Wood told newsmen, "I am reliably informed that investigations have been under way at Soledad for some time, both by members of the Attorney General's staff and officials of the Department of Corrections." Unfortunately, he added, what was not known was that the deputy attorney general who was in charge of the Soledad investigation was killed in an automobile accident several weeks before.

He expressed concern that the "often perilous plight of prison guards and other staff personnel not be forgotten in the rush to respond to the complaints of the inmates." Pointing out that "considerable notoriety has been given to the situation at Soledad by the statements attributed to certain of my legislative colleagues," whose intent he said was "sincere," he asserted that the report showed the "need for an immediate impartial study of current conditions in the prison before the truth is obliterated by further irresponsible charges and counter-charges."

For some months Warden Fitzharris had been disturbed by the kind of publicity Soledad was receiving in the newspapers and on newscasts in the region. He decided that the best way to counter the adverse reports would be to host a Soledad "News Media Open House" to which he would invite selected newsmen. With the help of a local television official, a list of acceptable newsmen was drawn up and invitations were mailed out. Word of the open house spread quickly, however, when one of the few San Francisco invitees telephoned other reporters to ask for a ride to the prison. The following day, August 25, more than fifty showed up at Soledad. "This is about five times the turnout we expected," a prison official confessed, "but no problem, we'll get you all in."

Veteran penal workers joked with reporters and offered coffee and doughnuts. It was the first time in their memory, they said, that the press had been invited to tour such a facility. No area would be off limits. As it turned out, one area was restricted. Reporters were

barred from the O-wing yard and from the gun tower from which
O. G. Miller fired the fatal shots on January 13. Admittance to the gun
tower would have revealed the extremely close range at which the
guard shot the three black inmates.

Prison officials greeted the arriving newsmen warmly, handing each
a bundle of papers wrapped in an attractive yellow folder entitled
"SOLTAC News Report." The bundle, prepared by the Soledad
Technical Advisory Council, included the program from a recent
prison high school graduation; several mimeographed sheets of
menus; an eight-page stencil on the purpose of the prison (". . .
each in pursuit of study . . . some who have difficulty in finding
themselves; some in search of personal counsel and religions . . .");
and a twenty-three-page report crammed with the complete criminal
and psychiatric background of more than one hundred inmates ("extremely assaultive individual . . . effeminate homosexual . . . defiance towards authority . . . racist . . . a racial agitator . . .").

Unknown to prison officials, as they handed out their literature, a
reporter from a Berkeley radio station distributed copies of the Black
Caucus Report, the twenty-six-page black legislators' indictment,
which bore the official state seal.

Newsmen were driven around the institution to a conference room
in North Facility. Television crews set up their cameras and tested
their lights. Fitzharris approached a small podium which had been
set up in front of the room. "Cue the whitewash," a television
cameraman joked. The reporters laughed. Fitzharris gave a tentative
smile. "I got so damned tired of taking it on the chin from the Fay
Stender–Angela Davis group," he said, "that I had to see that the
truth got out." He assured us "there would be no place you can't go
and no one you can't talk with." We would start, he said, with North
Facility, the wood shops, metal shops, toilet paper factory, cooking
facilities, and then meet in the employees' dining room for lunch.

The television crews asked when they would be allowed to visit
and film in O-wing. When they were told that O-wing was scheduled

last, they complained. The story, they pointed out, was in O-wing, the O-wing yard, and Y-wing, where the first guard was killed. Late-afternoon filming meant they would not be able to supply footage for their evening newscasts. Fitzharris said the schedule had already been made. The newsmen persisted, however, and the program was changed. Fitzharris said reporters would not be allowed in the O-wing yard or in the gun tower. And although he was pressed to do so by a number of reporters, the warden declined comment on specific events and refused to explain what happened that catalytic January 13.

The press was there, he reminded them, to see the conditions at Soledad. "This is not a prison," he said as they started the tour. "This is a correctional training facility. We don't have guards here. We have correctional officers." He said his men would show us around.

They moved quickly and efficiently. "O.K., that's about it," a program administrator said after the group had been in O-wing for about fifteen minutes. "There are a lot of other things to see." Indeed there were. The reporters were shown how carefully the prison kitchen prepared food: no ground glass, urine or fecal matter in that. They visited the classrooms: inmate students listened attentively. They walked into the main-line recreation yard, noticing that hundreds were out playing and exercising.

The prisoners were frank in their remarks but most of them declined to give their names. "The bulls keep harping on the race trip," a group of writers was told by a young white inmate who had been busted for possession of four ounces of marijuana. "They [the guards] say that it's imported from the outside. Actually, the race problem is something they created themselves." Two reporters asked if they could quote him on that. "I'd rather have you write that I said this was Palm Springs," he answered.

When the visitors were ushered into one of the industry shops, the gray-haired instructor, a Soledad official, greeted the first arrivals with a hearty "Here come de shuck! Here come de shuck!" He laughed. "Why do you say that?" Rick Davis, a correspondent with KNXT-

TV, a CBS affiliate in Los Angeles, asked. The official laughed again, did an about-face and walked away. "They do good work, don't they?" said one official, commenting on the prisoners hunched over their machines. "Damned good—for seven cents an hour," one worker said. "We have some people earning twenty-five cents an hour," the staffer rejoined.

After the walking tour, Fitzharris met again with the reporters. Someone asked if the warden thought "all the tragedy goes back to that event in the O-wing yard in January." "No, I don't—" Fitzharris began, but abruptly changed his answer to, "Well, I don't know." A reporter said O-wing inmates complained of a number of things, like racial prejudice. "That's mostly brought in from the outside," Fitzharris answered. "If there is racial prejudice on the part of the staff, it's pretty well hidden because we haven't come across it." Homosexuality: "It'd be silly to deny that. That's true in the Army and Navy." Beatings: "I've never known a beating to take place in this institution." Later, Fitzharris again commented on the race question. "Would it be plausible for us to agitate racial strife and then have to go in and stop it?"

Fitzharris sat casually as he talked with the press. Above his blue eyes, streaks of gray tapered back over his auburn hair. He seemed relaxed in his Irish green suit, yellow shirt and green tie. He said there were a few changes he'd like to make at Soledad. He wanted to modernize the staff. He wanted to stop using guards at gate towers. Electronics and modern technical devices could perform that job. He said the telephone-pole architectural design of the prison was inadequate and inefficient. "All that traffic in the central corridor with jostling and fighting in lines is an irritant." He said he would like to hire a psychiatrist to sit on the prison disciplinary panel.

"And"—Fitzharris paused, as if to get attention—"I can't think of anything more antiquated than a man with a gun." The reporters leaned forward. Far out. The warden wanted to get rid of guns. A reporter asked what he meant. "Well," said Fitzharris, "I've heard that they're experimenting with ultraviolet-ray guns in the Army. Maybe we could try some of those."

By August, the CDC was almost reeling from the gathering inmate strength in clandestine prison organizations, from an impressive array of court petitions filed against prison conditions, even from the sympathetic media coverage which the prisoners were getting. Reporters were hounding Soledad for information about the latest killing and every week brought more press inquiries about civil actions filed on censorship and mailing privileges or an inmate hunger strike or petitions demanding better food, greater access to periodicals and books, even petitions asking for personal items such as toothbrushes and more shower time. The prison system was buffeted by one blow after another.

What the prison was up against, besides oppressed prisoners, was a determined and dedicated group of reform-minded individuals who gathered together in the legal defense of Jackson, Clutchette and Drumgo. Calling itself the Soledad Brothers Defense Committee, the group had actually formed as early as March. It planned to publicize the case and assist in raising funds for the Brothers' legal defense, and that alone.

The prime mover, initially, was Fay Stender, the tall, raven-haired Berkeley radical lawyer who represented George Jackson. A graduate of the University of Chicago Law School, Fay Stender had been a legal assistant of Black Panther attorney Charles Garry for many years. Months before she agreed to take on Jackson's case, she had left the Garry law firm and formed a collective law partnership in Berkeley. Under Stender's guidance, the Defense Committee hired one full-time worker, a media-savvy woman named Lynne Hollander, who had recently moved west after working on various movement causes in New York. Together, the two enlisted the volunteer efforts of a wide range of liberals, New Left radicals and revolutionaries. It didn't matter what a person's politics were, really, as long as they believed in the cause of dignity, justice and humane treatment for all prisoners. As the drumbeat of publicity increased in the summer months of 1970, the cause became *célèbre* and it was easier for the Defense Committee to elicit help from even the establishment attorneys.

The attitudes and statements emanating from the Salinas courthouse and from Soledad Prison also helped the cause. One staid San Francisco attorney joined the growing prison reform movement for just those negative reasons. Fay Stender had called Edwin Caldwell to ask if he would help defend five white inmates who were charged with assaulting a guard and holding him hostage. She had asked this of him because they had gone to law school together. "At first, I couldn't believe what Fay and the others were saying about Salinas and Soledad," Caldwell explained in his penthouse offices in the San Franciscan Hotel. "I'm not in any movements. I'm pretty much an establishment lawyer. I'm a registered Republican. I have a home in Terra Linda. The whole bit. Just to get her off my back I thought I'd go down there, look around and get out of it some way. But then, when I saw the pressures in the Salinas community and heard the court officials and prison administrators talk, saying things like 'Don't tell me you're another one of those nigger-lovin' attorneys' and 'Those animals don't deserve a trial' and 'What are you nigger lawyers doing down here?' I took the case. Hell, it's more than a hundred miles, but I'd pedal down there on a rubber bicycle now."

Others joined. Law students offered to help with legal research in the Soledad Brothers case and when there were more than enough law students and attorneys to go around, they worked on other cases: prison brutality, mail censorship, appeals on former convictions, appeals for medical treatment, defending additional clients as more riots broke out and more guards died.

The famous also joined the cause. They were listed on the Defense Committee letterhead as sponsors. It was a cross-section of liberals and the New Left: from the world of politics came Julian Bond and Ron Dellums; from arts and letters, the sponsors included Pete Seeger, Jane Fonda, Jean Genêt (who would write a most eloquent foreword to Jackson's book of prison letters), Barbara McNair, Herbert Gold, Terry Southern, Jack Newfield, Noam Chomsky, Benjamin Spock, Lawrence Ferlinghetti, Ralph Gleason, Beniamino Bufano and Allen Ginsberg; from the more radical left, Huey Newton, Robert Scheer, Tom Hayden, Mario Savio and Angela Davis.

As Huey Newton declared when he was freed from prison, the courts didn't do it, the people did. The Defense Committee believed in that principle. They saw their mission as one of informing and educating the public and the press. Their thrust went in two directions. The focus on the defense of the Brothers would be maintained. And from this focus, a corollary attack would be constantly reporting conditions in the entire prison system. "The thousands of black youth trapped in the prison systems through poverty and racial prejudice," an early committee leaflet concluded, "stand before us in the persons of Fleeta Drumgo, John Clutchette and George Jackson. The wasted lives, the brutal inhumanity inherent in the prison system is here on trial. These three young men are being routed to the gas chamber for refusing to bow down, for trying to save their identities and self-respect. Their lives are in jeopardy for who they are, not for what they have done."

By June, the Defense Committee had gathered so much support in manpower that it split into seven different subcommittees: office staff, legal, prison, mobilization, publicity, fund raising and community organizing. Office staff volunteers answered telephones, typed legal briefs and press releases, ran errands and operated a constantly humming mimeograph machine. Lawyers and law students who worked on the legal committee researched various aspects of the Brothers case, from surveys of the makeup of the Monterey County grand jury to a block-by-block survey of the biases and prejudices of the Salinas and Monterey citizenry. All of the results would be used in court. The prison committee was set to the task of researching, organizing and publicizing information about conditions in the prisons. It was also charged with mobilizing prison support groups for visits and contacting inmates, lobbying in the state legislature for prison reform (one result was the Black Caucus Report) and pressing for political organizing within the prisons. Working from a growing "telephone tree" of names, the mobilization committee tried to urge a massive number of supporters to appear at court hearings and rallies. This committee was also responsible for a complete card file on all contributors.

In visibility, the two most important subcommittees were publicity and fund-raising. The former handled all contact with the media, from arranging press conferences and interviews with George Jackson (personally through Stender or Thorne) to producing leaflets, posters, news releases, lapel buttons, bumper strips and fund-raising letters. The fund-raisers organized all of the events, from small parties to large benefit concerts and speaking engagements with donations from various rock groups, such as the Grateful Dead, and such speakers as Jane Fonda and Angela Davis. To raise money, the group tried everything from poetry readings to art auctions to bake sales. It was months before Jackson's book of prison letters was published, and except for a small advance from Bantam Books, which Jackson mostly applied to the Brothers case, the Defense Committee relied solely on contributions.

The money question—how much there was, where it went and who controlled it—caused great friction in the committee. A relative of one of the Soledad Brothers walked into the Defense Committee offices one day and was dumbfounded to see a committee member sitting on the floor counting and neatly stacking thousands of dollars. To the relative, the question was who could tell if the white volunteer was counting one-two for the committee and one for her own pocketbook? How much was there? Where was it all going? the relative asked. The volunteer didn't know. She was just counting it prior to depositing it in the bank. The relative stormed out.

For weeks there had been complaints, growing in intensity, from relatives of the Brothers that too much of the money was unaccounted for, that there were too many white volunteer freeloaders hanging around the committee "house" in the San Francisco Mission district, ripping off food, sleeping quarters and supplies. The relatives were poor. They felt, rightly or wrongly, that some of the funds should go toward their own family expenses. And they felt, rightly, that too much of the funds raised for their brothers' and sons' defense was being squandered on the petitions and defenses of other black and white prisoners. This and other matters came to a head after the Marin Courthouse tragedy, an event which frightened politicians, liberals and some radicals from the defense cause—an event which triggered the more active participation of the Black Panther party and an ensuing struggle within the committee over a very basic question: reform or revolution?

VII

Guerrillas at the Marin County Courthouse

The Marin County Civic Center, designed late in his career by Frank Lloyd Wright, was once described by an architectural critic as "one of the great works of environmental design in the West." Nearly a quarter-mile long, with open archways that seem to spring across the low San Rafael hills, it magically enhances the landscape with its peach brown stucco, shiny powder blue roof and endlessly restated decorative circles and arcs and spheres. Underneath the domes and curvilinear roof lines, the interiors are a soft, comfortable mosaic of bright earth red concrete floors, beige walls and golden anodized aluminum trim around dark woodwork paneling. Monstrously wonderful, it is like some great space machine from the land of Oz or Xanadu.

Like other August days, it was sunny and drowsy in Marin that Friday morning, August 7, 1970. The vast parking lot was almost empty of cars and official vehicles. There had been such a hot spell that many of the county office workers had taken the day off to begin a three-day weekend. On the second floor of the Hall of Justice, located near the middle of the oblong structure, a small, seemingly insignificant trial was under way. A San Quentin inmate, a black named James D. McClain, was acting as his own attorney, defending himself against charges of stabbing a white guard. A small scattering of spectators lounged indifferently in their seats. Nearby, in holding cells, were three witnesses who were scheduled to testify, Willie Reddic, Mark Cisneros and William Christmas. McClain, the defendant, was seated at the defense table. He was beginning to question a black inmate witness named Ruchell Magee. It was 10:43 A.M. The jury had just returned to the courtroom; they had been excluded while McClain and the assistant district attorney, Gary Thomas, were arguing a point of law.

At ten forty-five, a tall, thin young man in a baggy raincoat entered the room. He carried a small flight bag and a paper bundle. He sat down near the rear of the room. The courtroom bailiff, Deputy Sheriff James Layne, remembered that the lanky youth, a black with a light brown Afro, had attended the trial the day before but at that time he wasn't carrying anything. He was just a kid, Layne observed. The "kid" nodded at Layne and sat down. But the deputy sheriff had another thought. He remembered thinking that it was odd to be wearing a coat in August, particularly on such a hot day, and that he ought to get a better look at this young man. He started walking toward the rear of the courtroom but it was too late. The youth had pulled a .38 caliber revolver out of his flight bag and pointed it at Layne.

"This is it. Everybody freeze," the youth ordered. "We don't intend to hurt anybody."

The youth, Jonathan Jackson, walked over to McClain and handed him an automatic. Then he opened his raincoat and brought out a carbine. Someone muttered something in the courtroom and the young Jackson wheeled around. "Freeze, just freeze," he ordered once again, and repeated, "We don't intend to hurt anybody."

McClain trained his pistol on the judge, Harold Haley, demanded that his handcuffs be removed and then turned to the jury. "I have been unjustly accused," McClain told them. "I want to be a free man."

"Hit the floor," Jackson shouted, and everyone did, even the judge.

"I don't want no shooting," McClain admonished.

McClain handed Magee a revolver and told him to go out and get the other inmate witnesses.

Outside, Magee ran into Tim and Sandra Wylie, who had taken their seven-month-old son with them to the Civic Center to pay a traffic ticket. They said they "didn't argue" with Magee when he ordered them into the courtroom. Indeed, they later claimed that it was Magee who "saved" them and their baby by insisting that the young couple not be used as hostages. Magee spoke gently, Wylie said. "He didn't touch us once. He didn't touch anyone. The other men were pretty violent. They kicked the sheriffs on the floor. They yanked and pulled the judge and told him to shut up." Magee told Wylie, "We don't want to hurt you or your wife or the baby. Get on out of here." But Jackson disagreed. Wylie said Magee insisted and won the argument.

Christmas returned with Magee but the two other prisoners, Reddic and Cisneros, refused to take part. Inside the courtroom, Christmas rushed up to a San Quentin guard. "You've held me for a long time," he said, his voice quavering. "For the love of God, take these cuffs off me. I want to be free, so help me God, I want to be free." The guard quickly removed the handcuffs.

While the twelve jurors and several clerks and bailiffs cowered, many of them praying, the four armed men huddled together in the middle of the courtroom, trying to formulate a plan. Some witnesses said they seemed confused, even frantic at times. Finally, they said, McClain took charge. He ordered the sixty-five-year-old judge to telephone the sheriff and describe the peril in his courtroom.

"We have an emergency situation," the judge told the sheriff. "There are armed convicts here. There are a number of lives at stake. We do not want interference at this time."

When the judge had finished, McClain grabbed the phone and

shouted, "Call off your dogs, pig, or we'll kill everyone in the room." And he told the sheriff, "We want the Soledad Brothers freed or we'll kill the judge."

The prisoners then argued over the hostages. A woman juror said McClain told young Jackson to "calm down and leave the jurors alone." Another witness said it was Magee who stopped Jackson from taking the young couple with the baby and an elderly woman juror as hostages. Eventually, the prisoners selected five hostages: three suburban housewives, the judge and the assistant district attorney. Using cloth and tape, McClain fashioned a crude yoke around Judge Haley's neck and attached a sawed-off 12-gauge shotgun to the yoke, pressing the barrel up against the underside of the judge's mouth. A few minutes later, the five hostages and the four revolutionaries walked into the hallway.

Deputy Sheriff Art Wiggins, the second-floor security guard, was making his casual rounds when Claudia Gallagher, Judge Haley's court reporter, ran down the hall toward him shouting, "They're in there with guns. They've got guns on the judge. They're taking over." Sitting near the rear door, she had dashed out unnoticed the moment Jackson produced the gun. Wiggins peeked into the courtroom and saw the armed cons. He ran downstairs and out of the building to a sheriff's car, seized the shotgun from it and scrambled back to the main north exit of the building.

Christmas clung tightly to one of the women hostages, a pistol barrel jammed in her ear. As the prisoners headed for the elevator, Magee and Jackson moved up and down the hallway, disarming police and sheriff's deputies. Christmas told McClain there was a photographer taking pictures. "Hey, be sure you get a good picture of the judge," McClain yelled at Jim Kean, " 'cause you probably won't see him again."

Jim Kean had been with the *San Rafael Independent Journal,* the county's major daily, since 1937. He was returning to the paper from a routine assignment when he heard Condition Red flash on his police radio calling for "all available units" to respond to the Civic

Center. He was uncertain where the action was but he instinctively headed for the Hall of Justice and took an elevator to the second floor. When he stepped out of the elevator, he saw some lawmen crouched against the corridor leading to the courtroom. He aimed his camera down the length of the corridor and snapped his first picture. It was of Judge Haley held hostage by McClain. After McClain told the photographer to get a good one of the judge, Christmas told Kean to "take all the pictures you want."

"We are the revolutionaries," Jackson added.

Kean kept squeezing his shutter on the extraordinary scene: the judge with the muzzle of a gun to his neck; the hostages herded together, terror in their eyes; the desperate armed men. Kean made a point, though, of telling Magee, whose back was turned to him, whenever he was shifting position. "I'm going to move now," Kean would say, and continue shooting. The hostage party disappeared into an elevator, but just before the door closed someone yelled once more, "We want the Soledad Brothers freed by twelve-thirty today."

Wiggins stood behind a waist-high concrete wall waiting for the fugitives to emerge. As they came out, McClain spotted the deputy. "Get that motherfucker," McClain shouted at Jackson. "Kill the bastard." Wiggins ducked behind the wall but when he peered over it again, a carbine was pointed at him. "All right," McClain ordered, "come over here and put that gun down right at my feet. We want that gun." Wiggins obeyed. As he straightened out, the gunman told him, "Now, you motherfucker. I'm going to take care of you." He aimed at Wiggins's head. But suddenly there was a sound of police sirens and screeches of braking tires and this distracted the inmates momentarily. Wiggins took that moment to vault a wall and run.

McClain led his comrades and the five hostages away from the arches of the building and into the hot sunshine of the parking lot, wielding guns and highway flares disguised to look like dynamite. They covered the two hundred feet to a yellow Hertz van at a brisk pace. En route they encountered another *Independent Journal* photographer, Roger Bockrath, who was snapping photographs while crouched behind a car. "Stand up, you motherfucker," someone yelled at the young photographer. Bockrath did as ordered, raising his cameras in the air, thinking that if they saw the cameras instead of a gun, they wouldn't harm him. He was right. They told him to "get moving."

Out of sight in the parking lot and along the roadway were more than a hundred policemen. Many were local police from nearby towns and sheriff's deputies, but others were guards from San Quentin. "We were going to play it by ear," one official said. "We were very concerned about the hostages. There was no telling what the prisoners were going to do. They were heavily armed."

The hostages were prodded to walk quickly. Jackson walked sideways, sometimes backwards, carrying an automatic rifle and covering the rear. When the group reached the yellow panel truck, the hostages were packed into the back, guarded by McClain, who still held the shotgun to Haley's throat, and Magee.

Inside the van, McClain drove a little way, then decided against it and moved to the passenger seat while Jackson drove. According to one hostage, Assistant District Attorney Thomas sat on the floor of the van on the passenger's side, directly behind McClain; juror Maria Graham was behind Thomas, followed by Ruchell Magee and Judge Haley. Jurors Joyce Rodoni and Doris Wittmer sat behind McClain and William Christmas sat in the rear, directly opposite Judge Haley. When the hostages entered the van, one of the women asked if they could untie themselves. One convict said yes, another said no, but they untied themselves anyway. The gun was still taped to the judge's neck. The judge turned to one of the jurors and said he was sorry they had to "go through this." The van moved slowly heading for the main north-south coastal highway, U.S. 101.

In their path, about forty feet away, stood a roadblock manned by a group of five or six unidentified San Quentin guards. Nearer, fifteen feet off on the driver's side of the road, stood a San Quentin guard named John Matthews, who was armed with a .30 caliber rifle. As the van approached him, Matthews leveled his rifle at the front window of the van and fired, apparently killing Jackson. The van lurched to a stop. Other police opened fire. Almost at once, a muffled blast of a shotgun roared from inside the van, knocking out a rear window. Then, also from the inside, came a series of pistol shots. Finally, a second shotgun blast from inside, killing Judge Haley. Meanwhile, the San Quentin guards continued firing with a murderous nineteen-second barrage of gunfire.

"I don't know how many shots were fired or where the first shot came from," one of the jurors said. She flattened herself on the floor and the next thing she heard was Gary Thomas yelling, "Stop shooting. You've shot me." All of a sudden it was very quiet.

What the lawmen could not see or know was that the tall, beefy assistant district attorney had lunged over the front seat, grabbed Jackson's pistol and started shooting inside the van. When the gunfire finally stopped and police flung open the van's rear door, Jackson, McClain and Christmas were dead. Magee and Thomas were badly wounded and one of the women hostages had been shot through the upper arm. The judge was also dead, half his face blown away by the shotgun that McClain had fastened around his neck. McClain was found on the floor in the front of the van in a kneeling position, his head and right shoulder almost on top of the accelerator pedal. Jackson was found in the rear of the van, having been flipped over the driver's seat by the impact of the initial blast, the one that killed him. Christmas was found lying next to Haley on the floor of the van.

When they pulled the assistant district attorney out, Thomas said, "I grabbed the gun from the driver and shot three of them. I hope I killed them."

It's not clear who fired first: whether Gary Thomas started shooting in the van, causing the guards to believe they were being shot at, or whether the San Quentin guards started firing, distracting the kidnappers so that Thomas could grab a gun and start firing inside. Of twenty-two eyewitnesses, thirteen stated that they could not discern who started firing. The remaining nine witnesses declared that the police, particularly the San Quentin guards, began the shooting barrage. Of the nine, several said that the San Quentin guard who was later identified as John Matthews fired the first shot. Another said the San Quentin guards at the roadblock triggered the initial shots.

Certainly the convicts didn't open fire. They had absolutely no reason to. They wanted the hostages to remain alive. That was their sole bargaining point. If even one of the hostages was harmed, there was a good bet that the kidnap attempt would have failed at that moment. Then, too, the law enforcement officials who were supposed to control zealous guards and deputies also failed. There were reports, later substantiated, that the sheriff's order was that no one was to open fire. In fact, a police helicopter was ready to take off and follow the yellow van, wherever it went. Later reports said it was headed first for a San Francisco radio station, where a talk show was in progress, so the revolutionaries could make their demands on the air to the general public. Then, the group was to head for the airport, wait for the arrival of the Soledad Brothers and take off with the hostages for a foreign country, Cuba or Algiers. Once they landed safely, the hostages were to have been released.

A spokesman for the Marin County sheriff's department refused to agree that the hostages would be returned after the kidnappers had achieved foreign asylum. Rather myopically, he kept insisting that this was a simple "escape attempt" rather than acknowledging the possibility of its being part of a wider political revolution. Officials would not consider the possibility of Latin American cooperation in the guerrilla kidnap action and, very probably, for good reason. If they conceded that, other black groups on other occasions might have the same idea.

Later, investigators said the prison guards who opened fire were on their way back from a session at a nearby rifle range when they heard broadcasts of the daring escape attempt. These guards did not hear an order by Sheriff Louis Mountanos to allow the van to leave the area. Authorities added that the two guards were the only police officers who fired weapons during the deadly exchange.

San Quentin guards don't recognize hostage situations. In prison, they're told that if they're ever taken hostage, they can consider themselves, for all practical purposes, dead. "It's our policy not to acknowledge hostages," Associate Warden James Park explained to reporters after the shooting. "If you let them get away with hostages once, they'll do it again and again. You'll be plagued with it forever, like airplane hijackings." He continued, "If our men report to an emergency, then they are under the direction of local police authorities." Then he gave his men a way out: "But Friday things were confused."

In an angry, emotion-laden conference, Jonathan Jackson's mother declared that her son was "only seeking justice" when he tried the hostage attempt to free his brother George. Bitterly denouncing "white justice," Mrs. Georgia Jackson said her seventeen-year-old son was certain he couldn't get justice any other way. "I think," she said slowly, "he did what every black man—or white man—who cared about his country would do. If you can't get justice one way, you take it in another."

For years, Jonathan Jackson had been obsessed with his brother George's imprisonment. He believed that George was being held illegally and being treated inhumanely. Jonathan was a strong-minded youth. He listened most to the man he admired, his older brother George, though sometimes he did not fully agree with him.

Georgia Jackson said that his older brother's imprisonment had begun affecting young Jonathan about four years earlier, when the youth was thirteen. "Ever since George has been there [in prison], we've been trying to do something for him but we've never been able to," she said. "Jonathan heard all of this and saw all this and he saw the way the courts worked. Frankly, I think that the so-called justice in this country and the so-called law courts in this country are the cause of my son being dead today. I don't know if you went to any of the hearings in Salinas or not, but just to go to one of those hearings and sit there, even if you weren't concerned with the people who were being tried, would just tear you apart. I mean, for someone who's never been involved in the courts or never been to a court for anything, it's incredible. Even I didn't believe it was that bad—and I've always had a very pessimistic attitude about what went on in this country.

"What really tore Jonathan apart in the last two or three months," Mrs. Jackson continued, "was that, when this first happened with George at Soledad [the murder charge], he went to two of his instructors that he had a lot of respect for and he told them what was happening. I know he really liked one of them especially, because he thought this man understood what was going on in this country with black people, and this [high school] teacher said to Jonathan, 'Oh, if I were you I wouldn't get too upset about it. You mightn't know all the facts.' After that he just seemed not to be interested in school anymore. All he would think about was George. All he would talk about was George. I would tell him I thought that if there was anything possible to be done for George, Mrs. Stender would see that it was done. I told him it wasn't like it was before when we were just alone with this and nobody cared.

"Jonathan," his mother said late in that 1970 August, "felt that George was going to be killed—if he wasn't killed by the courts he would be killed in prison. That's the way he felt. And he felt like Mrs. Stender was a good lawyer and he told me, 'Mama, she works hard night and day, but no matter how hard she works, don't you see what happens in court?' He said, 'I just don't know about the judge. That judge just sits there and he says no to everything. He doesn't even stop to think before he says no.' A lot of the time when we'd be at the hearings he'd get up and go out and he'd be crying. So would my husband. You feel so helpless and frustrated. You say to yourself, 'In this country, you're supposed to have justice from the law. If you can't get justice from the courts, where can you get it!' "

Fearing at first that Jonathan might follow in his brother's foot-steps, Mrs. Jackson had sheltered the youth in a quiet home life and Catholic schools. A sensitive, alert young man, he did so well in school that his mother fondly recalls one of the Catholic lay teachers asking her how Jonathan "got so smart." Jokingly, Mrs. Jackson said Jonathan took after her. "Well, sister," the teacher came back, "he has a good chance of being President some day, smart as he is."

George, however, was fearful of such a sheltered existence for his younger brother. This comes through clearly in his early letters. "You know that I love my mother dearly for many reasons," he wrote his father in 1964, when Jonathan was thirteen, "she always . . . pro-vided for me materially the best she knew how, but she failed me bit-terly in matters of the mind and spirit. My education she put in the hands of the arch foes of my kind. . . . I would not be in prison now if she hadn't been reading life through those rose-colored glasses of hers."

His later letters were replete with criticisms and advice on the proper upbringing of young Jon. "How could I, . . . Jon or any of the men of our kind accomplish what we must as men if we think like bourgeois women, or let our women think for us?" George asked his mother.

"Jon should be the main concern now," he wrote when his brother was thirteen. George complained that his brother didn't "look too healthy to me," suggesting that he should work out with weights because he appeared "thin, pale, and soft." Catholic school, George said, wouldn't teach Jonathan "anything except possibly a few Latin prayers." Help Jon become a man, teach him the "truth." George wanted his family to release Jon from what he felt was a black bourgeois cocoon which the family was weaving around its only other son. He railed against his father for objecting to Jon's membership in a black social club, reminding his father that Jonathan "can only benefit from contact with people he might learn from."

George's fears about his brother's development lessened somewhat after a family visit in the summer of 1968. "Jon is an admirable man-child," he wrote home after the visit. "You sired a man without question. I just know that you are training him to be a benefit and a credit to his kind, and to act out his historical, obligatory duty. I know you are teaching him to love just us, and protecting him from this alien ideology. I am certain that you are doing this since you remember clearly the failure of your father, and his father, and so on as far back as it goes."

At the same time, George started participating in his brother's upbringing, sending Jonathan ethnic and political books (some of which Georgia took away); describing how to make a bench for weight lifting; suggesting that Jon, like himself, learn five new words a day; advising him to reject his father's philosophy, the "credo of the slave"; offering some advice for Jonathan's self-direction: "Decide now what you would like to specialize in, *one thing* that you will drive at. Do you get it? *Decide now.* There are several things that we as a group, a revolutionary group, need badly: chemists, electronic engineers, surgeons, etc. Choose one and give it special attention at a certain time each day. . . . the thing that you plan to carry through this war of life." By now, Jonathan was fifteen and George was writing more letters to him than to his parents.

Meanwhile, Jonathan attended Pasadena High School briefly, his stay cut short by his mother after he became involved in his first fist-fight. Georgia transferred Jon to Blair High, where there was more of a mixture of blacks and Chicanos. He took up karate and played some basketball but he wasn't really interested in school. He attended the desegregation hearings in Pasadena and wandered around the courts in Los Angeles, watched on occasions when judges would order angry blacks to be bound and gagged in courtrooms. This convinced him that "all judges are racists" and he came to the conclusion even before attending his brother's hearings in Salinas that "there wasn't any justice in court."

At Blair High, his teachers and friends spoke highly of him. "I was very fond of him," said the principal, Sam Schwartz. "Everything I knew about him was positive. He played basketball on the

junior varsity and had an IQ of 117. He was a smart kid." A class-
mate named Laura Treister described Jon as "desperate . . . articulate . . . really intense. . . . He was very devoted to his brother,"
she said. "He seemed to feel the whole thing was very urgent. He'd
go to the hearings and he'd come back and seem very uptight and
depressed." Robert Salley, a teacher, said the black youth was "in-
telligent, articulate and at times warm and capable of much good
humor. He was also obsessed. His obsession, which determined his
view of this country, was the plight of an imprisoned brother he
could not really have known. . . . Jonathan Jackson's 'revolution'
was so absolutely absurd, so tragic, so wasteful. Deceived into believing a thousand others would follow, he was undoubtedly prepared
to die on the barricades."

Jonathan was "obsessed." He wrote about that obsession in the
Blair High School underground newspaper, *Iskra* ("The Spark," the
name of Lenin's newspaper), seven weeks before he died:

This is the era of the pig and has been for 190 years. Ever since the
Second Continental Congress, the American system has been ripping off
the people under the protective cloak of so-called "law and order." The
imperialistic dogs have not only coerced their own people into servitude
to capitalism (for who really cannot be coerced with death?) but have
rammed it down the throats of almost all of the people on earth. The
voracious monster must be stopped. The people must rise up and crush it.

But the majority of the people in this country are too involved with
themselves to be concerned with the struggle. In some ways these people
are worse than the genuine right-wing reactionaries. The reactionaries can
be dealt with effectively. But what do you do with a person who refuses to
open his eyes and observe the repression that is going on all around him?
You either have to educate him in the ways and means of the revolution or
deal with him. There can be no middle ground.

People have said that I am obsessed with my brother's case and the
Movement in general. A person that was close to me once said that my
life was too wrapped up in my brother's case and that I wasn't cheerful
enough for her. It's true. I don't laugh very much any more. I have but
one question to ask all of you people that think like you, what would
you do if it was your brother?

"Mama," Jonathan said to Georgia one night in June, "if I die—
or if I die in any way that makes you sad—I want you to know that
I died the way I wanted to die."

Jonathan's death and the revolutionary action in Marin frightened
the do-good liberals who were more a part of what he called "the
middle ground" than they were part of the revolution. Almost like a
thunderclap, his death moved his mother and his sister Penny from
the middle ground and into the revolution. Georgia's change of
mind and heart overwhelmed her only surviving son. "Go over all the
letters I've sent you," he wrote two days after Jonathan died, "any
reference to Georgia being less than a perfect revolutionary's mama
must be removed. Do it now! I want no possibility of anyone misunderstanding her as I did. She didn't cry a tear. She is, as I am,
very proud. She read two things into his rage, love and loyalty."

With their change in attitude and approach, both Georgia and
Penny became increasingly more involved in the affairs of the Defense
Committee. Up until Marin, the legal defense of the Soledad Brothers
had been handled by the four attorneys in concert with three defense
committees which had formed in San Francisco, Santa Cruz and San
Jose. The committees were using the case as a basis for political
organizing and education among ghetto blacks and any whites who
were willing to listen. In addition to the rallies, the fund-raisers, leaflets and posters, the committees had produced a film which was being
circulated in various metropolitan areas and coalitions were being
formed with defense groups supporting Angela Davis, who was the
subject of a nationwide FBI search and arrested as part of the Marin
County Courthouse kidnap conspiracy, and Ruchell Magee.

Questions about money, personal control and political direction
became a friction point between the whites in the San Francisco
committee and the Jackson family. The friction was played down,
however, for a number of reasons. There was desire on either side
not to make things more difficult for the three defendants. Each side

continued to maintain an air of secretiveness, particularly the whites, out of fear of embarrassment and retribution.

The disagreements came to a critical head one week in the early summer of 1971 when committee members arrived at the San Francisco headquarters to find that the storefront office was padlocked. The landlord had been informed that it was no longer being rented by the committee. The members were bewildered. During the days that followed, members of the San Francisco chapter met with counterparts from San Jose and both sides sat down and drafted a letter that set forth the San Francisco chapter's side of the dispute, mailing a copy to each of the three defendants.

The Jackson family's reaction was swift and angry. Penny Jackson arrived at the San Jose office, backed by a group of Black Panthers, and told them flatly that the members of the San Francisco chapter were no longer involved in the defense of the Brothers and that henceforth the Central Committee of the Black Panther party would direct all the affairs of the various defense committees. She also revealed to them that she had been a member of the party for six months, since shortly after Jonathan's death.

Her declaration was later affirmed in a letter written by George and published in the Black Panther party newspaper. The letter confirmed what Penny said about the party, charged that the San Francisco chapter had been infiltrated by opportunists and revealed for the first time that George, too, was a member of the Black Panther party. He held the rank of field marshal.

George's position was that the ousted committee members were taking "reformist, reactionary steps backward to the techniques of the 1930s." He accused them of having "been led to believe that negotiations with a pig are possible, and that an appeal to arms is just taking life too seriously." "The objective of ALL our activity," Jackson declared, "is in the end the creation of the people's army— not an acquittal here and there—our case was intended to be used by you as a springboard for revolution, nothing else. I'm the foco-motor, the dragon."

The committee members disagreed with that. They thought the Soledad case should have been used as a basis for mass organizing. They claimed that trying to organize a military venture from the case was not only foolish but impossible. For one thing, the committee was under close scrutiny by law enforcement officials; it was probably even infiltrated. In fact, the committee members defended themselves, they already had to counter the negative acts of several provocateurs who were suggesting militant ventures that bordered on conspiracy. For another, they felt that militant revolution, as George suggested for the committee, would drive away mass support instead of increase it. In short, people weren't ready for revolution.

The crux of the matter was the interpretation of and attitudes toward Jonathan's tragic death at the Marin Courthouse. To George and other revolutionaries, the shootout was a dramatic, heroic and historic revolutionary assault upon a court system that was blatantly racist and unjust. The guerrilla act failed only because the police, indifferent to the safety of the hostages, were so determined that this act should not succeed that they fired a fusillade of bullets into the van of hostages.

The committee members, on the other hand, said merely that the "incident grew out of the historical failure and obvious injustice of the American judicial system." In this analysis, Jonathan is no longer the heroic revolutionary actor on the stage of history but a victim, and a blind one at that, who struggled against oppressive forces but destroyed himself in the process. "You took the wrong position on August 7th, public and *private,*" George wrote a month before he died. "I've heard all of the cowardly remarks bearing on my brother's judgment and sanity. Revolution is aggressive. The only reason some of you were allowed anywhere near any of our operations was in the hopes that you would mature to an understanding of this. . . . I know who all the opportunists are. I have you all listed. You have made the very worst enemy you could have—when actually you could have had the very best comrades and friends. . . . You all sound like Utopian anarchists! This is 1971—Fascist Amerika, ruled over by a gang of insecure, threatened vicious mad-dog gunslingers. Baby brain friends and innocents and you pigs, too, we will not be co-opted. The war will go on."

Jackson's ideological conflict with the committee resulted in some mystifying contradictions. If he was loyal to Huey Newton and the Black Panther party, while at the same time he was advocating in the party newspaper the "creation of a people's army," asserting that "the revolution has begun," then ideologically this cast Jackson closer to Eldrige Cleaver than to Newton. Six months earlier, Newton had broken with Cleaver over this sort of ideological conflict. From Algeria, Cleaver was calling for immediate revolution through armed uprising. From Oakland, Newton was proclaiming a new, and immensely successful, program of "survival, pending the revolution." Indeed, he had pressed forward with it, giving away ten thousand bags of groceries and twenty-five hundred pairs of shoes in a "Survival Conference" which culminated with Party Chairman Bobby Seale's announcement that he, Bobby, would run for mayor of that Bay city. Not only were the new tactics an overwhelming success; for the first time the party had conducted a massive rally which was overwhelmingly black.

Where did all this leave Jackson? Presumably, contradictory or contrary tactics could be realized if the overt ideological line was building a mass base within the black community, while the covert ideological line was to build a people's army underground within the community. The strategic and ideological link would be loyalty to the Black Panther party.

Jackson also accused the committee of a number of other misdeeds. He specifically mentioned the spending of money on fancy clothes. The problem, as committee members countered, was that no one was living lavishly; Penny held the postal box key in Berkeley where contributions were sent; and the committee had no access to the royalties from George's book.

A committee member charged that members of the family destroyed the San Francisco branch because it was not in their control.

Believing that George would have agreed with them if he could have heard their side of the story, they claim that George acquiesced to family wishes because, aside from his attorney, only members of the family could visit him in prison. Understandably, no one wants to talk about it openly. Some former members are simply afraid to talk; others say talk would have hurt the defense effort and the cause as a whole. The timing of the committee confrontation was also tragic: although it had been building for almost a year, it came one month before Jackson died. As a result of the committee struggle and Jackson's death, effective political work of the committee ceased and everyone went their own way to pick up the pieces of reform and revolution and try to start over again.

VIII

The Abortion of Reform:
The Birth of Revolution

Frank Rundle was intrigued. The ad in the psychiatric trade journal was enticing: decent pay, interesting work and calm, casual California living in nearby Monterey, Carmel or Big Sur. He had heard very little about the place mentioned in the ad, Soledad Prison, and he wasn't very familiar with prison psychiatric work. Except for a brief period when he worked as a medical student at the House of Corrections in Chicago, Frank Rundle had been engaged for more than a decade in private practice in Wisconsin and other places in the Midwest. Still, he was intrigued enough to write a letter.

The reply was almost instantaneous. First came a telephone call from a Dr. Kenneth Francis, who said he was the prison's chief psychiatrist. After explaining that he was retiring, Dr. Francis said he was impressed with Dr. Rundle's letter. He wondered if Rundle could fly out to meet with him. Then came a second call. The man identified himself as Dr. Daniel W. Boone, the prison's chief medical officer. Dr. Boone said he, too, was impressed with Rundle's credentials and reiterated the initial invitation. Dr. Boone added something else. You can have the job if you want it, he told Rundle. Come on out.

The offer surprised Rundle. The prison staff had not met him and he had not really spelled out his qualifications in his letter. Nevertheless, he was motivated to fly out because he thought he would be helping men to rebuild their lives and ministering to some real needs, something different from the middle-class Midwesterners who had been relaxing and anguishing on his black leather couch.

He was met at the prison gates by Dr. Francis, an elderly man who greeted Rundle warmly, speaking with an English accent that was still rather thick, even after many years in this country. Rundle was quickly disturbed, however, because Dr. Francis seemed primarily interested in the inmates' sexual problems and discoursed frequently and at some length on the psychological aspects of masturbation.

Dr. Francis took Rundle on a quick tour of the prison. The first stop was the hospital. The young psychiatrist peered into a hospital cell and saw a tall, slender black standing naked in a dark, windowless concrete box which was empty except for the man and the putrid litter around him. There was a hole in the floor, a toilet, which was flushed from the outside. The black convict was immobile, mute, and his eyes said something to Rundle of "unspeakable anguish." "Catatonic," said Dr. Francis quickly, and walked on. Rundle followed, knowing that the black would continue to stand alone, isolated and comfortless in his waxy catatonic state, completely cut off from human contact. Rundle would learn later that this kind of cell had been prohibited by a federal court order in the *Jordan* v. *Fitzharris* case. It was only the first of his observations of illegal practices in Soledad.

Out on the main-line corridor, the two men paused before the solid steel red door which led into O-wing. Francis explained that O-wing was for especially "difficult" cases, men who would not respond to authority. He whispered that Rundle should stay out of there as much as possible. They did not go in. The psychiatrists continued down the corridor, stopping to glance at the prison chapel, the gymnasium, then they walked outside into the main recreation yard and returned to the administration building, where Dr. Francis introduced Rundle to his new boss, Warden Fitzharris. The warden struck the newcomer as a "seemingly innocuous, pleasant, rather insipid man" whom Rundle was quite certain was "not the real power in the institution." Then, walking next door with Dr. Francis into the business office, where salary and fringe benefits were explained, Rundle filled out the brief application forms and was hired.

The sandy-haired young psychiatrist left the prison that afternoon feeling depressed. He was disturbed not only by what he had seen of the place and the treatment he had witnessed of the catatonic black, but also by his general impression that the professional work being done was "second rate." He was troubled, too, by the fact that he had been hired after such a cursory examination of him and his credentials. It told him that they were desperate to have someone. Six months later, they would be desperate to be rid of him.

Rundle reported to work on Pearl Harbor Day, 1970, and within a week he was spending most of his time in O and X wings. He found them "filled with the most concentrated human misery to which I had ever been exposed." He couldn't believe that human beings were treated in such a manner, locked in their cells often twenty-four hours daily, totally shut off from the world, "abandoned to desperate fantasies, torturing loneliness and yearning to meet another human being on equal terms, talk as man to man, pass the time of day, perhaps just touch someone on an arm."

Rundle wondered why these men—some of them locked there for ten or twelve years, and doomed to a lifetime there unless something drastic happened—didn't kill themselves. Why did they want to live? It seemed that the only motivation for many prisoners was the bitter pleasure of continued spiteful defiance of all prison efforts to crush their spirit and individuality. Some would later declare openly to Rundle that they lived for the day when they would have the chance to kill some guards and take one or more of the officers with them. "On that day," Rundle observed, "they would declare the day of their death and that of the officer as well. Living so as to expend his life in taking the life of a symbol of the system which was crushing him." To Rundle, it was appalling.

At the end of his first week, Rundle was invited to attend a conference sponsored by a group of police officers from Oakland. The Oakland police had arrived at Soledad to describe the method they had developed for identifying the "problem cops," those who loved to split skulls and shoot runaways, and how they had been working in Oakland to change them. The conference shifted to a discussion of "problem prisoners" and Rundle mentioned that he had been "appalled" by the conditions he had observed in the Adjustment Center wings. A kind of embarrassed, slightly hostile hush hung on the air for a moment and then one of the deputy wardens smiled and suggested that maybe everyone could benefit by looking through Rundle's "fresh eyes." The administrator suggested that Rundle be assigned to study the A/C for two weeks and report on the matter.

He was working on that study, sitting in the sergeant's office in O-wing, when he was caught up in a great commotion. Guards were dashing in and out, telephones were ringing, prison photographers rushed by and someone paused to tell Rundle that a black inmate named Yogi Pinell had just stabbed a guard named Monaghan. Rundle could make no sense of the confusion and the conflicting information he heard, but he recalled clearly that when he saw the inmate Pinell, he was "struck by his extraordinary calm, poise and grace, such a contrast with the frenetic behavior of the staff." Rundle would come to know Pinell as "Commandant" or "General," titles which were conferred on him by other black inmates. Monaghan lived but within months Pinell would be charged with killing another white guard, Robert J. McCarthy. Months after that, when Pinell was transferred to San Quentin for neurological and psychiatric testing at the University of California Medical Center, he would be one of several defendants charged with the deaths of three more white guards and two white inmates, killings which took place the day George Jackson was slain.

From the day of the stabbing attack on Monaghan, Rundle concentrated on holding psychiatric interviews with the inmates of the Adjustment Center. He thought that was where the need was greatest. The rest of the prison administration grudgingly agreed but they warned him about his personal safety. The staff told Rundle that he should always sit with his desk between the inmate and himself and be prepared to shove it hard with his feet to pin the convict against the wall if he should attack. Rundle was also reminded to be sure to carry his police whistle, which was issued to him upon accepting the job, and blow it loudly if he was ever attacked. Rundle wondered how he was going to do that if a pair of hands were compressing his trachea. The psychiatrist was also told that if he took the telephone off the hook, this would signal an emergency in Central Control and help would be there almost immediately. Rundle, however, was never afraid of the Adjustment Center inmates and soon left his whistle at home.

"How hungry they all were," Rundle reflected, "just to sit and talk, be listened to seriously, to be believed, to be respected, to be cared about, to be liked, even to be loved—though most of them would never say the latter. They were so hungry to be dealt with honestly, to know where they stood. So needful of everything human beings everywhere are needful, but here in much more massive doses."

Eventually, Dr. Rundle became intrigued with the recent tragic history of Soledad. Going through the files left by his predecessor, the psychiatrist ran across the photographs of the three black inmates who were shot and killed on January 13. The file also held photographs of each inmate who had been in the O-wing yard at the time of the shooting. "I remember thinking to myself," he said later, "with what deadly accuracy the shots had been placed. In the heart of the great vessel area in two, avulsing the femoral artery in the third, through the testicle of the lone survivor." He could not reconcile the photos with what he was told by the prison staff, that the men had been killed by missiles ricocheting off the yard cement. Nor could Rundle reconcile what he heard from inmates with the staff version, since the prisoners uniformly swore that there had been no warning whistle, that the three blacks had been carefully picked and set up and that the shooting was planned and deliberate murder.

Even after he left his Soledad employment, he said he still was unable to reconcile the two versions. However, an incident occurred in January 1971 which caused him to lean toward the inmates' version. The date was the thirteenth, the first "anniversary" of the yard killings. For the entire year, Billie Harris, the virulent admitted racist who helped provoke the yard fight, had not been allowed out of his cell if any black inmates were on the tier, nor had he been allowed to mix with blacks under any circumstances. Somehow, on this January 13, Harris was ushered into a shower with a group of black inmates. There was a melee as soon as Harris got there. He was stabbed in the chest and a prison weapon was fired to stop the fight. Afterward, Rundle heard many guards refer to Harris as a "rotten bastard" and express the opinion that he should have been killed. Of the shower incident, Rundle didn't know what to think. Was it carelessness? an accident? or a setup?

For Rundle, there were "daily examples of man's inhumanity to man" in the Adjustment Center. Inmates, filled with hate and with no other outlet, smashed toilets and sinks, burned their own mattresses, blankets and clothing and continued to throw urine and fecal matter on passing guards. The staff responded in this miniature war by spraying tear gas or water, leaving the men stinging and vomiting, or naked, wet and shivering in winter months. Sometimes the guards responded by not feeding the prisoners or not delivering mail or medication. Rundle never saw any indication that the guard staff had an inkling that they themselves might be responsible for the inmates' behavior.

A confrontation between Rundle and the Soledad administration was inevitable. It came during the third month. Dr. Boone had decreed that any inmate identified as a psychiatric patient and admitted to the prison hospital would be locked in an isolation cell at all times unless a guard was present. Since it was very difficult to get an officer to go to the hospital, the order essentially meant twenty-four-hour confinement for the inmate, no showers, no exercise, no recreation, no contact with people. Exactly the conditions to drive a man further into a psychosis, or make his recovery more difficult. Of course, the use of such isolation cells had already been declared illegal by U.S. District Judge George Harris in *Jordan* v. *Fitzharris*. Rundle, who disagreed with Dr. Boone's order, took his case to Warden Fitzharris. The warden declared that Dr. Boone must be right because he was administratively in charge of the prison hospital. "It was," said Rundle, "a strange way to determine proper treatment, but characteristic of administrators lacking in courage." Rundle wouldn't give up. He wrote a letter, with copies to various CDC people and professional organizations, declaring that under such treatment circumstances he, Rundle, would not be responsible for the care of patients in the prison hospital.

The letter provoked much anger and led CDC director Procunier to summon Rundle to Sacramento. The two men had a long discussion. Rundle, who "liked" Procunier, was fascinated by the CDC director's penchant for administrating "according to his own sensitivities and personal feelings rather than relying primarily on rational reflection." The director, Rundle observed, "was obviously comfortable with power, realistic about its use, of which he wasn't afraid." What surprised Rundle at first was that Procunier told him "secrets," but the psychiatrist later understood the meaning of this: it bound Rundle to Procunier in a kind of forced loyalty. Procunier told Rundle he would intercede for him with the Soledad staff and a few days later went to Soledad for a staff conference. There Procunier tried hard to get the other staff members openly to express their feelings about Rundle and what they objected to in the young psychiatrist's methods and procedures. Few said much, probably because they were intimidated by Procunier's opening statement that he wanted Rundle to stay on, that everyone should work together to resolve any conflicts. There was a warm glow from the meeting. The good will between the staff and Rundle, now supported by "Pro," lasted two weeks.

Near the end of March, Rundle was subpoenaed to testify at a preliminary hearing for Yogi Pinell, who was on trial for killing Guard Robert J. McCarthy. Rundle testified that Pinell's history suggested the possibility of an organic brain lesion and that special examinations should be done outside the Department of Corrections. Also, in response to questions regarding the conditions under which Pinell lived in O-wing, Dr. Rundle replied that the area in front of Yogi's cell was usually littered with garbage and that, generally, it was a "miserable and unwholesome" place.

When Rundle went to work the following day, the front gate tower guard shouted down to him that he was wanted in the associate warden's office immediately. A ninety-minute conference ensued, the associate warden, a Japanese-American named Jerry Enomoto, making it clear to Rundle that the psychiatrist had given improper answers in court the preceding day. The staff was angry because they believed Rundle may have provided Yogi with a way to beat the rap of killing a guard: "diminished responsibility." Two days later, an inmate informed Rundle that a guard had told him "no one should be surprised if they found him [Rundle] in a dark alley."

From there, the slide for Rundle was rapidly downhill. In mid-May he testified in the "Soledad Seven" case—the trial of seven black inmates charged with the stabbing of William Shull, the second guard killed at Soledad—and again his testimony was seen as unfavorable to the institution and favorable to inmates. He testified once more in a hearing on the Pinell case. And again Rundle's testimony was considered damaging.

Then, a final incident and Rundle was fired. One of the prison's program administrators, Kenneth Conant, had been sitting in a prison office on the morning of May 19 talking with an official from CDC headquarters in Sacramento. Suddenly, two white inmates burst into the room and in a scuffle in which the events are still unclear, stabbed

Conant to death. At the time of Conant's death, Dr. Rundle was in his own office waiting for the inmate who was later accused of killing the program administrator. The accused prisoner, Eric Hilton, had had an appointment to see Rundle. Rundle, hearing of the stabbing, sat at his desk thinking that this would probably finish him at the institution. He went home.

He dreaded going to work the next day. The flags were at half-mast. The entire prison was in a "lock-down" condition, every prisoner in his cell. About midafternoon, an administrative assistant of the warden's asked Rundle for his confidential psychiatric file on the accused inmate. Apparently, the official had no idea that his request was out of the ordinary. He seemed startled when Rundle told him that he would not release the file to anyone unless the inmate requested or approved. The staffer walked out. Soon there was a phone call from Associate Warden Enomoto, who asked for the file. Rundle refused. "I don't like to do this," Enomoto said, "but I'm giving you a direct order to produce the file." Rundle suggested that perhaps one way out of this impasse would be for him to talk with the accused inmate and see whether he would give Rundle permission to release the file. "Wait a minute!" said Enomoto. "That would mean that every time the warden wanted one of those files, we'd have to get the inmate's permission. Nothing doing!" Rundle asked for ten minutes to think over the matter and the associate warden said all right. Rundle raced to a phone in another office and called the state attorney general's office to ask about the law regarding confidentiality of patient communication. He explained his situation to one of the attorneys and the state lawyer said he didn't know, but he'd look it up immediately. Rundle said he had about five minutes. "Wow," the voice came back over the phone. "Try to stall them off and I'll call right back."

As Rundle emerged from the office where he had made the telephone call, he was surrounded by two associate wardens and a guard captain. The trio were obviously angry and their manner, demeanor and tone of voice seemed threatening. Associate Warden Clem

Swagerty took a firm grip on Rundle's arm. "C'mon, Frank, you're coming with us." The psychiatrist refused to move. He tried to explain he was waiting for a phone call. "There's no time," Swagerty said. "Are you coming with us or are we going to take you?" At this, the guard captain chimed in, "Let's take him." As they walked down the corridor, a group of uniformed officers ran up to the group. They were waved to a halt by one of Rundle's escorts with an "It's all right." The men walked a little farther and another group came running up. One of the guards carried manacles and leather restraining belts. It suddenly dawned on Rundle that they were coming for him. "Were those manacles and belts for me?" he asked. "Uh, no," the guard answered. "It was a mistake." But the guard followed Rundle and his escorts into Warden Fitzharris's office.

Fitzharris reiterated the request that Rundle hand over Hilton's file. Rundle refused. The warden told Rundle he was fired—as of that moment. The psychiatrist returned to his office, noticed that the Hilton file was now missing, picked up his few private possessions and was escorted out of the prison.

Frank Rundle had tried in his own way, given the limitations of his position, to change things at Soledad. He had found himself sliding into a new reformist attitude which, while a very few of the staff appreciated it, most either ignored or fought against. Asked about the Rundle firing, a high-ranking CDC official told me, "Well, the dumb bastard wasn't doing his job. Those files are our files. He was supposed to get to know the inmates and tell us which ones were dangerous. He just didn't know what he was there for."

Even after he left, Soledad wasn't finished with Rundle. Seven months after his departure, a group of Soledad guards tried to frame him for murder. The bungled frame-up attempt began one mid-December evening when a smartly dressed young man and his fiancée rang the doorbell of Rundle's house in Monterey. Rundle greeted the couple warmly because he had known the young man, who was named Tom Pewitt, as an old and trusted inmate friend from Soledad. Rundle brought out some drinks and the three talked. Later, when the psychiatrist went into the kitchen to freshen the drinks, Pewitt followed. At the kitchen table, Pewitt grabbed a pencil and scribbled this startling note: "Do you realize that the CCOA [California Correctional Officers Association] is out to hang you at any expense? I'm bugged." Pewitt pulled open his shirt and revealed a network of wires strapped to his chest. Rundle was shocked but the two began exchanging notes, all the while making small talk for the invisible listeners, until Pewitt had informed Rundle that a miniature radio transmitter was in his cowboy boots; that a Soledad guard and a member of the state attorney general's office were a block away, sitting in a green Ford Torino, monitoring their conversation; that Pewitt, who had been transferred to Chino Prison, was on a fraudulent seventy-two-hour pass with promises of an early release if he cooperated; that CDC director Raymond Procunier was—like Rundle— under suspicion; that Pewitt's mission, as explained to the con by prison officials, was to set up Rundle as a conspirator in two Soledad murders; and that as far as Pewitt could tell, representatives of the attorney general, the CCOA, the Monterey County district attorney's office, the Kern County Homicide Division and staff members from at least two prisons were part of the plot. Moe Comacho, a Soledad guard sergeant who had been elected vice-president of the California Correctional Officers Association, had told Pewitt: "I believe that Rundle is involved with the Communist party and the radicals and so is Procunier. I believe that Rundle led these people to kill McCarthy and Conant and I want you to get the evidence." Pewitt had gulped hard and agreed.

In the process of his preparation for this strange scenario, the young white con met: Chino guard Lieutenant Roscoe Antrim, who arranged for his fraudulent pass; Moe Comacho, who seemed to be orchestrating the ploy; a Soledad O-wing guard named Loran Spoon, who drove Pewitt from Chino to Salinas; and Norman Gard, an investigator for the attorney general and the CII—the California Bureau of Investigation and Identification—who brought out the miniature bugging device and explained how to operate it. Later,

Gard was one of the chief investigators in the cases involving Angela Davis and Stephen Bingham. Pewitt was told that both Gard and Comacho would be nearby, monitoring the conversation. To get corroborating witnesses for his side, Rundle slipped out to "buy some Cokes," and telephoned two Monterey detectives. The pair arrived at the Rundle home, created a temporary malfunctioning of the recording device, took photographs and witnessed affidavits.

When Pewitt was returned to Chino Prison, he was interrogated by Comacho, who was upset about the mission's lack of success. Two days later, Pewitt was thrown into the Chino "hole," maximum security, under investigation for an unsolved four-year-old murder. In February, the parole board rescinded Pewitt's parole date. In late May 1972, Pewitt was finally released on parole, after the board dropped its investigation of the unsolved murder.

A frame-up of Rundle and perhaps even Procunier would have worked well with the line taken by ultraconservative correctional members that all of the troubles in California prisons are caused by "outside agitators." Since Rundle was the first insider to criticize conditions in the California prison system and was indirectly backed up by Procunier, the guards had a ready-made conspiracy theory to make public. It may be, too, that men like Comacho, Spoon and Gard believe such a conspiracy exists.

There were additional reformers and humanitarians whom men like Comacho, Governor Reagan and other conservative elements in the state damned and excoriated. One of the major groups to suffer the slings and arrows of this conservative outrage was the California Rural Legal Assistance. CRLA, a federally funded group of lawyers, has probably done more in legal assistance for the poor people of California than a legion of private attorneys. Representing the poor, however, has its political drawbacks, especially when the courtroom targets are businessmen, landlords, corporations, even prisons.

CRLA was mandated by its grant to provide legal services to the eligible poor in civil matters only within the rural areas served by its operational offices. To qualify for CRLA legal help, a prospective client had to ask for it, prove that his salary level was below $2,200 plus $500 per child, demonstrate that his case would not result in a court-awarded fee so that it could be presumed a private attorney would not be willing to represent the individual or group. When those three conditions were met, CRLA would be willing to accept the applicant as a client. The problem for Soledad Prison was that a CRLA office was in nearby Salinas and inmates qualified as "eligible poor," not in criminal matters, of course, but in civil cases.

In Salinas, CRLA filed two early civil actions on behalf of prisoners against Soledad. One suit challenged the prison's practice of mail censorship while the second action claimed that prisoners were denied due process at the prison's disciplinary hearings. This was all very disturbing to Soledad officials. They complained that the young CRLA attorneys were harassing the prison for publicity, that the young lawyers were visiting too many prisoners, and suggested that CRLA was "associating" with "movement" lawyers such as Fay Stender. Later, the prison callously lied and cast innuendos hinting at unethical conduct, intimidation of witnesses and possible perjury. When CRLA came up for refunding in 1971, Governor Reagan arm-twisted the Office of Economic Opportunity into holding off new funding, pending an "investigation" of CRLA. The final 283-page report, compiled by Lewis K. Uhler, who was hand-picked for the job, was a splendid updated version of the smear, innuendo, transfer and invisible witness techniques of the late senator from Wisconsin Joe McCarthy. Twenty pages of the study were devoted to CRLA's "activities and involvement" in the state's prisons.

For example, through the prison's censorship and Xeroxing facilities, the Uhler Report reprinted a letter from Patti Roberts, a legal assistant in George Jackson's case, which said that Dave Kirkpatrick, a CRLA attorney, had mentioned to her that someone had been "unjustly" placed in isolation. The report also noted that Ms. Roberts had addressed the prisoner in her salutation as "Dear Comrade." After pointing out that Ms. Roberts worked for Fay Stender and that Stender had written the "brief that secured Huey

Newton's release," after quoting a *San Francisco Chronicle* identification of Stender as a "radical or movement lawyer," after noting that Stender was a woman who had said she believed the U.S. court system is an "instrument of war against the oppressed," Uhler concluded that "our evidence shows that the association of Faye [*sic*] Stender with CRLA is close." The connecting link was that CRLA attorney Dave Kirkpatrick was mentioned in a letter by Stender's assistant to a Soledad prisoner. Was that Uhler's best shot? He tried others, such as claiming that CRLA attorneys had "visited" the three Soledad Brothers, but this was denied by CRLA and even prison officials could not come up with evidence to support Uhler's charge, though all prison visits are carefully logged.

One of the most potentially damaging criticisms levied against CRLA concerned visits which several CRLA attorneys had made to the Soledad Seven. The report also stated that some witnesses in the Soledad Seven case were visited by CRLA attorneys, and declared that the witnesses were being intimidated by CRLA. CRLA admitted visiting the seven blacks accused of killing Guard William Shull, but not in connection with any criminal case. The defendants had their own attorneys for that. They had asked CRLA for help in a civil suit, charging that they were being held in the Soledad Adjustment Center without explanation and without any charges being filed against them. The inmates simply wanted legal assistance in investigating what appeared to be a violation of their due process rights. The intimidation-of-witness charge was emphatically denied by CRLA.

The witness-intimidation charge backfired on the state in a most dramatic manner. The City of Salinas and the County of Monterey had stumbled through the early pretrial hearings in the Soledad Brothers case, but they were fully prepared for the trial of the Soledad Seven. Patrol cars cruised the city's streets. Outside the courthouse, several policemen, armed with rifles, stood on top of nearby buildings. More than a dozen deputies and policemen patrolled the courthouse grounds. Another dozen manned various guard positions inside the courtroom. The prisoners themselves arrived in two cars, accompanied by a small convoy of six California Highway Patrol cars. The convoy drove to a special basement entrance and the seven defendants were taken up to the courtroom by a guard contingent of a dozen more police.

The courtroom itself was sealed off from what had been normal access in the past. Entry during this trial was limited to a single door at the south side of the courthouse, a door which led to a small conference room adjoining the courtroom. The corridor usually used by spectators was locked and barred by a large wooden table, and large sheets of opaque plastic covered the corridor windows. Spectators, lawyers, reporters and members of the defendants' families walked into the small conference room by twos. Each was carefully frisked by men and women deputies. All packages, briefcases and camera bags were minutely scrutinized by hand and eye. Everything and everyone passed through a metal detector. An additional requirement applied to the defendants' families and relatives: they were led outside and photographed. Inside the courtroom, several spectators voiced concern about the large metal canister which protruded from beneath a table in front of the jury box. Nothing to worry about, a deputy explained; it was merely a large battery with two small floodlights. That was just in case a bomb blast blew out the court's power supply.

If that was bad, awaiting trial was worse. Roosevelt Williams, one of the defendants, later described his treatment in O-wing during the investigation which preceded the trial. "When I was first placed in the hole, I was stripped down and remained naked for three weeks. I had no shoes. I was given none of my personal property of letters and legal papers for over a month. Eating and sleeping was extremely difficult, and much of the time completely impossible. With no clothing and one skimpy blanket, the nights in the cell were too cold. Tear gas is frequently used in O-wing and when it's used in any cell on either of the two connecting tiers, all of the cells received the gas. Food served me by white inmates often had urine and excrement in it. Racial taunts and names were yelled at me day and night."

That was during July and August of 1970, just before and just after the Marin Courthouse shooting. The pretrial hearings took place in October, but they were adjourned for a later trial date. In February 1971, however, a new district attorney took office in Monterey and without giving any explanation, dropped the murder charges against four of the seven defendants. The remaining three—Roosevelt Williams, James Wagner and Jesse Phillips—came to be called the "Soledad Seven Minus Four."

The trial began in late May 1971. It lasted twelve days. The first inmate witness, Francis Indino, under questioning by Assistant District Attorney Ed Barnes, said he had overheard one of the black defendants talk about "offing a pig or bull," at a picnic table near the recreation shack where Shull's body was found. That established some kind of motive, perhaps, but upon cross-examination, Rich Hodge, one of the defense attorneys, elicited from Indino that the inmate had been threatened with a rubber hose.

Hodge: I take it at that time after you had been threatened, you were a little bit worried about your own welfare, were you not?

Indino: Yes, sir.

Hodge: As a matter of fact, at that time you thought it would be important for you, as a witness, to come up with something that would point the finger of suspicion away from yourself to someone else, did you not?

Indino: Yes, sir, I would have to say that.

Hodge: Isn't that the reason, Mr. Indino, that you mentioned to Mr. Barnes that you saw another person by the name of Jesse Phillips at the picnic table?

Indino: Yes, sir.

As Indino told the court of other threats, his own fear of doing the maximum or top part of his indeterminate sentence, and Captain Moody's intimidation of a witness named Brizendine, the prosecutor, Barnes, tried to object.

Hodge: You actually observed Captain Moody take a gun and put it to Mr. Brizendine's head?

Indino: No, chin.

Barnes: Objection, your honor. I ask that the defendant's answer
be stricken because there is no showing of any threats made
to this witness. . . . He said the gun was pointed at another witness's head.

Hodge: In his presence, I might add.

The Judge: In his presence.

Barnes: There is no showing as to whether this witness was intimidated by that or not.

The courtroom burst into laughter and the judge, suppressing a
smile, overruled Barnes's objection. The prosecution's case crumbled
when Thomas Brenson, the third state witness, was called. Brenson
testified that he had seen James Wagner, one of the defendants, leaving the recreation shack, presumably after Shull's death. Brenson
was asked to identify Wagner, who was sitting at the defense table.
After much hesitation, he picked out Jesse Phillips. After that error,
Brenson went on to testify that he had identified a second person who
had left the yard shack, then added, almost as an afterthought, "Oh,
excuse me, yes, but I lied about it." "Why did you do that?" he was
asked. "Just a grudge," Brenson said, shrugging. The witness tried
to explain that he held a grudge against another black inmate and
admitted that Wagner was not the man who had left the shack.
Indeed, Brenson said he had witnessed nothing. When Hodge asked
why Brenson waited six months before telling the truth, the witness
said it was "just something on my conscience." "And what part of
your conscience caused you to name Theo Williams and place him in
a position where he would be executed if he was convicted?" Brenson
was silent.

Patrick Hallinan, another defense attorney, began cross-examining
the witness.

Hallinan: You told [the officers interviewing you] that you are known
as a staff snitch and will tell anything you know, correct?

Brenson: Yes, sir.

Hallinan: Tell me, Mr. Brenson, was not the reason you were down
there because you were heavily in debt?

Brenson: Yes.

Hallinan: Now, what I would like you to do, Mr. Brenson, is tell the
jury what it means to incur heavy debts in prison.

Brenson: It is, let's see, I would be turned out, as the phrase is used,
stabbed.

Hallinan: Doesn't "turned out," Mr. Brenson, mean that whoever you
are obligated to or indebted to uses you as a male punk or
homosexual to have relations with other inmates?

Brenson: To a certain degree. It depends on the other individual, sir.

Larry Horan, the third defense attorney, followed Hallinan. Where
Hallinan and Hodge had been severe in their questioning, Horan was
gentle, compassionate. Brenson denied he had seen anyone come out
of the rec shack. "Mr. Brenson," Horan asked, "do you have any
idea what the effect of your testimony in this case can be?" Brenson
said he had wanted to get transferred out of Soledad, that his own
information was inadequate to achieve a transfer, so he invented
names to make the information more valuable. "It was so you would
get out of the institution, wasn't it?" Hallinan returned to ask. "Correct," said Brenson. Hallinan himself was a little stunned. "I—I
really have no further questions."

Barnes asked for a recess. The next day, Barnes's boss, District
Attorney William Curtis, asked that the charges against the inmates
be dropped. Curtis minced no words in understating his motion. "In
the last two days," he said, "the prosecution's case has suffered from
difficulties. In our considered opinion the state cannot present a case
that would end up in the conviction of the defendants." The judge
agreed. Later, in a press conference, Curtis acknowledged that his
office went into the trial knowing that their case "was not the strongest
in the world."

Curtis refused to answer any questions about Moody or any guards
putting guns to the heads or chins of inmates. He had no knowledge
on that subject. The inmates' charges of intimidation also came too
late to be helpful in the state hearings on the refunding of California
Rural Legal Assistance but it didn't matter; their testimony wasn't
needed.

At Governor Reagan's insistence, the Nixon administration had withheld funds for CRLA pending a quasi-judicial hearing. Three highly respected senior judges were asked to sit on the hearing panel and the results were disastrous for the conservatives. The media reported it all with a straight face but the Uhler forces were almost laughed out of court. CRLA was refunded. Still, the Comacho/ Reagan/Soledad purposes were served. CRLA is no longer as actively involved in prison cases. Their number of visits to inmates, their number of prisoner clients, their filing of civil actions have all diminished.

There were other civil suits filed, some of them quite shocking in their allegations. In mid-November, two white inmates—Carl J. Tsouras and Michael B. Huyck—asked a federal court to protect them because they had refused to kill a black Soledad inmate "at the request of prison officials." In their affidavit, the two prisoners said they were taken out of their third-tier cells in O-wing by three officers, one of whose name they gave, and escorted to the disciplinary committee room, where they were met by a guard lieutenant named Eads and a Mr. Huth. "Do you know a goddamn nigger name of Meneweather on max row?" the two whites were asked. After the two men said no, the guards explained "how they hated colored people and how they hated Meneweather especially because he was causing trouble for the staff by filing writs on them, and was snitching on Officer Miller for killing those niggers on the yard to these no good nigger-loving communist bastards trying to stir up trouble for the institution."

The guards told Tsouras and Huyck that Meneweather was in jail for assaulting a white man, that he was in the A/C for killing another white at San Quentin and that the black "only had three years and a few months" left on his sentence. The prison officials next told the two that "they would see that Meneweather came upstairs about five days from then and they said they would make it worth our while if we saw to it that Meneweather didn't live long enough to get off the tier.

"They told us if we didn't go through with it they would send us to Folsom or San Quentin and that the niggers are out to kill all the white dudes that were at Soledad Central and who were in O-wing when the shooting happened in January. They said if we could catch him [Meneweather] off guard and kill him they would be sure to see to it that nobody went to court for it and that we would be protected for three or four months and then transferred to CMC-East, Camp or Palm Hall and get paroled in a year."

In addition to asking the court for a transfer, Tsouras requested that he be granted an operation for a painful hernia. Tsouras had refused to kill Meneweather in July and had tried to forget the incident but now, he said, he feared for his life and believed the prison was withholding the needed operation to punish him.

At Soledad, Associate Warden Enomoto said that the inmates' charges had already been investigated and that he felt "really comfortable in saying that such allegations are totally without foundation." The press could not reach Officer William H. Monaghan, who was named in the suit, for comment. In the end, the two men were transferred and Meneweather received an early parole. Meneweather's parole, however, might have been due to the fact that Melvin Belli, one of San Francisco's most prominent trial attorneys, was following his case. Prison officials did admit that Huyck and Tsouras were assigned to cells next to Meneweather's but claimed that it was not for the purpose of killing Meneweather. The court refused to hear the case.

A similar suit was filed a month later, this time signed by both the alleged killer-to-be, a Caucasian inmate, and his target, a black prisoner who had also been out on the yard on January 13. The two men charged that guards named Vandike and Horton (they only knew them by their last names) were the conspirators. The targeted black inmate, Earl Satcher, said Guard Horton told him he would never leave prison alive. The white inmate, Oscar Craddock, swore that Vandike approached him in his cell and talked with him about killing Satcher. Pointing out that Satcher was a threat both to the guards and to white inmates because of his "subversive" political beliefs, Vandike said he was aware that Craddock was training in karate. What should be done? Craddock asked. "Kill Satcher; you're good enough," Vandike reportedly replied. Later the same day, November 20, 1970, while Satcher was out for an attorney visit, Officer Horton told Craddock to catch Satcher by surprise and kill him. However, Craddock decided not to kill Satcher and remained in his cell even though the door was left ajar so he could get at the black. The two men asked the court for transfers and requested that Warden Fitzharris be ordered "to submit to the court a plan demonstrating that he has the ability and intent and desire to control the guards at Soledad, to prevent further solicitations to injure or kill inmates by guards." Neither of the civil actions asked for monetary damages, only that court costs be covered. The courts declined to hear either one.

When the courts refused to hear the civil suits on murder charges and refused to consider prisoner complaints about prison conditions and unfair institutional regulations, the inmates began taking matters into their own hands. The first major move was an outbreak of violence at Soledad in which more than a thousand inmates broke windows, smashed furniture and fixtures, set fires and plugged shower drains in eight of the prison's housing wings. While the destruction was going on, one group of prisoners tacked a six-page mimeographed list of demands on all of the prison's bulletin boards. The list of demands, signed by the "Soledad Revolutionary Front," warned that "anyone who does not support the strike is opposed to it, that is, counter-revolutionary. Anyone who opposes it is an enemy and will be dealt with as such." The violence was coupled with a work strike.

In O-wing, Soledad prisoners declared their support for the work strike by going on a hunger strike until their own demands were "acknowledged as legitimate" with "some type of answer either yes, no or else you are considering it." The prisoners said they wanted a discussion of the demands, most of which involved prison conditions, with the Soledad staff. The inmates also insisted that CRLA attorneys be present to represent them in the discussions. On the tenth day of the hunger strike, Associate Warden Enomoto acceded to the demands for the meetings, one with inmates and one separate discussion with CRLA, explaining that they could have met earlier but "it is not our policy to have such a meeting, especially with a hunger strike going on. While inmates are in a state of insurrection, the administration doesn't deal with them." Enomoto said he had "mixed feelings about a proposal like" a joint meeting. "I think these attorneys are acting in good faith," he said, "but they don't really understand the kind of men we have in O-wing and we do, we think."

In their demands, the prisoners wanted Soledad to abolish the requirement that six months' acquaintance with inmates precede corresponding and visiting privileges for people "outside." They demanded that the prison stop subjecting inmates to "double punishments" for infractions against prison rules, the first punishment being a stay in the "hole" and the second occurring when the parole board reads about the first and adds six months or a year to a man's sentence. They asked that they be given a hot breakfast and a noon meal (the noon meal had been taken away and sandwiches substituted as routine); that the guards stop stealing magazines, newspapers and other publications which are mailed in; that prison officials mail all writs and legal documents that are "duly deposited in the U.S. mails from O-wing"; that each inmate be informed why he is being punished; that the inmates be given tennis shoes; and that "something be done immediately about the bug-infested cells in O- and X-wings."

Enomoto wrote a memo reply to the demands. The six-month-acquaintance requirement for visits and correspondence was prison regulation. There is no such thing as double punishment because assignment to the "hole" is a "classification assignment" and not a "disciplinary assignment." "The problem with serving a full noon meal is that the time taken for such serving would seriously affect the time presently used for exercise and yard." He said he would try to alter the variety of sandwiches. Magazines and newspapers *are* being delivered. The mail is being sent out after censorship. They were trying to get tennis shoes and a contract was signed with a pest-control company a week after the strike began. The prisoners were surprised: not all of their demands were met, but some were and that was more than they had expected. They ended their hunger strike. It was a cruel twist but not one of the promises was kept. For one thing, Enomoto, who had acceded to the demands, was promoted and transferred to an institution upstate. As the weeks and months passed, the hunger strike was forgotten: it was no longer hot news.

Simultaneously, and in conjunction with the Soledad strike, most of the inmates at Folsom Prison declared a general prison strike. The eighteen-day Folsom strike—in which inmates refused to work (they carry out most of the prison's daily operations)—was the largest and longest in California history. In addition to demands for better treatment, Folsom inmates called for the freedom of Reis Tijerina, the New Mexico Chicano leader; Angela Davis and the Soledad Brothers; and Chip Fitzgerald, a little-known Los Angeles militant. The general prison demands focused on ending the state's indeterminate-sentence law and fairer treatment of prisoners, particularly those in the Folsom Adjustment Center. Not one of the demands was acted upon by prison authorities.

The waves of prison strikes and the outbreaks of violence which are now periodically washing over various institutions are seen by many as a new "revolutionary movement" of "political prisoners" in the nation's prisons. California prison authorities have remarked that they are receiving a "more violent breed of inmate, inmates from the streets smoldering with revolutionary rhetoric." That's not surprising. Anyone with a little common sense can deduce from the national statistics that most of the crimes which send men to prison can be traced to social and economic conditions of poor whites and poor blacks. It's not hard to steal if you're turned out of one job after another, if you're refused work or laid off first because of the color of your skin, if you bear the brunt of social indignation for accepting a welfare check whose amount has been carefully calculated to help you survive and that's about all, when courts mete out harsher sentences because you're black and when you have to cop a plea because the public defender is very busy and you can't afford your own attorney. Aware of that and aware of the snail's progress in acquiring more equal opportunities in the nation's cities, many inmates have taken to calling themselves "political prisoners," feeling, honestly, that they have been the *victims,* not the *villains,* of American society and justice.

When CDC director Raymond Procunier attended a meeting of the nation's prison officials in Florida, he was constantly asked the same question. "What those other wardens and superintendents really wanted to know," Procunier said, "was our 'revolutionary' thing out here. They said there's nothing like it anywhere else, but they're afraid it's coming." Within two weeks, Attica occurred. And there followed revolutionary prison riots in other prisons in New York and in New Jersey, Maryland and Louisiana.

The catalyst in California was the January 13 shootings, but veteran prison workers say that there have been undercurrents of such a revolution for almost a decade. They think that the "movement" may go back to a mess hall riot in Folsom Prison in 1961 when some black inmates tried to integrate the prison dining facility. The incident was first blamed on Folsom's Black Muslim group, but Folsom Warden Robert A. Heinze expressed a different kind of worry in 1961. "It isn't just the Muslims anymore," he said. "It's gone beyond that. The other colored boys have joined up and this thing is getting out of hand." As a result of the incident, twenty-four blacks, eleven of whom were described as Black Muslim leaders, were transferred to the Soledad Adjustment Center. Later, a report by the then state attorney general Stanley Mosk blamed Folsom prison authorities for "racial segregation policies" which led to the rioting. The Soledad Adjustment Center was little known then and no one questioned conditions in the heavily barred steel-meshed cells where eight years later the prison revolutionary movement would be born. To the inmates, it is clear that prison officials will not accede to reformist demands of more humane treatment and better living conditions. To them, it is clear that society's forces of law enforcement will do anything, even break their own laws, to gain a conviction. And for black prisoners especially, it is clear that prison officials will stop at nothing, even murder, to stifle a voice of protest.

"No human being deserves the treatment we receive," Hugo Pinell wrote exactly one year before the multiple tragedy at San Quentin. "Twenty-four hours of psychological torture is enough to disturb the strongest mind. . . . These staff members don't show us cooperation, respect, they don't show us anything but the fact that they aim to destroy us—either physically or mentally. There is no fear in our behavior. Then, again, there is no violence in our behavior. But my question is, what good does it do to withstand all these injustices if we remain in the same dungeons day after day? We are cautious! We are well behaved and yet nothing is granted. We simply don't want to remain here anymore. . . . All we do is think, how strong is our resistance?"

And, as George Jackson put it a year before he died, "I don't think we can afford to be nice much longer, the very last of our protection is eroding from under us. There will be no means of detecting when that last right is gone. You'll only know when they start shooting you. The process must be checked somewhere between now and then, or we'll be fighting from a position of weakness with our backs against the wall."

The time was ripe for violent revolution.

IX

The Death of George Jackson: The State's Case

The California State Prison at San Quentin sits on a flattened promontory in San Francisco Bay, a barren, wind-swept headland some ten miles across the choppy waters from the city of San Francisco. Much of the prison land is surrounded by water. Off to the north and northwest of the high-walled compound, the ground rises sharply in rolling earthen hills which lead to the city limits of San Rafael, the Marin County seat. In summer, the hills are a tawny brown, their high grasses dry and brittle from lack of rainfall and a scorching sun. Both the prison and the town took their names from the promontory point on the bay. The small rural village of San Quentin is a three-street assemblage of wood-framed houses, a white adobe post office and a snack bar. In numbers, the two hundred residents of the community are dwarfed by the prison population of 2,500 and a correctional staff of more than six hundred.

The prison is California's oldest. Because it has the only gas chamber in the state, it also became the most famous. It was here in the late spring of 1960 that Caryl Chessman lost his ninth stay of execution and was strapped into a steel chair to inhale the bitter almond stench of two cyanide capsules. It is here that Robert Kennedy's assassin, Sirhan Sirhan, and the Tate murderers Charles Manson and Charles Watson sit and sleep their life away. It was here that Ruchell Magee awaited trial for his involvement in the Marin County Courthouse tragedy. And it was here, on a plaza of flower beds and walkways, that George Jackson met his death on a late August Saturday in 1971.

Except for a gusty wind that funneled in through the Golden Gate, the day George Jackson died was sunny and warm. He had expected at least one visitor that August 21 and inside the Adjustment Center he kept asking the guards whether his visitor had arrived. The guards said no, even though they knew otherwise. Two people were waiting to see Jackson but the visiting room officer had told the guards on the telephone that they had not been "cleared."

The two visitors, a young white radical attorney named Stephen Bingham and a female activist who said her name was Vanita Anderson, had signed in at the prison's East Gate at 10:15 A.M. They were not required to produce identification at the gate, but Lloyd Hine, the guard who manned the desk there, recalled that they arrived and left together and that Bingham was male and Caucasian and Anderson was female and "colored."*

Inside the East Gate, the two walked about two hundred yards to the prison's security fence, where all visitors are required to pass through a metal detector. Purses, bags, tape recorders, briefcases and similar large objects, while not passing through the "inspectoscope" detector, are examined routinely by the guard at that gate.

That Saturday, Correctional Officer Bernard C. Betts processed more than 225 visitors through his metal detector. It was not his

* Although I do not believe that Vanita Anderson was in fact the woman who accompanied Bingham on this visit, I will continue to refer to her as Ms. Anderson because law enforcement officials do. No one knows who accompanied Bingham or whether the woman was black or a Caucasian woman who was disguised as a black.

normal duty station but he had manned the machine before. It was another routine day for Betts. A man wearing a leg brace set the metal detector off. So did a woman wearing a Naugahyde coat with three-inch metallic buttons.

Steve Bingham passed through the inspectoscope at about 10:20 A.M. Betts remembered that the young attorney was wearing a mod necktie and a corduroy jacket, his long hair combed neatly. Betts could not recall that the Berkeley attorney carried anything.

Vanita Anderson walked up to the inspectoscope carrying what looked to Betts like a portable typewriter case. Light-complexioned, with a mild Afro and wearing a pair of finely handcrafted copper earrings, Ms. Anderson was dressed in a three-piece checkerboard suit.

"What's your title?" Betts asked.

"I'm a legal investigator," she answered.

"Who are you going to visit?" Betts inquired.

"George Jackson," the woman who identified herself as Ms. Anderson replied.

Betts instructed her to pass him the bluish-gray metallic case, holding it away from the metal detector so the case would not set the machine off. She thrust the case toward him "in a contemptuous manner" and Betts began examining the contents. The case was about twenty inches long, sixteen inches wide and some four or five inches deep. Inside, Betts found several inches of yellow legal-sized paper and a tape recorder. The recorder was nine to ten inches long, five or six inches wide and almost four inches thick. The guard carefully removed the back of the recorder and saw four C-size batteries, various diodes and transistorized parts and a speaker. Betts did not try to turn the recorder on to see if it worked. He said later that there were about three inches of the recorder which he could not see. He also said that the tape recorder and the attaché case belonging to Ms. Anderson were the only ones which passed through his gate that day.

"You're clear," Betts said to the woman, returning the case. He picked up his phone and called the visiting room to inform guards there that the black female visitor was carrying a tape recorder inside her attaché case.

Betts did not really take notice of Bingham until later in the afternoon, when he saw the young attorney sitting with the black woman on a bench about sixty feet from his station. Observing that Bingham made "numerous" calls from a public telephone, Betts was prompted to call the visiting room to ask, "What gives with this guy?" The visiting room lieutenant told Betts he had denied Bingham permission to visit Jackson. The guard added that he also denied permission to the black woman.

The visiting room guard who prohibited the visit was Daniel P. Scarborough, a quiet, gangly officer who was well-liked by most of the prison's inmates, a feeling attributed to the fact that Scarborough rarely left the waiting and visiting rooms to work in the prison proper. Scarborough knew Bingham. He remembered him as the young radical lawyer who once brought in all that subversive literature. In an earlier visit, Scarborough had examined Bingham's briefcase and found "some pamphlets on guerrilla warfare in the United States" plus some "sealed envelopes." The guard opened the envelopes but found nothing which could be considered "prison contraband." On all previous visits to San Quentin, Bingham had visited with Jackson and no other inmate. Jackson, although his trial on charges of killing a Soledad guard was to begin in two days, had not been meeting with Bingham about that. The two men had been conferring about legal matters involving other black inmates who were Jackson's friends, men such as James Carr, a black militant ex-con who had been a cellmate of Jackson's. The Berkeley lawyer, with all his talk about what a nice guy Jackson was and how the prison tried to oppress George, quickly earned himself a reputation among San Quentin officials as "one of those bullshit dilettante radical attorneys."

Dan Scarborough wasn't about to bend over backward and be helpful. He denied Vanita Anderson's visit with Jackson because of a new prison regulation stipulating that legal investigators could only visit a client inmate once a week. She had seen Jackson a few days earlier. Scarborough denied Bingham's visit because there was "no prior authorization" for such a visit. He knew that Bingham was not Jackson's attorney of record. Bingham insisted that he had permission from Jackson's attorney, John Thorne, and an O.K. from Associate Warden James Park. Bingham asked to see Scarborough's supervisor, a raven-haired Irish lieutenant named Robert J. Milloy.

The two men, Bingham and Milloy, talked on the prison steps. After some moments, Milloy returned to tell Scarborough that Vanita Anderson was "denied for sure" but that Bingham could see Jackson if the attorney received approval for the visit from the associate warden. At noon, Milloy was relieved as the visiting room supervisor by Lieutenant William R. Sellmer. He briefed Sellmer on the Bingham/Jackson visiting situation. An hour later, Sellmer reached the associate warden by telephone at his home on the prison grounds. Park told Sellmer he concurred with the decision denying Vanita Anderson visiting privileges but said that Jackson's lawyer Thorne "had indicated that attorney Bingham had visited George Jackson on previous occasions and we go ahead and let him visit." Later, the implications of that decision may have so shaken Park that he asked to be relieved of his duties in the San Quentin front office.

Up to that point, it had been an unusual day inside the prison. Scarborough himself thought it was strange that the guard in charge of the Adjustment Center would telephone the visiting desk several times to ask whether Jackson had a visitor. The A/C sergeant, Kenneth McCray, told Scarborough that Jackson was "real hot" and that the black revolutionary was expecting a visit. Then, too, A/C inmate Yogi Pinell, twice asked the same question when he came into the visiting room to meet his mother and two other women. Pinell, charged with the third guard killing at Soledad, had been transferred to San Quentin some months earlier. Scarborough told Pinell that Jackson had no visitor.

The day didn't seem so routine in the A/C itself. Officer E. L. Osborne, who was working Death Row No. 2, on the third floor, heard what sounded like a shot at about 11:30 A.M. He telephoned down to the first tier floor officer, Urbano Rubiaco, and asked if he had heard it. Ruby looked down the tier corridor, returned to the phone and told Osborne two inmates were "out fooling around" and maybe that was the cause of the noise. Investigators later thought the noise might have been the test firing of a weapon. Osborne said he felt "uneasy and listened closely the rest of the day." At 1 P.M., he heard another loud clap, almost like a banging on metal. The second time he called down he talked with McCray. Aware that a new water heater had just been installed, Osborne wondered if that was making the noise. McCray said probably so.

Another guard said he heard some strange talk outside in the prison yard that morning. F. S. Chadwick was working the dominoes area in the "lower yard." He was watching some "Black Panthers" (a guard colloquialism for almost any prison black) playing dominoes and heard one of them say "it" was going to "cost them" seventy boxes—seventy cartons of cigarettes. That kind of "money" will buy life and death in prison. Chadwick didn't think too much about it at the time but two hours later, he saw the same black con sitting with a "high-ranking Panther," watched while "another inmate walked up and it looked like he was afraid to walk up on them. He stopped a few feet away and then they went through their handshake, a three-way handshake. This other inmate said Justin or Justice, I'm not sure, and Pinell. . . . I then heard 'as soon as possible.' The man sitting on the table said, 'Get back to the A/C and tell them I'll have it up there to them before two-twenty.' And at that the messenger replied, 'Yes, sir. O.K.' "

What did the contents of Chadwick's eavesdropping mean? Almost any black prisoner who doesn't smile and shuffle in the presence of guards could be considered a "Black Panther." Chadwick overheard nothing that would indicate what "it" was, whether a gun or a large cache of drugs. The price would have been too high for almost anything else. It is commonly rumored that there are at least seven guns in San Quentin, guns held by inmate leaders. The guns move around,

are sold from one "owner" to another, but they are rarely produced
and used. Guns make too much noise. A good sharp shank or knife
is much more efficient. If prison officials know more about the "Panther" conversation, they aren't saying. They deny that guns are inside
even though some turn up on occasion.

When Scarborough received word that the visit had been approved,
he asked Bingham if the attorney had a tape recorder with him.
Bingham answered no. Under later questioning by a Marin County
grand jury, Scarborough admitted that it was he himself who
initiated the conversation about the tape recorder. It was at this point
that Vanita Anderson stepped forward and told Scarborough that
Bingham could use hers.

Scarborough agreed that Bingham did not "at any time volunteer"
that he was going to use a tape recorder—at least until the visiting
room officer initiated the conversation and the black woman volun-
teered her own.

"I got a visit and you guys aren't giving it to me," Jackson yelled
in the Adjustment Center to two of the floor guards, McCray and
Rubiaco. Rubiaco, a tall, burly Chicano guard, had started working
in the A/C only three days earlier.*

It was to calm Jackson down that McCray twice called the visiting
desk. After making the calls, McCray told Jackson that there were
no visitors, even though he knew that two were waiting. He didn't
want to anger Jackson by telling him that the visits had initially been
denied.

At about 1 P.M., McCray received word that Jackson's visit had
been approved. The black revolutionary was released from his cell,

---

* The material in this chapter is a presentation of the events of the day of
George Jackson's death according to state prison official sources and is not to be
construed as a final, true statement of what actually happened.

No. 6, and he walked down the North Tier corridor toward the sliding grille gate which opens to the foyer of the Adjustment Center. There, McCray and Rubiaco began the routine skin search. All of Jackson's clothing was removed. The guards went through his trousers, shirt, shoes and the four reddish-brown Expandex envelopes containing Jackson's legal papers. They watched while he ran a "natural" comb through his hair, but they later admitted that they did not pay that much attention to Jackson's hair. Jackson was cleared for release from the A/C.

Outside the Adjustment Center front door, Jackson walked across the Portal Plaza area, a half acre of flower beds and walkways bounded by the A/C, the prison chapel building, two administration buildings and a gun balcony. After crossing the plaza, Jackson arrived at the "between gates," the main gate between the prison proper and the visiting room. He stood by for another search, this one by between gates officer E. H. Fleming. "What's happening, brother?" Jackson greeted Fleming. Fleming searched Jackson and led him down the narrow corridor which led to the visiting rooms. Because Jackson was a maximum security inmate, he was not allowed to enter the general visiting area but was required to meet family, friends and attorneys in special smaller rooms designed for security. Both visitor and inmate are locked in.

On the visitor's side of Room A, Sterling John Unangst, a relief guard, ushered Bingham in at about 1:20 P.M. "You can go in," he said to the attorney. Unangst said Bingham carried an attaché case in his left hand and a set of expando-type envelopes in his right. Unangst saw no tape recorder. Visiting Room A, roughly seven feet by six feet, is divided in the middle by a table. Affixed to the center of the side walls and dividing the room across the top is a metal screen which can be closed or opened during a visit. Guards said the screen was left open on this particular visit because Jackson was known as being "cooperative." This gesture by the guards meant that Bingham could have passed Jackson a gun in the visiting room. If guards had said the screen was closed, there would have been no way for Bingham to have passed a weapon to the black inmate. A single chair is on the inmate's side of the room, three chairs on the visitor's side. There is no other furniture, just bare walls and plain tile flooring. One door opens to the rear corridor which leads "between gates." Another door leads to the main visiting room. Both are locked during a visit.

First Unangst locked Bingham in. Then Fleming locked Jackson in. No one knows what went on between the two men in the room but after about twenty minutes Jackson shouted to Officer Unangst, "Say, Officer, my visitor has to get something in the other room. He's left some papers with his friend." And Unangst replied, "Well, you'll just have to wait a minute because I can't let him out until you're out of there." Fleming took Jackson out and Unangst unlocked the door for Bingham, allowing the attorney to go outside to the waiting room. Unangst said neither Jackson nor Bingham carried anything out of Visiting Room A during this pause in the meeting. The Berkeley attorney was gone about ten minutes. When he returned, he carried nothing in his hands. The two men continued their meeting and the visit concluded around 2:20 P.M. At the prison's East Gate, Lloyd Hine's visitors' register has it recorded that both Bingham and Vanita Anderson signed out at 2:30 P.M.

Notified that the visit was over, Officer Scarborough phoned over to the circular gazebo-like Yard Office located just outside the front door of the A/C and asked Carl Adams, the dispatcher there, to send an escort officer to return Jackson to the Adjustment Center. Adams sent Frank DeLeon, a stocky guard who would be dead in thirty minutes.

Curiously, Fleming, the between gates officer, who usually searches inmates coming into and going out of the visiting room, was too busy to search Jackson prior to releasing him from the visiting area.

"If the guy is escorted," Fleming explained later, "procedures are that the escorting officer will shake the man down for his own security." Presumably DeLeon did so but he didn't live to tell about it.

Walking into the A/C, Jackson entered the foyer area, which is separated from the two rows, or tiers, of cells by a sliding barred gate. On his immediate left was the North Tier, a row of seventeen one-man cells which run east and west along the length of the A/C. Farther along on the left was the South Tier corridor and its row of cells. The six rear or easternmost cells were used for isolation. With their double doors—an inner barred door and an outer solid steel door—the isolation cells are euphemistically called "quiet cells." It was into this area that inmates later retreated when a squad of guards rushed the Adjustment Center with shotgun and machine gun fire.

To the right of the foyer was the door to the kitchen. Next and adjacent to that was the sergeant's office. A rest room and utility room for cleaning equipment stood beyond, next to a locked stairway which led to the second and third floors of the A/C. At the far end of the foyer was a dining room.

Sergeant Ken McCray, a short, skinny, gutsy Scot, opened the A/C front door and let Jackson and DeLeon in. Two other guards were there at the time: the Chicano, Rubiaco, and stocky, heavy-set Paul Krasenes, whom black inmates described as a mean bull. Rubiaco was in the process of returning another black inmate, Larry Spain, to his cell. Spain, a tier tender, had just finished passing out food trays for the evening feeding. Prison regulations required that Spain be returned to his cell so that no two inmates would be on the corridor at the same time. Rubiaco then walked back to the foyer area to help with the skin search on Jackson. McCray began the search by looking through the expando envelopes which Jackson had placed on a foyer table. Jackson had opened two, maybe three buttons on his shirt when Rubiaco, as he came around Jackson's side, noticed a shiny object in Jackson's hair. He asked the black what it was. "Nothing," Jackson answered, and lightly ran his fingers over the top of his head.

Rubiaco said he wanted to see what it was. "When I touched it," he told state investigators, "I figured it was a plate inside his head or something." McCray, who had worked there much longer than the three days Rubiaco had been on the job, knew Jackson had no metal plate in his head. McCray ordered Jackson to produce the object.

"This is it, gentlemen," Jackson said. "The Dragon has come." The guards said Jackson took a step backward, reached toward his head, pulled off a wig with one hand and grabbed a pistol with the other. A bullet clip fell to the floor. Rubiaco said he started for the clip but Jackson had a second clip and shoved that into the butt of the automatic and slammed a round into the chamber. "All right, gentlemen," Jackson said calmly, "the Black Dragon has come."

The black revolutionary ordered the four guards to walk toward the front door of the Adjustment Center and lie face down. He told Sergeant McCray to release the rest of the inmates, twenty-six of them, from the north and south corridors of the first floor. McCray said he did not have the keys to the control boxes. Jackson turned to Rubiaco and told him to open the cells. The Chicano guard walked to the north bar box and began throwing the switches which separately slide open each cell door by remote control. McCray was told to open the sliding grille gates which connected the foyer area where the guards and Jackson were to the cell corridors. McCray opened the two gates. Jackson then forced the guards to walk inside the north corridor, where they once again were told to lie face down.

Turning his attention to the inmates, Jackson yelled for them to come out. Then, turning to the first black inmates who quietly approached him at the grille gate, Jackson explained, "The Black Dragon has arrived. He's here to free you."

"Our plans were messed up," a prison official quoted Jackson as saying. "I was caught off guard. They found it. But if we got to go, we all got to go together. It's got to be now or never. Whoever wants to come out, come out. The rest stay in your house."

According to McCray, Larry Spain, a militant black whom guards trusted enough to make a tier tender, and the mulatto from Nicaragua, Yogi Pinell, were the first two prisoners to come out. That was probably because their cells were near the front foyer area and were the first to be opened by Rubiaco. The Chicano guard continued to throw the bars on the rest of the cells on the north side but he was slow. "Rubiaco," Jackson warned, leveling his gun at the side of the burly guard's neck, "I'm real tired of telling you. Next time, I'm going to blow your brains out." Other inmates emerged from their cells. Altogether, there were thirty-four cells to be opened. Seven of them, however, were unoccupied. Some doors would not slide open because food trays were still in the slots. The inmates were told to remove them.

While this was going on, the two white kitchen attendants, Ronald Kane and John Lynn, noticed that Jackson had returned from his visit. They had prepared a tray of food for the black inmate but they were locked in the kitchen so the foyer could be clear for Jackson's return. They knocked on the door so they could come out and give Jackson his dinner. "Don't stand there, Rubiaco," Jackson said. "Get out of the way. Let them in." Kane and Lynn came into the foyer carrying the food but Jackson wasn't eating. Other inmates hustled the two into a cell on the north side and told them to sit on a bunk and wait.

Allan Mancino, a young, clean-cut white inmate, had been transferred to the San Quentin A/C just six days earlier. He was lying on his bunk reading a Nick Carter spy book when he heard someone yell, "Take your trays off the tray slots." Mancino, who had never been out of his cell since his arrival, was surprised. He thought it might be time for showers. "What's happening?" he asked a black who passed by his cell. "Oh"—the black inmate shrugged, smiling— "we're taking over."

Mulling that over, Mancino lay back on his bunk and remembered the time when he was in Palm Hall at the California Institution for Men in Southern California. It was eight or nine months before his transfer to San Quentin and he had heard rumors that there was a new gun in San Quentin. The reason he remembered, Mancino later told prison and state officials, was because "it was supposed to be George Jackson that had it." Mancino stepped out into the corridor and saw several guards tied up toward the front end of the tier. "It was real quiet," he said. "Everyone was out, tiptoeing around." He walked toward the foyer.

Cell doors continued to open. While the three guards were lying face down on the tier, someone covered their heads with pillowcases so they couldn't see who was trussing up their legs and tying their hands behind their backs, using the electrical cord which was supplied to each cell for the prison radio system.

Rubiaco returned to the north end of the foyer and saw McCray, DeLeon and Krasenes on the floor in front of the second cell. When Krasenes did "something" (Rubiaco never explained what), the Chicano guard said Fleeta Drumgo kicked him in the face. Rubiaco started for Drumgo but Jackson pressed the pistol to the guard's skull and declared, "You do that again and it's gonna be your last move." Jackson handed the gun to another inmate and told him to take Rubiaco to the south side to open the rest of the cells. "If he moves wrong, shoot him," Jackson yelled as the two left.

As soon as he was tied up, McCray felt a deep sharp cut on the right side of his throat. "It was painless and very swift," McCray said later. He began bleeding profusely. "I just lay limp." Due to the amount of blood McCray was losing he thought he would soon pass out or die.

Mancino, meanwhile, had been walking toward the front of the tier. When he approached the grille gate, he could see that the guards were tied up and that two of them lay bleeding from gaping throat wounds. He watched, he said, as Drumgo began strangling one of the guards with a radio cord. He said he recognized Drumgo because he had known him since juvenile hall days. As he passed an open cell, he noticed that both the white tier tenders, Kane and Lynn, were sitting inside. They looked terrified. Mancino said Rubiaco was in the sergeant's office.

Thinking McCray was dead, two inmates dragged him into a cell and left him on the floor face down, his head against the rear wall. A few minutes later, Krasenes was dragged into the cell and placed alongside the Scot. McCray continued to feign death. He could tell the next arrival was Krasenes because he caught a quick glimpse of a khaki uniform. The only guard wearing khaki that day was Paul Krasenes.

Krasenes began to cough and choke on his own blood. "Sounds like one of them is still alive," a voice said. Krasenes, between coughs, prayed. Two prisoners entered the cell and worked on Krasenes some more. McCray then heard the big man die, letting out one "last gasp and then I heard what sounded to me like defecation, like everything had just let go."

After Krasenes died, Frank DeLeon, the stocky older guard who had escorted Jackson back from the visiting room, was brought into the cell and the prisoners were trying to choke him. One of the inmates tied the cord around his throat into a Spanish windlass. McCray said he heard one inmate tell another that he had to twist harder. McCray said he heard a gasp and he did not hear DeLeon speak again.

By now, Rubiaco had opened most of the cells on the South Tier corridor. He was at the south bar box, throwing switches, when a young red-headed guard named Charles C. Breckenridge arrived at the A/C front door with John Clutchette, who had been visiting with his mother. The black con rang the bell while Rubiaco walked toward Breckenridge to open the door. Jackson, who was standing by the foyer table, walked toward the door with the Chicano guard. "You better be normal," Jackson whispered. "If you try to get anybody to give me away, I'll shoot Breckenridge and then I'll shoot you."

Some distance behind Breckenridge and Clutchette, Rubiaco could see Sergeant Jere Graham. Graham, a tough, solidly built guard who swaggered like a Marine drill sergeant, was standing about fifteen feet away next to an open section of the Yard Office just outside of the A/C. The crew-cut Graham, Rubiaco noticed, was looking directly at him so he gave Graham some "dirty looks . . . like there was trouble. I was feeling sick." Rubiaco did not raise Jere Graham's suspicions. Graham just looked puzzled. He would die minutes later.

Standing at the A/C front door and seeing Jackson walking toward him behind Rubiaco, Breckenridge blinked through his glasses and tried to protest. To take Clutchette into the foyer with another prisoner was against prison rules. The redhead got out four words, "What are you doing—" but by then the door was open, Jackson had pivoted around Rubiaco and had swung a pistol toward Breckenridge's red head. Jackson waved him inside the building. As he walked inside, Pinell came out of the sergeant's office with a penknife in his hand. "Put him in 62," Pinell said. Breckenridge said two other black inmates, Willie Tate and David Johnson, escorted him to No. 62—the second "quiet cell" in the rear of the south corridor—shoved him on the bunk and tied his hands and feet.

Rubiaco was returned to the south corridor also but the telephone rang. The caller asked for McCray. "He's in the plumbing area," Rubiaco told the caller, and hung up. The Chicano guard finished opening the rest of the cells. Jackson ordered him to walk toward the rear of the south corridor. While he was walking, Rubiaco tried to reach into his back pocket. "What's in your back pocket?" Jackson asked. "My handcuffs," the Chicano answered. "Let's have them," an inmate said, and grabbed the guard's arms, pinning them behind his back and clipping the cuffs on.

Rubiaco could have been reaching for a knife, a black-handled switchblade which he carried in his pocket. In fact, all the guards that day were armed with their own knives. Breckenridge carried a gray-handled pocket knife. Krasenes sported fingernail clippers with a knife attached. DeLeon carried a white metal money clip which held two folding blades, while McCray was armed with a bone-handled pocket knife. According to evidence later turned over to the California Bureau of Investigation and Identification (CII), Sergeant Graham, the last officer to go into the A/C, was the only guard who was not armed with a knife.

Rubiaco was led to No. 62. Breckenridge was already in the cell, hands and feet tied. The cons threw the burly guard at the foot of the bed. One tied his feet while another put a pillowcase over his head.

"Don't do it, ———," Rubiaco heard Breckenridge say. "You don't know who this is," a voice replied. Then Rubiaco's throat was cut. The first cut bit into the flesh just below his right ear. The second slash jammed into his throat near his windpipe and split the skin back toward the same ear. The third cut gouged into Rubiaco's throat beneath his left earlobe.

The killer started on Breckenridge, "———, there's no need for this," the red-headed guard said. Breckenridge was stabbed on both sides of his neck. Puncture wounds. One of the cuts went through the guard's esophagus and Breckenridge began to swallow blood. He was trying hard to swallow the blood as fast as possible so he wouldn't choke on it or cough and make noise. Several inmates were walking in and out of the cell. "These pigs aren't dead yet," one of them said. "Go in and strangle them," Breckenridge said he heard Pinell say. Breckenridge told state investigators a black inmate entered the cell and wrapped a sheet around his throat. As the inmate tried to strangle him, the redhead gagged, shuddered and made his body go limp. The inmates later untied him, took off his shirt, pants and boots. Then they retied him—just in case.

Gary Hetland and Glen Fisher were two white inmates who had barricaded their cells so their doors wouldn't slide open. "What are we going to do about the two guys that ain't coming out?" Mancino overheard one black inmate ask Pinell. "Dust 'em," Pinell answered. This got Mancino to worrying about himself and the two kitchen helpers, Kane and Lynn. He walked to the cell where they were sitting together. "What are we going to do?" Mancino asked the pair. They shrugged. Mancino pointed out that they were the only three whites out on the tier, since Hetland and Fisher had locked themselves in. He suggested that they come out and "make like you're doing something." Otherwise, he added, "they'll kill you." Come out and "make like you're keeping point, keeping watch or something," Mancino said. Kane walked out and said he wanted to work with Spain, probably because the two men were part of the tier-tending crew. Spain told them to go into the sergeant's office. Mancino walked in with them. As he walked in, he noticed that it was five minutes to three.

While they were in the office, the phones rang twice. The first time it rang Kane picked up the receiver and said, "No, I think he's upstairs." The second time it rang he said, "No, there's nobody in the kitchen." After the two calls were over, Kane crawled under the sergeant's desk and hid.

Outside the A/C, in the Yard Office, Sergeant Jere Graham was wondering what had happened to his two escort officers, DeLeon and Breckenridge. He asked Carl Adams, his stocky, hawk-nosed colleague in the Yard Office, to let him into the A/C and the two men walked over to the front door. Adams turned the lock, let Graham in and immediately locked the door behind Graham, returning to the Yard Office just fifteen feet away. When Graham entered the A/C he was met by Jackson. "Freeze," Jackson ordered. "Don't make a sound." "What is this?" Graham started to ask but an inmate punched him in the face. The three of them—Jackson, Spain and Graham—disappeared into Jackson's cell, where there were already three bodies on the floor. The floor of the cell itself was awash with blood. "It's time I found out if this piece really works," McCray heard Jackson say. "Good God, man, no!" Graham shouted. McCray heard the gun fire, felt the concussion within the small confines of the cell and continued to play dead while blood rushed down on top of him.

The shot was heard on both upper floors of the A/C. "What's that?" a corpulent guard named W. L. Hampton asked. "Something's wrong downstairs," Hampton's superior, Sergeant J. J. Kentzel, said. Kentzel asked Hampton and another guard, David Johnson,* to go downstairs and find out what was wrong. Johnson got there first. "Look out," he said, jumping back from the first floor stairwell window. "Everybody's out." Thinking there was a fight between guards and inmates and that maybe they could help, Hampton unlocked the stairwell door and took a couple of steps inside. "Hold it right there," an inmate said, pointing a revolver at Hampton. Behind him, another inmate picked up a bucket of garbage and threatened to throw it at the two guards. "You better get the hell out of here," Tate said. Hampton backed through the stairwell door and locked it.

(Hours after the tragedy, because a revolver was not found, Hampton was asked if he could "definitely" identify the weapon he saw as a revolver. "Yes, I'm certain it was a revolver," he told his superiors. "When he pointed the revolver at me and told me 'Hold it right there,' it drew my complete attention. I saw the barrel with the cylinders. I am sure. And knowing there is a marked difference between a revolver and a semiautomatic pistol, I'm definitely sure that this was a six-shot revolver, large caliber." The revolver was never found. Weeks later, when San Quentin guards testified before a Marin County grand jury, Hampton was not called as a witness.)

---

* David Johnson was the name of an inmate and a guard at San Quentin.

Just after Mancino and Kane heard the shot that killed Sergeant Graham, Mancino saw Jackson come out of the cell with the gun in his hand. Mancino turned around to talk with Kane when, suddenly, two figures rushed by him. After firing a shot through one of the windowpanes on the front door of the Adjustment Center, Jackson and Spain paused for a moment, opened the door and dashed out.

"George, come back," someone yelled.

About fifteen minutes before he died in the A/C with a bullet through the top of his head, Sergeant Jere Graham was in the Max Shack on the other side of North Block talking with a group of guards. He had wondered then what had become of his two escort officers, Breckenridge and DeLeon, whom he had sent into the A/C. He picked up the Max Shack phone, called the Yard Office and asked Carl Adams where the guards were. Adams said they were still in the A/C. "I'm coming down to the Yard Office," Graham said.

When Graham got there, he and Adams walked over to the A/C front door. They peeked into the windows at the top half of the door but saw no movement. "Let me in there," Graham ordered. "I want to see what they're doing." Adams opened the door, let Graham in and, as regulations required, quickly closed and locked it.

Back in the Yard Office, Adams paced back and forth, wondering now what had happened to Graham. He turned to one of the other four guards in the office with him and wondered out loud what was wrong in the A/C. He heard a shot. Adams strode the short distance to the A/C, again looked into the windows. This time he saw Jackson put a gun against the glass and heard him say, "Open this goddamned door or I'll blow your head off." Adams ducked while Jackson shot through a lower corner window, narrowly missing him. The gray-haired guard rolled away to one side, got up and ran into the Yard

Office. He was breathless. "I just—they tried to shoot me," he sputtered. "They're busting out of the A/C. Call for help." While other guards worked telephones, Adams himself picked up the intercom and sounded the alarm to the various gun positions nearby. "Jackson is loose in the Adjustment Center with a gun. George Jackson's got a gun. George Jackson's got a gun," Adams repeated over and over.

John George Frank, Jr., the man who would kill Jackson, was coming off duty as gun guard in the gymnasium. He was walking casually on an overhead gun rail walkway toward the A/C plaza area when he heard what sounded like a shot. "Sounds like a shot from Four Post [the Yard Office]," Frank said to another guard on the rail, and he started running toward the northwest corner of North Block, the housing wing adjacent to the A/C. He dropped to a prone position on the gun rail and aimed his 30/30 toward the yard. From his position, Frank commanded a view of a small part of the plaza and the "alley" which led past the chapel to the north wall.

Guard James Thorpe was in the Yard Office when Adams hit the panic button. He looked toward the nearby North Block gun rail and noticed that there were already two gunmen up on it. Having just come off duty in the prison gymnasium, Thorpe recognized one of them as his own gym gunman, John Frank. Thorpe ran past the A/C to the North Block corner where the two gunmen were lining up their sights on the yard. "George Jackson's got a gun and he's coming out of the Adjustment Center," Thorpe yelled to his gun guard. Officer Frank quickly looked away from Thorpe and toward the A/C. Thorpe walked cautiously back toward the Yard Office.

Frank Bortfeld, was manning the No. 1 gun balcony, about fifteen feet over the plaza, with a Winchester 30/30. From his position, Bortfeld could cover the entire Portal Plaza, the Yard Office, the front side of the A/C and part of the alley. Two other gun guards were on the balcony with Bortfeld when they heard the shots. They watched Adams duck and run for the Yard Office. Over the gun balcony intercom, they heard Adams's warning.

"He's got a gun. He's coming out," Bortfeld said to the two on the balcony. At that moment, the A/C door flew open and Jackson ran out, followed by Larry Spain. Jackson paused momentarily at the Yard Office. He could have gone inside and either wounded or killed the five guards who were inside. For some reason, he decided to run across the Portal Plaza and head down the alley toward the thirty-foot-high north wall.

"Jackson halt!" Bortfeld shouted from the gun balcony.

Jackson pointed his gun straight up in the air and fired off one round. He continued to run. Bortfeld squeezed off a round as Jackson reached the midground between the A/C and the chapel. The bullet glanced off the sidewalk, not too far behind Jackson's heels. The ricochet caught Jackson in the left ankle and calf. The black inmate seemed to lose his footing, his weight sagging to his left side. But he straightened himself up and turned down the alley toward the north wall.

"I had only a short time to get in a shot," Bortfeld said later, "and when I shot, he stumbled and went down on his knee. He regained his balance and continued to run." Before the guard could fire again, Jackson had turned the corner of the chapel and disappeared from Bortfeld's view.

Jackson ran into the sights of Frank's 30/30. When he came into the gym gunman's view, Jackson "seemed to stumble but he did not hit the ground." Frank said Jackson "started running again. I tried to aim for the legs of the running inmate but he was running in a crouched position. I fired one round and the inmate fell." Jackson bled profusely.

Like Bortfeld, Frank said he aimed at Jackson's legs. Each gunman said he fired only one shot. Other eyewitness guards said they heard more. Thorpe, for example, said he heard two shots fired from Frank's position.

William Carter, a former San Quentin inmate who was an eye-witness to the shooting from the fifth floor of North Block near

Frank's position, said Jackson was already wounded, lying motionless on the pavement of the alley, when the last shot was fired into his body. Carter watched the body "lurch forward."

Hospital workers who arrived at the scene to help the wounded noticed that even after Jackson was dead, the guards handcuffed him and left his body to lie there for nearly six hours.

Larry Spain, who had dashed out with Jackson, had run a straight line across the plaza and jumped into the bushes in front of the chapel. "Look out," Adams yelled. "There's another one in the bushes." Before moving toward Spain, Adams took a quick glance toward the open door of the A/C. He could see about a half dozen other inmates making moves as if they were also going to run out of the A/C but each time they did so they backed up. The acting captain of the San Quentin guards, Lieutenant W. H. Dixon, made the same observation. "Keep them in the A/C," he yelled to Bortfeld, his balcony gunman.

Led by Adams, several guards cautiously approached the bushes where Spain was hiding and ordered him to come out with his hands on his head. Spain got to the pavement edge, where a guard picked him up and threw him roughly onto the plaza concrete. They thought Spain had a gun but when they searched him all they found was a black-taped test tube containing some heavy liquid. "Don't shake it or you'll blow us all up," Spain said quickly.

Lieutenant Eugene Ziemer, a husky ex-submariner, said he got to Jackson's body first. "I ran up to Jackson, grabbed him by the shoulder and threw him over on his back," Ziemer said, adding that when he looked closely, he "could see that Jackson was dead." Carter, one of the inmate eyewitnesses, tells this part differently. He said Ziemer walked over to Jackson's body and kicked the black inmate twice. Perhaps that accounted for a large bruise found on Jackson's side during the autopsy.

In addition to the gun, which another guard pried away from Jackson's right hand, Ziemer found an extra clip in Jackson's pocket and a test tube of heavy liquid. "For Christ's sake, get it out of the sun," Spain, now handcuffed, yelled when he saw the second vial. Guards took both of the vials and carefully placed them in a laundry basket outside the adjacent building.

"They got him," a black inmate said quietly in the Adjustment Center just after the shots were fired.

Several inmates began herding the others toward the rear of the South Tier corridor. "Come on," one directed. "Let's move back to this side. Hurry up. Let's go." Mancino and Kane, after watching Jackson dash out of the A/C, were still in the sergeant's office. Lowering his head to talk with Kane, who was still under the desk, Mancino said, "You better come, man."

The group hunched low so they could move back without showing themselves through windows which ran the length of both corridors. They reached the quiet-cell area near the rear where Rubiaco and Breckenridge were bleeding profusely. A black inmate turned to Kane. "We gonna have to tie you up," he said to the white tier tender. He said it nicely enough. Kane shrugged. "O.K.," he said, but he was trembling. Two blacks took Kane into one of the double-door quiet cells. As soon as they stepped inside, one turned on Kane and smashed the white con with punches to the face and stomach. "No. Stop," one of the blacks cautioned. The punching continued. "Wait. Stop," the black asked again. By the time guards reached the cell, Kane was dead, his throat cut from ear to ear.

Mancino figured he was about the only white man left and he didn't put much on his own survival. "I'm going to go in the first cell," he said to the others, rising to leave, "and watch for the man and tell you when he's coming." Mancino jogged to one of the front cells and dived under a bunk. Whenever he thought the prisoners were coming toward his cell he would call out, "They're coming. They're coming." "And they stayed back," he said later. " 'Cause I figured I was next, you know."

By now, dozens of guards had gathered in the plaza, armed with an array of weapons including .45 caliber submachine guns, shotguns, M-1s, and 30/30s, to rush the Adjustment Center. Believing that there still was another gun in the A/C, they moved in cautiously. The operation to clear the A/C was not unlike similar attacks they had been part of in house-to-house fighting in the cities of Europe and in search-and-destroy missions in the villages of Korea and Vietnam. Moving carefully and quickly, one guard ran into the kitchen. He provided cover with his M-1 while another dashed into the sergeant's office. A third guard covered the foyer from his belly-down position at the front door of the A/C. They could hear movement and voices on the south side of the building but the north side was bathed in silence. From the foyer they could see the vast pools of blood which swamped the front half of the north corridor. The guards inched down that side first. When they got a few feet down the corridor, John Lynn, the second white tier tender, tumbled out of cell No. 6, Jackson's cell. Both sides of his throat were cut. Lynn was trying to say that he couldn't breathe because too much blood had got into his lungs. "He was mumbling something," one guard said, "but I wasn't paying that much attention to him."

The guard detachment was more concerned about the fate of their fellow officers. Lieutenant Ziemer led the group into Jackson's cell. They were stunned by the macabre scene. Two guards wept. The others shook their heads mutely. "There are four dead officers in this cell," Ziemer screamed.

Sergeant Graham, who had gone into the A/C to check on his escorting officers, was dead. He was found sitting on Jackson's bed, his head high against the rear cell wall. There was a bullet wound on the top of his head, clearly visible through the crew cut, and stab wounds on his chest and abdomen. "Looked like the top of his head was blown off," a guard said, shuddering.

The other three guards were stacked on the floor of the cell. Frank DeLeon, who had escorted Jackson back from his visit with Bingham, was found partially stuffed under the bed in the cell, an earphone wire wrapped around his neck, his face a deep purplish blue. "It looked like he had been judo-chopped on both sides of his head and under his nose and across his face and strangled," said a friend.

Paul Krasenes, partially under DeLeon's body, was in the middle of the stack. His face was smashed. His tongue was sticking out of his mouth, probably a result of the Spanish windlass garrote which guards found around his neck. A guard and a medical technical assistant jammed the tongue back in. Krasenes seemed to inhale a couple of times, then stopped breathing. On the way to the prison hospital, they tried to hold his mouth open and make him breathe. It was no use.

Ken McCray was alive, but barely. "Get me out of here," he whispered to Ziemer. "I'm drowning in the blood." "Get a gurney in here fast," Ziemer yelled. "McCray's still alive." They rushed McCray to the prison hospital and saved his life.

Meanwhile, Lieutenant William R. Sellmer, armed with a shotgun, and Lieutenant Richard A. Nelson, cradling a .45 Thompson sub-machine gun, had led a second group of guards to the South Tier corridor. From the foyer, they saw inmates darting from one cell to another and noticed a few arms waving from various other cells.

"Come out, one at a time," Sellmer ordered.

"Get out of the building. We got hostages," a voice answered.

"You ain't got shit," an officer rejoined. Then, turning to other guards nearby, he asked, "They ain't got hostages, have they? How many officers are missing?" A quick count determined that Rubiaco and Breckenridge were still missing.

"We have hostages, you motherfuckers," an inmate called from the quiet-cell area. "We're going to kill them."

Lieutenant Nelson fired a burst from the submachine gun down the corridor. Sellmer followed with a shotgun blast. "We're coming in after you," Nelson called out, "and when we come in after you, if you don't release those hostages, we'll kill you all."

"Fuck you, motherfuckers. We still have hostages and a gun."

Nelson fired another burst from the machine gun.

"We have hostages and they'll be dead."

Another burst of machine-gun fire raked the corridor.

Allan Mancino stepped out of the cell he was hiding in but Nelson ordered him back inside. The guards wanted the inmates in the rear to come out but all they saw was the fleeting waving of arms from a few cell doors. Noticing that the solid steel door on cell No. 62 was partly opened, Nelson fired a clip into the door. Suddenly, a couple of inmates raced out of that cell and ran toward the rear end of the corridor.

Rubiaco, alive, with his hands and feet tied and his throat slashed, heard the machine-gun fire. He had kept his head pinched against his chest to slow the bleeding from his throat. "I figured, well, I'm not going to sit here and die like a dog so I turned so I could see Breckenridge." It was the first time Ruby had lifted his head. He could see that Breckenridge had loosened his bonds. The red-headed guard tried to untie the sheet strippings which bound Rubiaco's legs but the process was slow. "We'll both get it if we stay here this long," Rubiaco said. The Chicano guard nodded toward a razor blade which had been left lying on the bed. Breckenridge tried the razor but the blade was too dull. "Let's go," Ruby kept urging. "We gotta go faster." Grabbing part of the Chicano's bonds, Breckenridge said, "There's only one way to do it—pull." Rubiaco's legs were freed.

Breckenridge started running toward the foyer. "Stop," the guards in front yelled. Dressed only in an undershirt and shorts and covered with blood, Breckenridge was not recognized by the guards in the front. Rubiaco was running behind Breckenridge but he fell down when he heard a shot fired over his head. Kicking his feet into the air, he tried to maneuver himself into a cell so he wouldn't be shot by his own men. By then, Breckenridge had been recognized and had made it to the front. "Rubiaco," the Chicano heard a voice call out, "it's all right. Come on out."

Rubiaco made it to the grille gate and fell at the feet of Sergeant J. T. Arms. "The motherfuckers have guns," he said. "Give me a gun," he begged Arms, "and I'll kill the motherfuckers." "Ruby," Arms said quietly, "let's get you out of here. We have twenty-six inmates loose in here.* Let's get you out." Two other guards led him out but Rubiaco continued cursing and screaming for his cuffs to be taken off and that he be given a gun.

With the escape, if it can be called that, of Rubiaco and Breckenridge, the prisoners no longer held hostages. Mancino was still convinced that he wanted to get out first. "Can I come out first? Can I get out?" he asked. The guards told him to come ahead and escorted him outside. Then, led by Nelson, they checked the first three cells next to the one Mancino was in. The cells were empty. Nelson fired down the corridor once again.

"We're coming out," a voice called.

"O.K. One at a time with your hands on your head."

A black inmate stepped out of a quiet cell into the corridor. He was told to remove his clothes, put his hands on top of his head and walk backward down the corridor toward the foyer. When he reached a point about seven feet from the guards, he was ordered to turn around for a visual weapons check and told to back out of the grille gate into the foyer.

Others came forward. They were asked how many were left. "I

* The guard calculated incorrectly. Twenty-seven inmates had been released; twenty-five were inside the prison, Jackson and Spain were outside.

don't know," was the usual reply. When they thought that all or nearly all were out, Nelson and his men began the careful process of check-ing each cell. They looked into 62, the one Rubiaco and Brecken-ridge had run out of. They only saw some boots, guards' uniforms and sheet stripping—and a lot of blood. Glancing into the next cell, 63, Nelson could see a pair of feet at the end of the bunk bed. He ordered the man out. There was no response. Nelson triggered a machine-gun burst into the cell, stepped inside the door and saw a white inmate who was either dead or dying. Ronald Kane lay on the bed with his throat cut. Nelson checked the few remaining cells on the corridor, firing a few protective bursts here and there, but he found no one else.

The Nelson squad walked around the foyer and began the same methodical search down the north corridor. The guards were still hearing "some voices on the tier." Again, they moved down the tier cautiously, firing machine gun bursts into various cells, until they came to No. 13, where they found the white inmate Gary Hetland. Het-land's cell door was locked and jammed shut. A guard called down to the prison fire station for bolt cutters to cut into the cell. Nelson told Hetland to back up toward the rear of the cell, remove his cloth-ing, place his hands on the wall and stay put until ordered out. Het-land was only too glad to comply. Four cells away, the guards found that Glen Fisher's cell was in the same barricaded condition, jammed shut. Fisher was happy to see the guards. "They tried to get me too," he told them, raising his hands.

All of the inmates were taken outside to the plaza, where they were bound hand and foot and forced to lie naked on the grass near the A/C front door and the Yard Office. Many, of course, were roughly handled and beaten in the process. Things got so bad that Associate Warden Park had to warn his men that he did not want a "head-whipping party." A short distance away, Jackson's body lay in the afternoon sun.

The A/C was cleared.

Word of the tragedy flashed quickly through San Quentin. The prisoners became unruly and hard to handle. In North Block, where several prisoners had witnessed the Jackson killing, inmates refused to be locked in their cells. They complied only after machine-gun and M-1 fire raked the building and windows. Inmates barricaded themselves into their cells, afraid that some ricochets would hit them. Two prisoners in North were wounded. The building's greatest casualty was its windows. Forty-six were shot out.

Prisoners in East Block were burning everything they could get their hands on to protest Jackson's death. "The smoke was so thick from burning paper, blankets and clothing that had been fired and thrown out of the cells," said one guard, "that I could hardly see or breathe." As the guards walked around East Block, prisoners were taunting, "Pig, you gonna die." And when a black officer walked by, they added, "You too, nigger pig."

Prisoners in several of the housing units cheered from their windows whenever wounded or dead guards were rolled below them on gurneys which moved through the South Block rotunda to the prison hospital. There was sporadic gunfire throughout the afternoon and evening. Sometimes there was so much confusion no one knew whom he was firing at or why. F. S. Chadwick, the guard who heard all that "Panther" talk earlier in the day, complained that inmate hospital orderlies and guards pushing stretcher gurneys to the hospital emergency room were shot at. "We were fired on three times very close," Chadwick said. "There were two other inmates carrying a gurney. They were fired on also."

Mike Killean, a white hospital worker, said he was not fired on when he transported the dead and the wounded but that may have been due to the fact that he "grabbed the biggest fucking uniformed guard" he could find, shoved a gurney at him and said, "Here, you go in front." By the time Killean reached the plaza, he saw so many guns it reminded him of the execution scene from the Zapata movie. "They were even hanging off the trees with guns."

There was so much confusion in the plaza that just the simple process of handling and preserving evidence was bungled time and again, like a montage from a detective farce. One guard placed his finger on the trigger guard of the gun found on Jackson, moving the trigger portion away from the dead black's hand. Two other guards later took the pistol to the prison armory, dropped the bullet clip out of the gun butt, ejected the live round from the chamber and placed the bullet on top of the remaining ones in the clip. They dry-fired the weapon out of a window to make certain it was clear and clean and then placed it in an envelope to await the arrival of state ballistics experts.

One of the more incredible foul-ups came with the disposal of the two vials of suspected explosives found on Spain and Jackson. A prison lieutenant asked two officers if they would take the bombs to the prison football field and dispose of them. The guards attached a long rope to the laundry basket where the vials had been placed and pulled it across the plaza. They'd gone only about twenty-five feet when the basket hit a "pretty good bump." The guards quickly flattened themselves on the ground but nothing happened. Deciding that the vials probably did not contain either nitroglycerin or a concussion fluid, they hand-carried the vials to the field. There, they shot at the test tubes with OO buckshot. Again, nothing happened. Exasperated, one guard removed one cork top and dumped the contents on the ground. He dumped the other one too. The liquid started foaming on the grass. The guard replaced the corks on the empty vials, wrapped them in his handkerchief and carried them back. Five days later, he was asked to dig up the plug of turf where he had emptied the vials and drive that dirt to the CII laboratory in Sacramento.

Another guard was given various clothing, mattresses, bloody sheets, inmates' blues and underclothes and piles of miscellaneous papers and cardboard boxes which had been taken out of the Adjustment Center and told to take them seven miles away and dump them.

Five days later, he was ordered back to the dump, where he asked the dump operator to excavate an area of about seventy-five feet by seventy-five feet by fifteen feet deep in the approximate vicinity where he had got rid of what should have been preserved as evidence. After a day's digging, the items could not be found. Some of it was found later.

The guards held on to the more interesting evidence which they said they found in Jackson's and Spain's cells. In Jackson's they found a .22 caliber gun barrel secreted in a block of Velveeta cheese. The weapon was loaded with a .22 magnum shell. In Spain's cell, they said they discovered an escape map hidden in a package of pipe cleaners and nineteen rounds of ammunition concealed in bars of Dial soap: 13 rounds of .38 Super Vels; five .410 shotgun shells and a .22 magnum cartridge. They said they also found a note on the floor of the cell which depicted the fourth-floor prison hospital layout of beds and assigned inmates, a map possibly used a month earlier when inmates tried to kill a snitch in the hospital but killed a guard instead.

Three days after the tragedy, prison guards said they made their biggest find. They had leaked to the press that they were searching for a wig. The A/C had been searched completely several times but no wig was turned up. At 10:30 A.M. on Tuesday, a guard found something which felt like steel wool in the drainpipe portion of the toilet in Yogi Pinell's cell. He couldn't pull it out so he called another guard over. The two of them finally worked out what looked like a wig. A label read, "A Japanese product made in Korea." Ray Klein, the guard who helped pull the wig out, said the earlier searches "should have" included toilets but did not know if that was done. According to guards, the so-called wig looked more like a part of a wig or what they described as a "wiglet."

The prison's most important find was not made public. When Jackson was returned to the Adjustment Center, he had placed his four Expando envelopes on the foyer table prior to his skin search and his producing the gun. After the shooting stopped and the killings were ended, these four envelopes and their contents were taken to the CII labs in Sacramento, where each page of each document was carefully examined. First, the lab technicians subjected each side of each page to a fluorescent black light reading, trying to "bring up" any writing not usually visible to the naked eye. When the investigators got to one four-page letter in a folder which otherwise carried only a picture of Jonathan Jackson, they noticed that the pages of the letter were out of sequence. This raised their suspicions and they looked closer. On the back of one page of this letter, they noticed some erasure marks and some writing which was barely visible. The black light, however, failed to bring out the writing. The criminologists took the page to the "Questioned Document Examiner" at CII and asked if he could determine the contents of the writing. Using oblique light, the examiner placed the letter under a stereoscopic microscope, a 3-D process, brought out the writing and, comparing it with other samples of Jackson's handwriting, said Jackson had scribbled it himself. He read the following startling message: "Take the bullets out of the bag. Hurry and give me the piece in the bag. Keep the bullets."

The guards handled the men about as roughly and awkwardly as they handled the evidence. While the inmates were tied hand and foot and lying naked on the grass, Mancino complained that the irons hurt his arms. A chain ran from his handcuffs to his leg shackles. A guard named V. J. Martin said Mancino rolled onto one shoulder and looked as if he was "halfway up" when Martin let go with a blast from his 30/30, firing one shot which the guard claimed "probably hit two or three feet in front of him and it ricocheted and caught him in the legs." At least, Martin added, leaving himself a way out,

"I think that's where it caught him." Because he shot Mancino, Martin was ordered to sit with the inmate, who by now was terrified, the rest of the night in the prison hospital. A white hospital worker who helped sew Mancino up described Officer Martin's statement as "simple bullshit." Describing Mancino's wound, the hospital attendant said "it looked like someone threw a hand grenade in his ass."

The prison's cover-up extended even to the institution's chief physician, Dr. P. J. McNamara, a balding, bespectacled retired Navy captain, who kept insisting that inmates simply don't enter the prison hospital with gunshot wounds. The doctor reiterated to those around him that Mancino must have been stabbed by another inmate because guards don't shoot prisoners—this even after Martin had admitted to his own superiors that he had pulled the trigger.

To cover up the beating in the yard, senior MTA Jack LaVelle signed an affidavit stating that he was on the plaza from about 4 P.M. to 11 P.M. and "saw no inmate shot" or "beaten."

Four hours after the tragedy, four guards, led by a clean-cut, short-haired lieutenant named D. W. Smith, began the interrogation of the surviving inmates of the Adjustment Center. Twenty-four men were interviewed. There seems to be no record of an interview with Luis Talamantes. Allan Mancino—who was described by hospital workers as "frightened out of his wits, just terrified"—was interrogated a day later. Mancino had quite a story to tell.

The twenty-four interviews were brief. The guards said they gave each prisoner the usual warning about his right to have an attorney present but no attorneys were called. Many lawyers, when they heard the news of the killings in the A/C on the radio, called the prison themselves and asked to be present during client interrogations or, barring that, that their clients not be questioned until they could be present.

The prisoners, however, knew their rights. Spain, the first called into the rough interviewing sessions, refused to speak until he had talked with his attorney. Earl Gibson was second. On their transcripts, the guards noted that Gibson had "muscle spasms" and was "unable to talk." Gibson was followed by Gary Hetland and Glen Fisher, the two white inmates who had barricaded their cells and did not come out. Both men said they knew nothing about what happened. Larry Justice, a radical black prisoner, said he had "nothing to say."

"I've got a headache," Yogi Pinell said.

Arthur Anderson was slightly more cooperative. "I don't know nothing. I was in my cell and the door opened. I saw a guy with a gun. I saw Jackson with a gun. I was told to come out of my cell or I'd be killed. I saw an officer open the cell doors. There was an inmate standing with him. I don't know what he had. I came out of my cell and stood against the wall." That's all he knew, he said.

Charles Gardner said he had nothing to say. Ray Carriger said he saw a Mexican officer pulling the bar to open the cells and noticed when he came out of his cell that "there were some officers fucked up" but he didn't "know who did the killing or who had the gun or knives." Larry Fields was shaken by the day's events. All he would say to his captors was "you all going to kill everybody."

"I don't have nothing to say," Fleeta Drumgo insisted. "I wasn't involved." Drumgo said he came out when his door was opened and that "the whole tier was running around. . . . I just saw one gun, in George's hand," he added. "He shot two or three rounds. I didn't see no knives." Drumgo said the first shot was fired before he left his cell. "You all can fuck me up or kill me," Drumgo told the guards, "but I ain't saying no more."

Arthur Marquez, Ken Divans and Jake Stokes refused to say anything.

John Clutchette said that when he was being returned by Officer Breckenridge, the Adjustment Center was already in an uproar. Inmates were running around, yelling for each other to "get down." Then another guard, Graham, entered and Clutchette heard him yelling, "No, no, no, no." Clutchette heard "something that sounded like a shot. I saw only one gun," said Clutchette. "George had it." Clutchette told his interrogators that Rubiaco was unlocking the doors on the south side of the tier when he walked in. He said he was afraid "they were going to start shooting" so he went into cell 55 with Gibson. Later, when Jackson walked down the tier looking out the windows on the south side, Clutchette told the guards he looked in George's hand and noticed that the gun appeared to be an automatic.

When asked if he would talk with the guards, Bobby Mabry replied, "About what?" Mabry said he had come out of his cell when ordered but ran back in and crawled under his bunk when he heard the first shot fired. Bernard Gordon, Barney Duran, Louie Lopez, Felton Cooper and Roberto Soto refused to talk with the guards. They insisted on having their lawyers present.

Ruchell Magee, already under indictment for the Marin Courthouse incident, told the guards Rubiaco opened his cell and he heard Jackson say, "Everyone come out of your cells." Through photographs shown him, Magee said Spain accompanied Jackson and Rubiaco when they were opening the cell doors.

Willie Tate and David Johnson said they wanted attorneys.

Later that night, autopsies were performed on the bodies of the deceased. Among the guard victims, there was only one surprise. Frank DeLeon, it was learned, died of a gunshot wound to the head. In all the recalls and interrogations, no one remembered hearing the shot which killed DeLeon.

For Jackson, the Marin County pathologist, Dr. John Manwaring, said the cause of death was a bullet which entered the back, coursed upward through the soft tissue of the back into the head, and exited from the top of the skull. In its journey, the slug broke off the ends of several ribs, one of which penetrated the lung. There was a great deal of internal bleeding into the chest cavity, the coroner said, but not enough to produce death. What produced death, according to Manwaring, was the bullet's passing through that area of the brain which pathologists refer to as "sudden death," before exiting almost precisely at the top of the head. The coroner said the shot nearly severed the lower portion of the brain from the upper portion.*

A second gunshot wound was found at Jackson's left heel, the bullet entering over the tendon near the top of the ankle. It exited near the bump on the inside of the ankle. This bullet, Manwaring said, fractured the tibia, which is the inner and larger of the two bones between the knee and the ankle. A large fragment of the copper jacket of the slug was found in the ligaments of the tibia. The leaded part of the slug was gone. Asked whether Jackson could run on the fractured tibia, Dr. Manwaring told reporters Jackson would have felt terrible pain if he did. Under normal circumstances, Manwaring guessed that no one could run, let alone stand up, because of the pain.

The pathologist added that Jackson also had tiny fragments of lead in the soft tissue over his entire left calf and a large bruise on one side of his chest.

Asked if he could tell whether Jackson was running at the time he was shot, Manwaring noted that it was an unusual way to run, if one were to put it that way. The coroner also said he could draw no conclusions about the distance the bullets traveled before they hit the black inmate because he was not able to examine the clothing, which may have been what prison officials were trying to find at the Richmond, California, dump. More than a month after the shooting Manwaring insisted that he had not seen the clothing.

Several days after Jackson's death, the A/C inmates had their own story to tell. It was an incomplete story but one that disputed the

---

* This information is contained in Manwaring's *revised* autopsy report.

prison version. In a petition reportedly signed by all twenty-six inmates of the A/C, including Mancino, Hetland and Fisher, the prisoners charged that the warden, associate warden and guards killed George Jackson and conspired to murder those who refused to join in the conspiracy against Jackson. They declared that "unknown" officers opened their cell doors and ordered them to come from their cells. When they did so they heard gunshots or what sounded like gunshots and fled to other cells in the rear of the south corridor to avoid being shot. Then other guards, armed with machine guns and shotguns, entered the building and ordered the prisoners to come out or be killed. They were then told to take off all their clothes and walk from the cells one at a time and they complied but after they did so they "received malicious physical beatings" from prison guards who wielded clubs, blackjacks and gun butts.

Fleeta Drumgo and John Clutchette, the two surviving Soledad Brothers, who would later be acquitted by an all-white jury of killing the guard at Soledad, penned separate affidavits stating they were burned with cigarettes and beaten. "You'll be dead in three days," one guard told Drumgo. "You're a dead nigger." Three days after the incident, when Drumgo and Clutchette appeared in court on what was supposed to be their first day of trial with Jackson, the two men could barely walk into the courtroom.* They told their defense lawyers, Richard Silver and Floyd Silliman, that they had been badly beaten. The attorneys asked the presiding judge, Carl Allen, to step down from the bench and examine the two defendants so he could see the bruises and burns himself. The lawyers wanted Allen to grant a cease-and-desist order stopping the beatings in San Quentin and a transfer order moving their clients from Quentin to the county jail in San Francisco. Judge Allen refused to examine the defendants or to

---

* The court proceedings were scheduled to start August 23. However, San Quentin officials did not appear in court with the accused. The court ordered them to do so on the following day. They did.

have a doctor examine them. With a swift motion of his hands, the judge turned down the defense motions. Drumgo quickly took off his shirt, baring a profusion of welts and bruises. The courtroom audience was stunned. Drumgo's mother, Inez Williams, wept, her loud cries of anguish filling the room. The judge threatened to have her removed.

During that courtroom session, John Clutchette hastily scribbled a note which was handed to me in the press section. The brief message made two points about Saturday's events: that Jackson was shot in the back and that the black revolutionary ran out of the Adjustment Center to draw gunfire away from the building, thus sacrificing his life to save his fellow inmates.

X

Speculations

Was there a plot to kill George Jackson? Except to its own investigators, San Quentin has refused to show evidence to anyone. It has refused to allow any member of the institution—guard, inmate or prison official—to talk with reporters, changing its rules on inmate interviews so that no prisoner can meet a reporter under any circumstances. It has barred access to the scene of the tragedy, the Adjustment Center itself, particularly during the time when prisoners were alleging, through their attorneys, that they were being brutally beaten. Nearly a week after the deaths, prison officials chose three reporters they were fond of and allowed them controlled but brief entry. With some hesitation and much couching of phrase, the reporters confirmed what the prisoners had said about being beaten. No one was allowed to talk about what happened.

But there is available essential evidence to discredit the critical points of the prison version, points concerning the "smuggled gun," the wig, the takeover of the A/C, the "escape plan," and the Jackson death itself. Taken in sequence, our inquiry begins with Jackson's visitors that day.

The Visitors

Why are there no warrants out for the arrest of Vanita Anderson? Why was there no indictment of Ms. Anderson forthcoming from the Marin County grand jury? The gate officer declared that she was the only person who carried in a briefcase and/or tape recorder. The waiting room officer stated that it was he and Ms. Anderson who had suggested to Steve Bingham that the Berkeley attorney use the black woman's recorder. Bingham himself carried a set of Expando folders, which, unlike the briefcase (which looked like a typewriter case), passed through the metallic detector.

Six months after the August tragedy, Vanita Anderson turned up in Houston, Texas, and was interviewed by *San Francisco Examiner* reporter Ed Montgomery. Law enforcement officials had supposedly been looking for her for some time. They had been claiming all along that they wanted her "for questioning." Thus, it seemed a bit out of the ordinary that Montgomery—whom many correspondents based in California feel does public relations work for the state attorney general's office and the CII through news stories in the Hearst paper —turned out to be the sleuth reporter who found her. If he interviewed Anderson, then the CII must have got there first.

Ms. Anderson told Montgomery that she was "fed up" with the militant black movement and that she had quit her former radical friends. She readily admitted having visited the prison on the day Jackson died but claimed, "I didn't go to San Quentin with Bingham. It is my recollection he already was in the visitor's room when I got there. They were not going to let me see Jackson because I had visited him earlier in the week." She added that because there were many visitors waiting, Jackson was not allowed in the big reception room.

"I knew Bingham," she said. "We were traveling in the same circles. I talked with him. He was having trouble getting to see Jackson because he was not an attorney of record. There was a lot of arguing about it and a long delay. I stayed there to see how he made out. When it appeared he was finally going to see Jackson, he said he would only take a few minutes and that I could have the remainder of his visiting time, which is normally one hour." But when Bingham came back, Anderson said, prison officials would not let her visit with Jackson, explaining that the black inmate had already been returned to his cell. "By that time," Anderson asserted, "Bingham had left. I never saw him again."

Ms. Anderson, who disclaimed any advance knowledge of the alleged smuggled gun or the tape recorder in which authorities say it was concealed, told the reporter that she planned to stay in Houston. "If the district attorney [Bruce Bales] from Marin wants to question me, he can come down here and talk with my attorney. I know there is no warrant out for my arrest. I remained in the East Bay for several days after the San Quentin episode but I didn't feel obligated to volunteer any information. I really got a kick out of the report back in January that I was suspected of taking part in hijacking that airplane to Cuba. I sat right here and laughed and laughed. I have no desire to go to Cuba."

District Attorney Bales, for his part, says that he would like to question Ms. Anderson but that she refused to talk with his investigators. He said he could, however, subpoena her if he wanted to. He may and he may not. He claims neither he nor his investigators have spoken with her.

There is conjecture, not fully substantiated, that Vanita Anderson did visit San Quentin on August 21 but that the woman who accompanied Bingham and claimed she was Vanita Anderson was actually someone else. This means that it is entirely possible that two visitors appeared at San Quentin, both claiming to be Vanita Anderson. Of course, the gate guard recalled that Bingham's companion was "colored." She may, however, have been a Caucasian woman in disguise. The possibility that she was someone other than Vanita Anderson would explain why District Attorney Bales is less than anxiously pursuing Ms. Anderson in Texas.

Well, someone probably lied—several times. Either she appeared at the outside East Gate with Bingham or she didn't. Either she carried the tape recorder in or she didn't. Either she offered the recorder to Bingham for his use or she didn't. Either she left with Bingham or she didn't. There are only four possible explanations: (1) Ms. Anderson lied and was not at the prison that day. Someone else was there and claimed she was Anderson. (2) The guards lied about her arriving with Bingham, about her carrying the recorder and the case in and about her accompanying Bingham upon departure. (3) Both Ms. Anderson and District Attorney Bales lied, she as part of a state conspiracy and he, also as part of that conspiracy, to explain how a gun got into the Adjustment Center in the first place. (4) Everyone told the truth.

All of the possibilities lead to three distinct theories about what was being plotted and planned for George Jackson and the Adjustment Center. One scenario concludes with a Jackson plot to build up arms for a black army within the prison and mass escape when expedient. A second version results in a state law enforcement conspiracy to kill George Jackson and perhaps other black inmates in the A/C. A third leads to an intricate weave of the two plans, a complicated arrangement in which the guards were aware of the first possibility—that Jackson was caching arms—and plotted on their own to control and manipulate that scheme. I choose the third.

This theory assumes that most of the principals in the drama told the truth; if anyone lied, the guards did. It assumes that Vanita Anderson did enter the prison about the time Bingham did, that she carried the tape recorder, that Betts examined it, that Betts observed the two visitors talking together, and that Bingham used the tape recorder. Jackson may have had one gun already. I believe he had two guns—a nine-millimeter semiautomatic and a .38 caliber revolver. The latter gun, the revolver, was never found. The former could only be traced to law enforcement officials, a detail that has yet to be explained. Let's examine this theory, point by point:

Stephen Mitchell Bingham

Bingham's friends—his college classmates, his co-workers in the civil rights movement in the South, his former colleagues in the Peace Corps, his legal associates in Berkeley, his family in Connecticut—all say that Steve could not have smuggled a gun in to Jackson. Bingham, they say, was deeply concerned about the plight of blacks and poor people. He was torn and anguished by brutal animalistic conditions in the prisons and by the oppressive dehumanizing treatment of convicts, particularly blacks. Despite this, they declare, Steve Bingham was a nonviolent man. But that is not enough to explain his innocence, innocent though he was.

During the months preceding Bingham's mysterious disappearance and the months afterward, various California officials have been trying desperately to legally "lynch" prisoners, attorneys and critics who have been active in the prison reform movement, as evidenced in: the killing of W. L. Nolen, writ-writer and militant; the blackboard manipulation of witnesses in the Soledad Brothers case; the rewards and physical threats brought to light in the trial of the Soledad Seven; the attempted character assassination of California Rural Legal Assistance; the death destruction which San Quentin guards and Assistant District Attorney Gary Thomas wrought at the Marin Civic Center; the arrest of Angela Davis on the skimpiest of evidence; and the attempt to frame the former Soledad chief psychiatrist, Frank Rundle. Now it was Bingham's turn, not because he was Steve Bingham but because he was a hated symbol. Bingham represented the many liberal and radical California attorneys, the "nigger-lovers," who were causing so much trouble.

In the summer of 1971, Bingham visited Jackson six times, on June 12, June 24, June 29, July 6, July 26 and that fateful August 21. Steve Bingham "disappeared" on August 21. That Saturday morning, after a breakfast conference with another attorney in a Berkeley restaurant, he had gone across the Richmond Bridge to San Quentin to visit Jackson, whom he had been seeing because he had once represented James Carr, Jackson's former cellmate and close friend, and was now going to represent a number of inmates who were planning to file writs against conditions at San Quentin. Carr had been arrested four months earlier for leaping a courtroom railing and throwing some roundhouse rights and lefts at San Francisco sheriff's deputies during one of Jackson's pretrial hearings.

When the interview with Jackson was completed, Bingham drove to the home of his uncle, Woodbridge Bingham. Steve was late for lunch, arriving at about four o'clock, but his uncle, a retired history professor at the University of California, didn't care. He was happy to see his nephew even if such visits were infrequent. A cousin and her husband, who were at the elder Bingham's home, invited Steve to dinner that evening but he declined, explaining that he was supposed to be in San Francisco at six for a political meeting. After lunch, Bingham returned to the north Oakland house where he was living collectively with a group of other young lawyers. He left his house after a brief stop and hasn't been seen since.

"I have reached the conclusion that there is no other way Jackson could have obtained the death gun except during his visit with attorney Stephen Bingham just before the killings started," District Attorney Bales stated on September 1. "The fact of Bingham's sudden and complete disappearance directly following the terrible and tragic events that he triggered at San Quentin Prison is not insignificant especially in view of my repeated public requests to talk to him."

The "death gun," as Bales described it (although most of the deaths were attributed to knives and razor blades), was probably already in the prison when Bingham got there. Bingham only carried papers into the prison. If the outside guards and Vanita Anderson were telling the truth, then she arrived on her own, unaccompanied by Bingham, carrying the briefcase and the tape recorder. If she wasn't telling the truth, Bales would have had her behind bars a few months after the event took place. To reporters who have tried to interview him about Ms. Anderson, Bales isn't talking.

When officials finally traced the gun, they found that it was purchased in El Cerrito, near Berkeley, two years ago by a Black Panther party member, and identified the buyer as Landon Robert Williams, twenty-seven, who at the time of the event was in a New Haven, Connecticut, jail awaiting trial in connection with an alleged party execution of an informer. Officials said Williams bought the gun on March 22, 1969, but had no comment about what happened to it after he purchased it. Williams was arrested in Denver in June 1969, then extradited to New Haven. He remained behind bars until well past the shooting. Police declined comment on the progress of the gun's possession from Williams's ownership until it appeared in San Quentin. There was also no comment from police about reports that Williams had been carrying the gun when arrested.

The easiest, most logical and usual way for a gun to enter San Quentin is by a guard. At Soledad, Captain Charles Moody had smuggled a gun in, was observed carrying it by Associate Warden Jerry Enomoto and reprimanded. Indeed, just a few months after the August 21 tragedy, a San Quentin guard was caught trying to smuggle a .22 rifle into that prison. The guard was suspended pending an investigation, but the prison officials have never announced the results. For a guard, smuggling a pistol into any prison in which he works is a simple matter: just wear it in or carry it in a case. The personal effects of guards have never been routinely examined. Of such thoughts District Attorney Bales said, "This is not a reasonable hypothesis at all." Nevertheless, it's the best there is.

Such an hypothesis leads to one other question. If Bingham did not carry a gun into San Quentin for George Jackson, where is he? Why is he in hiding? The acquittal of Angela Davis on conspiracy murder charges in the Marin County Courthouse shooting incident may be cited here as an analogous situation. Assuming that Bingham is alive, there is every reason to believe that he is awaiting the outcome of the trial. Like Ms. Davis and other defendants who have been acquitted in various "movement" cases, Bingham probably doesn't care to spend time in jail awaiting his own acquittal.

The Wig Theory

That Jackson smuggled a gun into the A/C by wearing it under a partial wig is almost impossible to believe. The gun was a Spanish-made Astra M-600, with an eight-and-a-half-inch length from barrel mouth to rear of stock, and a four-and-a-half-inch height from top of chamber to bottom of magazine butt. The gun is as large, if not larger, than most people's heads.

The *San Francisco Chronicle* found it hard to believe too. The newspaper assigned a reporter, Tim Findley, to go out, hire a black model, purchase a gun and a wig, and act out the gun-smuggling attempt. Even the grip handles were removed from the gun butt, as they reportedly had been removed from the "smuggled" automatic. In the *Chronicle* experiment, the model used a variety of ways to try to get the gun under the wig, but he could only do it with a full wig, after placing the gun inside the wig and then "forcing the hair piece back on his head with some struggle." The paper said the "wig was obviously askew and with every step he [the model] took, the gun wobbled dangerously, bringing his hands instinctively to his head. . . . If the wig theory is sound," the article concluded, "Jackson would have had to walk at least fifty yards under the eyes of a guard before he reached the Adjustment Center."

A day after the *Chronicle* experiment, the *San Francisco Examiner* reiterated reporter Ed Montgomery's claim of August 23, that the gun was really a five-and-three-quarter-inch Spanish Llama Corto and not the eight-inch Astra, as reported in all the other papers. Montgomery, punting well for the CII, was probably told that by officials and believed it. The solid evidence was that it was the Astra, as the Marin grand jury was told when it heard the case.

Even with the gun alone, the feat was impossible. Yet the *Chronicle* experiment did not include concealing two additional magazine clips of bullets which the guards claimed Jackson had under the wig.

The wig theory works best only from the standpoint of the guards. It is a scenario that protects them from the suspicion of bringing the guns in themselves, and it would explain how the "escape attempt" was forced by their stumbling onto the gun, rather taking credibility from other reports that guards held a gun on Jackson and he took it away. It should be remembered, too, that the wig theory evolved. First reports said that Jackson probably had the gun in his hair. A day later, prison officials were talking about a watch cap, which many reporters had seen Jackson wear to court. Finally, by the third day, investigators said they were looking for a wig. They would find one a day later, jammed into the toilet bowl of Pinell's cell, after several careful searches of the A/C had failed to produce one. Radical critics point out that the guards could easily have placed a wig in the A/C days later.

Not long before the tragedy, a *Newsweek* reporter interviewing Ruchell Magee offered the inmate several cigarettes to take back with him to his cell. Despite the fact that cigarettes are like gold, Magee refused, saying he would never be able to get them past the guards. "If Magee couldn't get a cigarette past the guards," Gerald Lubenow, *Newsweek*'s San Francisco bureau chief asked, "how could Jackson hope to get a gun with an eight-inch barrel into the A/C?"

"Indeed," asked Lubenow, who had interviewed some of the guards, "how could he even expect to get *to* the A/C with it? The guards around Jackson knew every inch of his body intimately. They had to look up his asshole at least twice a day. They knew the con-figuration of his scrotum, felt his ear canals, peered into his nose, massaged his scalp regularly. And yet they didn't notice anything unusual when Jackson clamped a black wig on top of a two-and-a-half-pound gun and strolled fifty yards from the visiting unit to the A/C."

It is clear that the prison version of how the gun was introduced is untenable. Evidently prison authorities and state investigators simply assumed that Jackson must have received the gun from anyone other than a guard and stitched together a very shaky scenario based on that premise. We don't know who smuggled the gun in: we may never know.

The Takeover of the A/C

Why would Jackson invite almost certain death by bolting across an open, sunlit prison courtyard in an escape attempt after all the emergency alarms had been sounded, and without any means to scale the twenty-five-foot walls that enclosed him, under at least three gun towers, then run at least a quarter mile to the prison's next barrier, twelve-foot-high chain-link fences topped with rows of barbed wire? And why should he do this two days before his trial was to start in San Francisco, a trial in which Jackson would be provided with a courtroom forum for explaining his case and denouncing the prison system? Does it matter now that both of his co-defendants, John Clutchette and Fleeta Drumgo, were acquitted? Could the guards have wanted Jackson dead, fearing an acquittal? And could guards who were part of a conspiracy to murder Jackson have planned his death and then initiated the beginnings of that plan —which backfired when Jackson gained the upper hand in the A/C and began releasing the inmates from their cells?

It is entirely conceivable, as one source claims—though not supportable by any evidence—that the guards had the drop on Jackson and told him they were going to kill him, whereupon Jackson took the pistol away from them and produced a second gun of his own. A third, gunlike weapon, a loaded .357 magnum barrel, was found later in Jackson's cell.

The prison explained the "escape attempt" two days after the tragedy by claiming that the Jackson family had made a dry run of the gun-smuggling venture by having a child tape a cap gun to his thighs inside a trouser leg. The metal detector went off, officials said, and this probably aborted entry of a weapon via that method. A letter written to Jackson's attorney John Thorne, dated August 2 and signed by Warden Louis Nelson and Associate Warden James Park, said that the prison was suspending the visiting privileges of Penny Jackson and Delora Ward, two of Jackson's sisters. The letter said there was an "attempt to introduce a concealed toy pistol via one of the children accompanying the women. We have no choice but to believe this was an attempt to test our defenses against smuggled weapons."

The Autopsy Report

It was not until a month after Jackson's death that a revised autopsy report was released on the black revolutionary's death. The first report had stated that Jackson suffered "a gunshot wound in the head with a fracture of the skull." The second report completely reversed the path of the bullet, claiming that it struck Jackson in the middle of his back, broke three ribs and coursed upward, breaking ribs, until it exited at the top of the skull.

Why the report was changed is unclear. Jackson's body had been released to the family weeks earlier; the state had made its studies and released its findings. John Manwaring, the Marin pathologist who changed his report, was conveniently away on vacation when the revision was made public. The county coroner, Donovan O. Cooke, said Manwaring revised his conclusions after consultation with state ballistics experts. To a television reporter's question, Cooke said the path of the bullet was "obvious, given the coning effect on the skull." He didn't explain why that was more obvious in September than in August.

The revisions conformed with the Jackson family version and that of other prisoners. When Jackson's mother first viewed her son's body, she said George had been shot in the back of the head and charged that her son's face had been beaten beyond recognition. "I could only recognize his hands and his nose," she said at the time. The revised report also reflected what John Clutchette had shouted the first time he appeared in court, three days after the event: "He was shot in the back," the defendant yelled through a bulletproof screen dividing spectators from judge and attorneys, "and when they saw he still wasn't dead, they shot him in the head."

The Jackson Conspiracy and James Carr

Several days after the tragedy, police officials produced a letter which they declared proved the existence of a conspiracy to help Jackson escape. They said they had come into possession of the letter, written by Jackson's friend James Carr, when it was left in the back pocket of a pair of slacks which Carr's wife, Betsy Hammer Carr, had taken to a San Jose cleaners. The cleaning operator had pulled the letter out, glanced at it quickly and found that the contents urged him to read on. Eventually, he turned it over to the police, who said they Xeroxed the original before replacing it. This letter, according to police, was written by Carr and was an offer to help Jackson plan an escape. Jackson supposedly replied on the back of the envelope by drawing a diagram of an escape plan, suggesting that the scheme take place at night when he could knock out the prison's one power line by pounding a metal stake into the ground, attaching a metal chain and tossing it over the wires. Jackson reportedly further urged that women visitors smuggle explosives into the prison in plastic vials hidden in their vaginas and secreting derringers in hollowed-out heels.

Carr thought the letter a frame-up and a ludicrous one at that. He denied writing it and added, "Assume that I did write it. I would never hand-write it. I would have typed it. And I would never have put my name on it or whom it was going to."

He was interviewed about a week after the event. He had been in the San Francisco County Jail for five months, charged with disturbing the peace and assault on a police officer in a courtroom brawl which had erupted during an April pretrial hearing in the Soledad Brothers case. He had been paroled from the California Men's Colony in San Luis Obispo in July 1970, moving to Santa Cruz, where he became a teaching assistant at the University of California, correcting calculus papers, no mean feat for a self-taught convict who had only made it to junior high school. He was assisting in a spring semester course on prison reform when he was arrested. That was when he met Bingham. But Carr claimed that his relationship with Bingham was a distant one. He said Bingham was assisting another attorney and that the two men never talked much. He also said that Bingham never told him he was going to visit on his behalf and added that there was no logical reason to do so.

So, according to Carr, whatever Bingham was talking about with Jackson, it did not involve Carr. Carr says he couldn't conceive of Bingham and Jackson planning an escape, both from what he knew about the Berkeley attorney and from how well he understood his former cellmate. "My impression of Bingham," Carr said, "is that he was a lawyer struggling to become a better lawyer. I don't think he'd be likely to smuggle a gun in. He was a mighty good dude and he wasn't into that kind of action. He didn't have it in him. It was a conspiracy to kill Jackson, but this time they made a mistake. The truth will come out eventually and when it does, someone is going to have to make a mighty big apology to Stephen Bingham. . . .

"I loved George Jackson," Carr added. "There is no way I would let anyone send him a gun or explosives because it would be suicide. And I knew him well enough to know that he had too much intelligence and love for the people to commit suicide."

James Carr would have little else to add to that. Seven months later, he was gunned down on a lawn in San Jose. Police said two men, one black and one white, were waiting in ambush when Carr started out of the Hammer home (where he was living with his white wife and mother-in-law and where Angela Davis stayed when she was freed on bail) and blasted the teaching assistant with six shots from a shotgun and a rifle. Carr staggered across the dirt driveway, collapsing on the driver's seat of his jeep, where he died.

Weeks before his death, two unexploded Molotov cocktails had been found on the front lawn of the Hammer home. There were crude arrows drawn in the turf, pointing from the baseline of the bombs to the house. They had complained to police about this and other similar threats, but were ignored.

It was a mysterious tragedy and all kinds of rumors played havoc to muddle it even more. Some radicals believed Carr was a police agent. Other people thought he was an extremely militant radical, and was killed by a Los Angeles police contract. A few charged that Carr was killed because he was skimming funds from the Angela Davis Defense Committee. Still others thought his death was the result of a Black Panther vendetta. There were rumors in the Santa Clara County Courthouse, where the Angela Davis trial was under way, that Carr was going to be a surprise witness for the prosecution. The Santa Clara district attorney said Carr was the victim of a $540 contract.

There was no substantiating evidence for any of this, but it was public knowledge that Carr had been linked to the killing of Black Panther captain Fred Bennett at a reported bomb factory in the Santa Cruz Mountains. A police informer told investigators that Carr killed Bennett and burned his body, even adding the grisly detail that Carr kicked a loose leg which had dislodged from the body back into the fire. The white informer, Thomas Mosher, speculated that Bennett was killed because he was having an affair with the wife of another Black Panther. Bennett's remains were found near a group of cabins which police said contained 149 sticks of dynamite. Officials believed that the explosive devices were similar to those used in the bombing of the Marin Courthouse which occurred two months after Jonathan Jackson's death.

Because Carr was never arrested for the alleged murder, Carr's critics claimed this was more "evidence" that he was an agent. Of course, the critics also pointed out that if law enforcement officials believed that Carr helped plan Jackson's "escape," why hadn't he been charged? In addition, Carr was freed only five months after his indictment in the courtroom brawl and given a two-year suspended sentence, very light considering that he was charged with assaulting a police officer.

Then, there was one more curious touch in Carr's life. In October 1971, a young black named Louis Tackwood revealed to the press in Los Angeles that, as a police agent, he had been spying on various radical groups. Tackwood implicated himself in the police assault on Black Panther headquarters in Los Angeles and even declared that state officials had been forewarned about the attempt to take hostages at the Marin Civic Center. There was one other thing: Tackwood was linked to James Carr by marriage. Police added the final comment. The two men arrested for the Carr murder were identified as Richard Rodriguez, a Los Angeles Chicano, and Lamarr Lloyd Mims, who turned out to be a "fugitive" sought in that Los Angeles Panther shootout with police which Tackwood had talked about.

The Grand Jury Indictments

The Marin County grand jury met late in September to consider murder indictments against San Quentin inmates for the deaths of three guards and two white prisoners. After hearing two days of prison-directed testimony, the jurors voted to indict seven men— Stephen Bingham and six inmates—with the minimum amount of votes required, twelve.

One of the nineteen grand jurors resigned on the spot. Two others angrily denounced the indictments. Jerry Hawes, a thirty-seven-year-old San Rafael resident, resigned, he said, because the grand jury was unwilling "to seek impartial legal advice during indicting sessions and makes impossible a fair and just procedure which can mete out genuine justice." Hawes said the indictment process was "vulnerable when the members of a jury . . . are unwilling to surrender their independence to the public prosecutor."

"It was not justice, but vengeance," declared another juror, Richard Beban, who said he was considering his resignation. Beban, a student at the College of Marin, explained that security procedures adopted at the Marin Civic Center after the courthouse shooting had created a "paranoid frame of mind in the community." This grand jury, he added, reflected the "racism, paranoia and economic bias" of the county. "We're responsible for what goes on in that room," Beban said, "and I don't think we have the ability to deal with questions of crime inside San Quentin."

A week after the indictments were handed down, John Thorne, George Jackson's attorney, released an affidavit that was signed by the liberal juror. In the affidavit, Beban declared that when he first heard about the deaths at the prison he felt that, as a member of the grand jury's justice committee which was investigating the administration of the Marin prison, he should go to the prison and find out what happened and whether he could help. According to ground rules which had been agreed upon between the prison and the grand jury, Beban telephoned first to state that he would be there within minutes. He arrived at the prison at 8:10 P.M. on the night of the tragedy and was met by a guard at the outside East Gate. When he walked into the lobby of the prison administration building, he said he had the following exchange with James Park, the associate warden:

"What the hell are you doing here?" Park asked.

"I came to see what is going on and whether you have need of our services," Beban answered.

"Why don't you go investigate the Communist party?" Park suggested.

"What?"

"It's them and people like you who are causing what has happened today," Park said.

"What do you mean?" Beban asked.

"We lost three guards, three good men," Park explained. "The only good thing that happened all day was that we got George Jackson. Killed him. Shot him through the head."

The associate warden then paused, looked the grand juror square in the face and asked if he wanted to go in. Beban did not answer, but Park continued, "I'll let you go in, but the guards would kill you and I wouldn't stop them." Beban left the prison.

Allan Mancino

According to prison officials, Allan Mancino, the surviving white inmate in the A/C, was an excellent witness. To protect him and what he was expected to say in court, the prison quietly transferred him out of state to a Nevada prison. Although San Quentin hospital workers had whispered that Mancino had been badly wounded while lying on the Portal Plaza, prison spokesmen kept insisting that he was just grazed. And the guard who shot Mancino declared to state investigators that he had fired into the grass and the bullet must have hit a rock and ricocheted into Mancino's buttocks and legs. There was no word from Mancino, who was not allowed press interviews or meetings with attorneys either in California or in Nevada.

However, Mancino did have something to say to an attorney a little over five months *before* the San Quentin tragedy. He was in Palm Hall, at Chino Prison in San Luis Obispo at the time, and he had dictated and signed a startling affidavit. He declared that at the end of January 1970, a week or so after Officer John Mills was killed,

several guards including one Officer Spoon [Loran Spoon, an O-wing guard whom the former Soledad chief psychiatrist, Frank Rundle, charged was part of a conspiracy to frame him for two murders] came to my cell which was the next to the last cell on the tier, the last cell being empty. Apparently they entered the tier through the back way, through the "tunnel," so that they did not pass in front of any other cells on the tier. They came at night, about 10:00 P.M., and told me to come to the bars. They told me to strip which I did and they examined me with a flashlight without yet opening the door. They then had me dress.

Officer Spoon then cracked open the cell about six or eight inches and told me to turn around. Spoon then handcuffed me with my hands behind my back which is not unusual. He then placed a blindfold over my eyes so that I was unable to see and this struck me as unusual and scared me. When I asked why I was blindfolded, I was told by Spoon that somebody wanted to talk to me and gave me a cigarette.

They then took me out of my cell and out the back door of the tier a short distance into the "tunnel" from where they had apparently entered the tier earlier. During the move, I did not have to pass in front of any other inmates' cells.

As soon as I left the tier and I was in the "tunnel," I recognized several other voices being present nearby. One of these I recognized as Captain Moody's voice, since he often frequented O-wing because of the troubled status in that part of the prison.

Moody began to address me and asked how I liked being among the "niggers" on the second tier, and asked how I felt about George Jackson specifically. He asked if I would care if anything might happen to George Jackson, to which I answered that I didn't care one way or another. Moody then asked me directly if I would kill George Jackson. He said that he did not want another Eldridge Cleaver.

I thought that this was very strange, possibly a set-up for further criminal charges if I agreed. I didn't really understand what Moody was trying to do at this point. I was on the second tier and Jackson was on max row [the first tier]. Moody then hypothesized of a situation where I would be taken out in the yard one night to locate a knife. He said that it would be unfortunate if I should break toward the fence and be shot if such an event actually happened. I understood this hypothetical [sic] to be a direct threat on my life if I did not kill George Jackson. I realized that Moody was completely serious.

When I refused to join in this plot to kill George Jackson, I was taken back to my cell. A few days after this incident with Moody and Spoon and the others, I was transferred out of O-wing in Soledad to Palm Hall, Chino.

The affidavit was sworn, signed and dated March 19, 1971.

Five months later, when Jackson died, the attorney who took the affidavit and witnessed it was worried about Mancino. He tried to meet with the white inmate to find out if he was in any trouble or if he wanted to talk with an attorney. Prison officials refused his overtures, and Mancino was not heard from, not until a year after the tragedy, when, after his release on parole, he filed a damage suit against the prison, charging that the guards had brutally shot and beaten him and had coached every answer he gave to state investigators. Everything was untrue, he declared, but he did not say what did happen.

∎

On the morning of George Jackson's funeral, explosions ripped into three offices of the CDC in three different cities. Two of the bombings were attributed to the Weathermen, who declared in notes that they were acting "in defense of George Jackson."

A more tragic revolutionary act occurred the following Sunday. Shortly before nine o'clock in the evening, a bomb went off inside the Bank of America Ingleside branch in San Francisco. The blast brought most of the men on duty at the Ingleside police station to the scene. Police said the station had just emptied when a woman telephoned to report a stolen purse. They suggested she come to the station to fill out a report but their suspicions were raised when she refused to give her name and turned down a sergeant's offer of a squad car escort.

The woman appeared at the station, gave her name as Carol George, and the desk officer, a lanky sergeant named John V. Young, took her report and went back to work. Less than thirty minutes later, the station calm was shattered when several men burst through the station house door and opened up with three shotguns and a semi-automatic pistol. A woman dispatcher, who was wounded in the arm, said a tall, slender black man thrust a shotgun through a small round aperture in the bulletproof glass shield protecting the desk sergeant and fired several rounds at Young, killing him.

The following day, identical letters were received by the *San Francisco Chronicle*, the *Examiner* and the city's major black weekly, the *Sun-Reporter*. The letters, Xeroxed on a piece of binder paper, declared that the attack on the Ingleside police station was in retaliation for George Jackson's death. The declaration read:

On the night of August 29, 1971, revolutionary violence was committed against the Ingleside Pig Sty as one political consequence for the recent intolerable political assassination of Comrade George L. Jackson in particular and the inhumane torture in P.O.W. [prisoner-of-war] camps in general.

We retaliate against these acts along with the constant murder and brutality of black people in their communities.

We must not forget nor allow our oppressors to continue brutalizing families and friends of our incarcerated comrades.

The statement was signed by the "George L. Jackson Assault Squad of the Black Liberation Army."

War was declared, a war without terms.

In April 1972, the two surviving Soledad Brothers—John Clutchette and Fleeta Drumgo—were acquitted. An all-white jury found them innocent of all charges. When the acquittal was announced, the trial of Angela Davis was in its twenty-first day. After forty-nine days of trial and thirteen hours of deliberation, she too, was found innocent. By August, Ms. Davis was in Moscow and Clutchette was out on work furlough. Fleeta Drumgo was still in prison facing general murder conspiracy charges but only a single charge of assault on Officer Paul Krasenes during the San Quentin tragedy.

Epilogue

We arrested them because they had nothing. We jailed them because they threatened the bounty of our existence. We forgot about them because they had been banished from our presence until they paid their debts and learned our rules. When they complained, our guardians protected us with billy clubs, dungeons, tear gas, false testimony and bullets. Some men died because they were black. Others died because they were white. But that angered the men more and they rose, like a brotherhood, with one voice. Roaring from their cages, they protested, damned us, and died. We stirred. Who killed George Jackson? God, isn't it awful about those San Quentin guards?

Finally, we realized that *we* had killed them, killed them all, and we cried.

This monster—the monster they've engendered in me will return to torment its maker, from the grave, the pit, the profoundest pit. Hurl me into the next existence, the descent into hell won't turn me. I'll crawl back to dog his trail forever. They won't delay my revenge, never, never. I'm part of a righteous people who anger slowly, but rage undammed. We'll gather at his door in such a number that the rumbling of our feet will make the earth tremble. I'm going to charge them for this, twenty-eight years without gratification. I'm going to charge them reparations in blood. I'm going to charge them like a maddened, wounded, rogue male elephant, ears flared, trunk railed, trumpet blaring. I'll do my dance on his chest, and the only thing he'll ever see in my eyes is a dagger to pierce his cruel heart. This is one nigger who is positively displeased. I'll never forgive. I'll never forget, and if I'm guilty of anything at all it's of not leaning on them hard enough. War without terms.

GEORGE JACKSON, *Prison Letters*

Index